Managing Tourism

Managing Tourism

Edited by Professor S. Medlik

BUTTERWORTH
HEINEMANN

Butterworth-Heinemann Ltd
Linacre House, Jordan Hill, Oxford OX2 8DP

�toⱤ A member of the Reed Elsevier plc group

OXFORD   LONDON   BOSTON   MUNICH
NEW DELHI   SINGAPORE   SYDNEY   TOKYO
TORONTO   WELLINGTON

First published 1991
Reprinted 1993
Paperback edition 1995

© S. Medlik 1991

British Library Cataloguing in Publication Data
Managing tourism
    1. Tourism
    I. Medlik, S. (Slavoj) *1928–*   II. Tourism Management
    338.4791

ISBN 0 7506 2355 1

Printed and bound in Great Britain
by Redwood Books, Trowbridge, Wiltshire

Contents

Preface

The *Tourism Management* journal was launched in March 1980 and published ten volumes of quarterly issues in the 1980s. This book of selected contributions, which appeared over the ten years, marks the end of another decade for tourism and of the first decade for the journal.

The 1980s were eventful times for tourism. The early life of the journal coincided with the worst recession the world had experienced for fifty years; international terrorism and other problems were present throughout. But tourism demonstrated a remarkable resilience, a major growth and development in volume and diversity, as well as much ingenuity and enterprise on the part of business and other organizations. In that time, and this has continued, tourism has increasingly become the concern of governments and also of academic institutions. Its economic, social, cultural and environmental impacts and significance in particular have come to be questioned and critically examined and analysed.

Tourism Management has sought to provide a forum and to serve the needs of policymakers and managers, as well as students, teachers and researchers. It has attracted contributions from academic, business and other communities from around the world. Not only the authorship but also many of the writings have had an international flavour, and both are reflected in this book. About one-half of the contributions included come from the UK and the rest of Europe, and one-half from North America and elsewhere. Irrespective of where the authors come from, the selected articles range widely in their orientation, and are divided in similar proportions between those which address issues of common concern and those which deal with different parts of the world.

In *Managing Tourism* the aim has been to bring together some of the significant material of longer-term value and interest to a wide readership, which those concerned with tourism would find valid long after it had first appeared in the journal and wish to retain for future reference. The view taken has been that the selection should have something to say to readers in the 1990s, wherever they may be. Articles of passing interest and those with a predominantly localized focus, whatever their methodological or other merits, did not qualify. Nor did those intelligible to relatively few, because of their mathematical content or exposition. What is included straddles theory, concepts and practice, for it may be argued that in this field in particular practice without concepts is barren, and that theory should be the best practice selected.

This volume comprises thirty articles and they are grouped in ten parts.

Brief notes at the beginning of each part are intended to serve as introductions to what follows. Many more quality journal articles had to be left out, often for no other reason than limitations of space. However, in order to compensate, each part of the book includes also a list of further articles published in *Tourism Management* on the same or related topic as 'Further reading', and more than 300 articles have been so listed. No regular reader of the journal can be expected to agree entirely with the selection of material or its grouping. But it is hoped that most of the repertoire offered will appeal to all and especially to those for whom this book will be their first contact with the journal.

As much as possible of the original journal text has been retained in each chapter. However, all authors were invited to edit their original contributions for inclusion and, more often than not, were also asked to shorten them, in order to fit into the overall format of the book. An appendix shows for each chapter the journal issue, in which the original version of the article appeared, and also whether it has been edited, shortened and/or whether a postscript has been added.

Managing Tourism is intended for:

● international, national, regional and local tourism organizations;
● tourist attractions, transportation, accommodation, tour operations, travel agencies and other sectors;
● teachers and students in higher education; and
● other walks of life where an understanding of tourism is important.

This volume would not have been possible without the ready cooperation of the authors and publishers and their help is gratefully acknowledged. The editor is also indebted to Howard Green, whose wordprocessor transferred with great speed and efficiency drafts of articles and supporting material on to a disk, from which the book was typeset. The idea of the book was conceived as a joint venture between Butterworth Scientific Ltd and Heinemann Professional Publishing in the Spring of 1990; that the book was in print by the end of the same year, is a tribute to them all.

S. Medlik
Guildford

Publisher's note

Tourism Management is a quarterly international journal, which publishes original research in tourism, analysis of current trends, and information on the wide spectrum of tourism activities and industries.

The journal aims to meet the needs of both academics and practitioners for authoritative material on policies, issues and practices and to serve as a source of long-term reference and as a practical tool.

Articles cover economic, social, cultural and environmental impacts and significance of tourism; tourist attractions, transportation, accommodation and other sectors; management, marketing and planning of tourism.

Butterworth-Heinemann Ltd was created in April 1990 to bring together Butterworth Scientific Ltd (the publishers of *Tourism Management* amongst other journals and books in the technology, medical and policy areas) and Heinemann Professional Publishing (book publishers in the management, medical and technical areas). Butterworth-Heinemann Ltd is the Scientific, Technical, Management and Medical (STMM) group within the Professional Division of Reed International Books and aims to publish quality books and journals for an international and professional readership.

Professor S. Medlik is an author, consultant and educator. Between 1967 and 1977 he was Head of the Department of Hotel, Catering and *Tourism Management* at the University of Surrey, UK, where he also served as Dean of the Faculty of Human Studies.

Since then he held several senior academic appointments overseas in the USA, Canada, the West Indies and Australia; advised a number of companies as well as tourism, educational and other bodies; lectured widely in Britain and abroad.

His published work includes twenty books and other separate publications and in the region of 100 contributions to the professional and technical press.

Contributors

Affiliations of contributors shown are those at the time when each chapter first appeared as an article in *Tourism Management*.

Part One

Futures – Analysis – Planning

In recent years the growth of tourism has been accompanied by an increasing volume of research. Forecasting the future of tourism and assessing its impacts and significance have been important concerns of the research, which has been providing inputs into tourism planning. Three articles selected for this part of the book illustrate the wide range of writings on these matters in *Tourism Management* in its first ten years.

Jozef van Doorn, at the time of writing at the Twente University of Technology in the Netherlands and latterly partner in the advertising agency Young & Rubicam in Amsterdam, asks 'Can futures research contribute to tourism policy?' The author examines the interrelationships between planning, policymaking and forecasting, describes forecasting methods and techniques, and puts forward criteria by which the usefulness of forecasts may be assessed.

Brian Archer of the University of Surrey, UK, writes on 'The value of multipliers and their policy implications'. The author examines the nature of tourism multipliers, their origins and evolution, their misuse, weaknesses and limitations, and their value for policymaking and planning.

Michael Haywood of the University of Guelph, Canada, asks 'Can the tourist-area life cycle be made operational?' The author reviews major decisions necessary to accomplish this and discusses the adequacy of the life cycle concept in the planning and management of a tourist area as it evolves.

Further articles related to the themes of this part of the book published in *Tourism Management* from 1980–9 are listed at the end as follows: on forecasting the future of tourism on page 39, on tourism impacts and significance on page 39, and on tourism planning and development on page 40.

1 Can futures research contribute to tourism policy?

Jozef W. M. van Doorn

In the title of this paper an assumption is made which specialists in the field of futures research now safely take for granted, but which, nevertheless, may raise legitimate doubts in the fields of tourism and recreation. The assumption is that scientific research can be, and in fact has been, extended from past and present to future events.

With the first societal grouping man's concern was directed towards the preservation of his possessions and the acquisition of new ones, which both implied risk-taking and hence an interest in the outcome of the actions to be undertaken. Similar to what happened in the field of medicine, where the witchdoctor had to give way to the anatomist and the physician, and where the art of healing became science, the futures researcher has had to do away with the superstition and occultism, with oracles, prophets, astrologers and fortune tellers. His tools are no longer the crystal ball, dice, entrails of animals, the stars or cards, but statistics, hard evidence and facts, and computers.

The missing link between the ambiguous and paramountly applicable predictions of the oracle and our present day 'failure-prone' forecasts is to be sought in the still pre-scientific approaches to insight into the future; especially into the future of whole societies, such as Thomas More's *Utopia* (1517), Bacon's *New Atlantis* (seventeenth century), Condorcet's idea of conditional probability, and Gilfillan's thesis (early twentieth century) with regard to the methodology of futures research.[1]

In the field of policymaking at governmental or industrial level the futures scientist still encounters obstacles in the form of certain deep-rooted views that tend to prevail despite all theoretical advances:

● *The future cannot be known.* Science as such has to rely on empirical facts, which are available from the past and the present, but not from an as yet non-existent future.

- *Insight into the future is possible only by means of non-scientific methods,* such as the crystal ball, astrology, intuition, rules of thumb and hand-reading.
- *The future can be known if we view it ideologically as the strict realization of ideas conceived in the past,* e.g. the realization of an ideal state of society in conformity with definite political ideas.

The above notions, while they prevail, have an inhibiting effect on the futures researcher's genuine commitment. Although it is true that there are certain unpredictable events, such as natural disasters, and although tacit knowledge and political ideas have a timely bearing on futures research, e.g. in the Delphi method, the only way for scientists to overcome the problem of acceptance is by converting policymakers to their credo:

- *The future can be partially known by way of scientific methods and techniques.* Thus the assumption we implied initially is not only a challenge for the scientist, it also makes a promise to the user in the sense of partially deleting risk from any venture. So in this paper I play the role of the devil's advocate and try to make planners and users of forecasts, with regard to tourism and recreation policies, keep both their feet on the ground, by pointing out some caveats, complexities and promising possibilities in futures research.

Futures research, planning and policymaking: a triad

Policies are the consequence of a decision-making process which has the objective of modifying the present in view of the future. This is why decision-making bodies do need valid information about the future and the positive and negative impact of potential decisions. This information-gathering can only be done by careful research, research which will then support the policymaking processes.

Let us consider an example that is common practice in many resorts – the building of an hotel. Such accommodation already has something to do with the future: the expected flow of tourists, the necessary bed capacities, the market share etc. Building an hotel means talking about objectives, involves data-collection and processing, and concerns several government departments and sectors at a local, regional, or national level.

Policymaking should display cohesion between multi-sectoral aspects and should strive to achieve coherent and viable coordination between multi-level objectives. The objectives may differ widely. They may aim at the creation of jobs, attracting congresses or certain kind of public relations exercise for the community.

And who is to coordinate all those objectives, interest groups and powers? The planner. The systematic support of policymaking by research takes place in the planning process. Planning is the basis of policymaking. Thus futures research becomes a fundamental part of the planning process.[2]

In tourism, policies have to rely on a coherent set of economic, political, sociocultural and spatial objectives. These objectives have to be placed into a decision framework whose primary function is the achievement of aims with specified means in a certain period of time. Policymaking in tourism is not an exclusive task of government, but grows along the lines of cooperation with the policymaking tourist organizations (national tourist organizations, information offices, consumer associations) and the tourist industry (hotels, restaurants, tour operators, travel agencies); even pressure groups might have a say in the policymaking process.

Futures research and forecasting: methods and techniques

Two methods of approach can be distinguished:

● The database is taken from the past and the present and gives rise to 'exploratory futures research'.
● The desired future itself constitutes the database, decisions being shaped by working backwards – the 'normative approach' to futures research.

On the basis of this almost classical distinction we can distinguish four different forms of forecasting. They have in common that they elicit conditional probability statements, based on either of the rational models of analysis. This means that forecasts, irrespective of their form (or modality) are obtained systematically and are subject to control and testing.

In *exploratory forecasting* the scientist is concerned with the extrapolation of trends and the search for the logical development of alternative possibilities.

Apart from this form it is also scientifically sound to base one's forecasts on a blend of intuition, expertise, and generally accepted assumptions – *speculative forecasting*. Whereas in exploratory techniques it is hardly possible to include expectations about future policy decisions, speculative techniques offer the advantage to do so by means of method-implicit procedures.

Table 1.1   Type of forecasting technique and methodological tools

	Type description	Methodological tools
Explorative	Extrapolation of trends	Trend setting – time series analysis
	Search for logical alternative possibilities	Regression analysis Gravity models Historical analogy method Scenario writing Morphological analysis
Speculative	Probability estimates of event occurrence Implicit expectations in policy decisions	Brainstorming Delbecq and Impasse Delphi
Normative	Explicit description of desired future states and the routes that lead to them	Normative scenario writing Bayesian statistics Pattern
Integrative	Research into the implications of options Establishment of relational patterns among hitherto isolated forecasts	Input–output models Cross-impact analysis Mapping

Source: van Doorn and van Vught, text reference 3

Here it comes close to the ideas of *normative forecasting,* although in normative forecasting the scientist starts out explicitly with the formulation of norms and values that are to be valid in the future. The procedure involves constructing a series of consistent images of the future and subsequently tracing the route of attainment of (access to) these images.[3]

Matters become even more complex when dealing with *integrative forecasting,* since its procedural capacity covers all the techniques customary in the three preceding forms. The aim of these techniques is to set up consistent relational patterns among isolated forecasts to enhance the plausibility of pronouncements deriving from any other technique. Thanks to this procedurally-comprehensive approach, a functional accumulation of knowledge, time, types and sectors is achieved.

In Table 1.1 we offer a typological synthesis view over the four forms of forecasting and methodological tools applied in each.

Exploratory forecasting in tourism

Time series analysis

One of the most important data for recreation as well as for tourism is to know how many people are involved. Information about flows of recreationists or tourists are the inputs into policy decisions. It is not surprising that the majority of forecasting studies so far in tourism are devoted to demand.

Demand depends on a range of factors (or variables). Several explorative forecasting techniques are used to foresee the developments with regard to demand in tourism. Those techniques differ, among other things, with respect to the number of factors that are taken into account. Time series analysis merely focuses on the historical developments of one variable so as to forecast its (near) future developments; linear regression models do the same for two variables, while the multi-regression models (like the gravity model) consider demand in relation to three or more variables.

Thus time series would start with just one variable: tourist arrivals, recreational receipts, or aircraft sales, etc. The forecaster can choose one of the various time series analysis techniques: Box-Jenkins, Census II, Leading Indicator, etc. All these are used to break down, in one way or another, a time series into seasonal, trend, cycle and random elements.

I want to emphasize that forecasts tend to become less accurate and less reliable the longer the time period they range over. Although the techniques mentioned are widely used in tourism planning, they do not seem to be of too much help to the tourism forecaster who focuses on the medium and long term. Several authors like BarOn and Vanhove have mentioned this problem.[4]

Regression models

The second type of exploratory forecasting considers two or more variables in correlation. A well known technique here is the linear regression model, used for a two-variable relationship, e.g. income and holiday participation, based on the least squares method. For more than two-variable calculations, multi-variable regression models will be required. Vanhove recommends for this purpose the Artus model, while Archer presents the Askari model.[5] As examples, or better, slight deviations from the multi-variable regression models, we could mention the so-called trip-generation models and gravity models.

In the literature a long list of models is presented. To mention a few with the name of the author: Armstrong, Crampon and Lesceux (gravity), Gordon (trip generation), Jud (linear regression).[6]

In the Armstrong model the following variables were used to forecast tourist flows to several tourist destinations:

- size of the population of the tourist generating country;
- income per capita (in each of the generating countries);
- distance from generating country to tourist destination;
- travel time;
- special relation variable, e.g. a common language between a generating and a destination country;
- a parameter for the relative appeal of the destination countries.

Using his model for comparison with actual data, the results are not very encouraging. This model shows the weakness of any extrapolation method:

- useful in the short term;
- losing power very quickly in the medium term;
- practically useless in the long term.

Scenarios

In the preceding forecasting techniques, arithmetic and mathematics were used. The variables were quantifiable and the results were forecasts about a certain point in time, or points in time. Nothing or little could be said about qualitative variables, such as the influence of the policymaking process itself, and the changes of variables being subject to time. For medium- and long-term forecasts to be of any practical value to the planner, we must adjust our techniques to handle a bundle of qualitative variables denoting the expected turning points in a policy framework along a timescale as a result and extension of quantitative data processing.

This is what the scenarios are intended to be. In the classical sense scenarios are hypothetical sequences of events. They pretend to trace possible designs of the future and the routes that subsequently would lead towards them. In exploratory forecasting, scenario writing means moving along the scale from past-present to future, while in normative forecasting the procedure is more sophisticated: the forecaster moves from the future backwards-forwards to the desired state. To date no normative scenario exists in tourism.

Table 1.2 Scenarios based on alternative assumptions (Tourism to Thailand: scenarios 1975–80).

Field	Optimistic	Intermediate	Pessimistic
Political			
1 International	Improved détente	As 1975	Increased tension, local wars
Economic			
2 Prices of oil and air transport	Relative reductions	As 1975 (relatively)	Further relative increases
Air transport			
3 Fare structure	More fare reductions, scheduled and charter	As 1975	Decreased availability of charter and promotional fares
Forecasts of visitors arrivals (000)			
1975	1,185	1,165	1,135
1978	1,895	1,575	1,375
1980	2,550	1,900	1,550
Actual number of arrivals (000)			
1975		1,180	
1978		1,475	
1980		1,850	

Source: BarOn, text reference 4

To quote only a few examples of these 'preparatory stage scenarios', we could mention MacGregor's, Koster's and Kahn's contributions to the conference 'Tourism in the Next Decade' (Washington, DC, 1979).[7]

Examples that overtly point in the direction of scenarios as we defined them, are found in BarOn's paper presented at the tenth annual Tourism and Travel Research Association (TTRA) conference in 1979. Here it must suffice to skim through just one of the examples to illustrate what kind of alternative assumptions are made and how they are arrived at (see Table 1.2). The assumptions made explicitly (e.g. the relative reduction of oil prices) and the underlying, implicit but less obvious, assumptions (e.g. the balance of powers in the world remaining unchanged), are always the weakest points of the exercise. The assumptions can be considered a result of a time serialization of the database, the alternatives being triggered by means of factorization towards negative or positive developments. But there is a lack of hypothetical grading or stepwise progression towards one of the alternatives. Thus the scenario-writing business needs to be supported by more elaborate techniques that will enable the forecaster to improve his assumptions, to strengthen their predictive power, and to widen their scope to range over qualitative data.

For this purpose we turn to the second area of forecasting – speculative forecasting.

Speculative forecasting

This type puts a series of tools into the hands of the scientist that allows him to move towards a less quantifiable terrain and become more independent of the influence from his past-present database, thus enhancing the accuracy of his studies. We are now ready to abandon the somewhat casual assumptions made in the Thai example in Table 1.2 and take a look at some of these tools. In passing we mention a few names from the list of (already) conventional techniques, such as SIG (Subjective Integrated Group Processors), JAM (Judgement Aided Models) and GDST (Group Discussion Structuring Techniques). The common objective in all these procedures is the pooling of the expertise and skills of people proficient in highly unstructured fields (e.g. tourism). The most famous among these techniques and perhaps the one that has been subject to the most passionate discussion and criticism is the Delphi method.

The Delphi method

In a Delphi study, a questionnaire dealing with a specific problem is presented to the group of experts in the field. They will answer questions, for example, about the probability and/or desirability of certain events occurring, e.g. the likelihood of a 100 per cent computerized reservation system for the leading hotel chains and travel agencies by a given year.

Characteristic of Delphi studies is their striving towards consensus. In several written rounds the – most of the time anonymous – experts try to convince each other, by their arguments, that certain answers are more likely than others. The result for each statement is then a statistically aggregated collective answer on which consensus was reached. A Delphi example focusing on tourism might be found in the report on the results of the international symposium, 'Tourism and the Next Decade'.[8] The validity of this method may be questioned and subjected to serious criticism.[9]

Two Delphi studies relevant to tourism were undertaken in Austria and Switzerland, respectively.[10]

Integrative forecasting

As was mentioned above, normative forecasting studies are almost completely absent in tourism research. This can be attributed partly to the vagueness of the concept of tourism. If one does not know exactly what tourism stands for, how can one develop a policy strategy for it? Second, in various Western European countries tourism is not attached to one single ministry but to several. Last but not least the sector is denied political importance, notwithstanding its vital economic importance. Even in the USA this is the case. This attitude can be held partly responsible for the non-existence of normative forecasting.

Remembering what was said above, this form of forecasting contains integrated forecasts from various sectors, from different forecasting methods, preferably long-term studies. Yet in the course of my paper reference has been made to the poor feasibility of long-term studies in tourism. However, there are a few good studies that comply with some criteria that define integrative forecasting. Falani's study on forecasting part of the air traffic between fourteen US cities through an input–output model has turned out to be so important for airport directors, airlines, pressure groups, catering and fuel suppliers, that it could be characterized as integrative at least in a sense.[11]

Taylor, Edgell and BarOn[12] similarly emphasize the need for integrating several techniques in one comprehensive method. The combination preferred by them and myself is the triad 'Time Series–Delphi- –Scenario writing', in that order.

Results

Despite the growing file of reports on tourism forecasting, surprisingly little attention is paid to the comparison of actual data with the corresponding forecasts; and this despite the existence of a considerable number of criteria to assess/evaluate these results. The scope of my paper only allows for a brief mention of a few of these.

Particularly in short-term forecasting, one should be happy when forecasts materialize. That should be proof that the technique used was valid to some extent. Other criteria to assess the usefulness of forecasting results could be the number of alternatives presented, the contextual stability of the forecast, the presentation itself and last, but not least, the costs.

So the policymaker in tourism, whatever his place, in government, industry or elsewhere, always has to counterweigh different criteria against his own objectives and preferences – he will have to ask questions like:

- What will the forecast cost me?
- What is the term of application and what is the relative value of this term?
- What data are available?
- How valid is the technique proposed?
- Do I need alternatives or just one answer?
- Are the results plausible?
- Can I use this forecast to impress my electorate or can it be used to manipulate investors, political leaders or the public?
- Do I really need a forecaster? Or could I do it better myself?

Doubtless in most cases policymakers need the forecaster, but they should not blindly depend on his rulings. Decisions ought to be the result of communication, perhaps even directly embedded in a communicative or negotiation-type of planning, before both parties will benefit from one another in an optimal way.

Conclusions: the bearing of forecasting on tourism

In this paper we have presented a typology of futures research (i.e. forecasting). Most studies, briefly mentioned or quoted, focused on exploratory forecasting.

On the whole, forecasting in tourism has not yet received universal recognition as a vital aspect of planning and/or policymaking in tourism. The greater part of research in tourism refers to short-term exploratory forecasting and therefore will not substantiate the necessary support to strategic planning, while on the other hand the new 'pre-stage' scenarios presented to date move more along the lines of contingency planning than in conformity with scenarios proper.

Recreation stands and falls with society and the forms of tourism developed in this context. It is determined by factors such as income level, leisure time, energy supply and prices, processes of individualization and social segregation, as well as by inflation, demographic structures and ecological imbalances such as pollution – and, not least, by the changes in all those factors or variables through time.

All those aspects and factors will grow in complexity and dynamism. Besides, there is an increasing interdependence of the elements that make up the tourism and recreation system. In the decade to come tourism is bound to remain a fuzzy set. Forecasting has proved to be valid to some extent in economics, technology, demographics and a few other fields. I have tried to demonstrate in the course of the paper that it is also a handsome tool for planning and policymaking in tourism.

References

1   Good introductions to the history of futures research are: Cornish, Edward, *The Study of the Future*, Washington, DC: World Future Society, 1977, and Fowles, Jib, *Handbook of Futures Research*, London: Greenwood Press, 1978.
2   van Doorn, J. W. M. and van Vught, F. A., *Planning*, Assen: van Gorcum, 1978.
3   van Doorn, J. W. M. and van Vught, F.A., *Forecasting*, Assen: van Gorcum, 1978.
4   BarOn, R. R., 'Forecasting, theory and practice', *Tenth Annual Conference Proceedings of the Travel and Tourism Research Association* (1979); Vanhove, N., 'Forecasting in tourism', *Revue de Tourisme*, 35 (3), 1980.
5   Archer, Brian H., 'Forecasting demand: quantitative and intuitive techniques', *International Journal of Tourism Management*, 1 (1), 1980; and Vanhove, *op cit*, reference 4.
6   Armstrong, C., 'International tourism, coming or going: the methodological problems of forecasting', *Futures*, 4 (2), June 1972, pages 115–25; Crampon, L., 'Gravitational model approach to travel market analysis', *Journal of Marketing, 30*, April 1966; Lesceux, D., *La Demande Touristique en Mediterranée* (Aix-en-Provence, 1977); Jud, G. and Joseph, H., 'International demand for Latin American tourism', *Growth and Change*, Jan 1974.
7   Kosters, M., 'Holland and tourism in the next decade', in *Tourism Planning and Development Issues*, Hawkins, Shafer and Rovelstad (eds), Washington, DC: George Washington University, 1980; MacGregor, J. R., 'Latin America: future scenario forecasting for the tourism industry in some of its developing nations', *Tourism Planning Development Issues*, pp. 429–43; Kahn, H., *Travel Trade News Edition*, section one XCVI (6), 1979.
8   Robinson, A. E., 'A return to Delphi', in 'A decade of achievement', *Tenth Annual Conference Proceedings of the TTRA*, 1979.
9   Sackman, Harold, *Delphi Critique*, Toronto: Lexington Books, 1975; Linstone, H. and Turoff, M. (eds), *The Delphi-Method: Techniques and Applications*, Reading, MA: Addison-Wesley, 1975.
10 *Delphi-SEER-Expertenbefragung 1978–1980 über Fremdenverkehrsentwicklung in Österreich*, Vienna: Institut für Fremdenverkehrstechnik, 1980; Krippendorf,

J., *Eine Delphi-Umfrage über die zukunftige Entwicklung des Tourismus in der Schweiz*, Bern: 1979.

11 Falani, M. O., 'Air traffic forecasting: an input–output technique approach', *Regional Studies, 7*, 1973.

12 BarOn, R. R., *op cit*, reference 4; Taylor, G. and Doctoroff, M., 'An approach to an integrated forecasting system for a national tourist office', in IUOTO, *The Measurement of Tourism*, London: British Tourist Authority, 1975; Edgell, D. and Seely, R., 'Tourism policy: a two-stage model for the development of international tourism flow forecast estimates', paper presented to the Symposium, 'Tourism in the next decade', Washington, DC, 1979, see also reference 7.

Acknowledgement

This article is an edited version of a paper given to the International Conference on Winter Recreation in Ottawa, Canada, in February 1981. The author wishes to thank Dr B. Otto Schneider, Associate Professor in English and Linguistics, University of Barcelona, Spain, for reading, commenting and criticizing this paper.

2 The value of multipliers and their policy implications

Brian H. Archer

There is perhaps more misunderstanding about multiplier analysis than almost any other aspect of tourism research. The blame for this unfortunate situation must lie with tourism researchers themselves. Not only have we (and I accept my share of the blame) failed to explain adequately to non-economists the theoretical basis and practical nature of multiplier analysis, but we have used different and conflicting concepts of the multiplier itself. Furthermore, some researchers have brought the technique into disrepute by misusing the methodology and producing nonsensical results with disastrous implications for policymaking.

This paper tries to set the record straight by examining the nature of tourism multipliers, their origins and evolution, their misuse, their strengths, weaknesses and limitations and finally their value for policymaking and planning.

A tourist income multiplier is basically a coefficient which expresses the amount of income generated in an area by an additional unit of tourist spending. In other words, if tourists spend an extra £1m in a holiday region and this generates, say £800,000 of income in that area, the value of the income multiplier is 0.8. Because of data difficulties, however, it is normal practice (though not conceptually correct) to measure income generation in terms of average rather than marginal units of tourist spending. Unfortunately, insufficient evidence exists so far in the field of tourism to judge what differences might exist between multipliers measured at the margin and those assessed on an average basis.

Although this paper is concerned primarily with the 'value' of multipliers in terms of both their possible numerical limits and their usefulness for policy and planning purposes, it might be useful first to examine the nature of a tourism multiplier to see how the effects of tourist spending ripple through an economy.

The nature of tourism multipliers

Tourism expenditure is an invisible export in that it creates a flow of foreign currency into the economy of the destination country. Like most other forms of export, this inflow of revenue creates additional business turnover, household income and government revenue. The initial tourist spending is received as revenue by hoteliers, shopkeepers, taxi-drivers and others.

Thus, for example, £10m of additional tourism expenditure forms £10m of *direct revenue* within the region concerned. Not all of this money, however, forms *income* to the resident population. Hoteliers, shopkeepers and others must restock their inventories to provide for future sales, they must maintain their buildings, fittings and equipment, and must pay land taxes, profit taxes, licence fees etc. to the central and local governments, and insurance premiums and other payments to private sector organizations. In addition, some profits from these firms may be paid to people and organizations outside the area. Thus, as businesses respend the money which they have received from tourists, some of this direct revenue 'leaks' out of the economy.

Some money, however, remains in the area. Tourism establishments pay out wages and salaries to local employees and in addition replenish some of their stocks from local wholesalers and manufacturers, whose turnovers are thereby increased. To meet this additional demand, extra employees may be taken on and/or higher wages paid to the existing labour force. The local business firms which form the secondary recipients of the tourist spending themselves respend the money and thereby set in motion a further chain of economic activity.

As the tourist spending seeps its way through the economy, the general output of the area rises (assuming that sufficient resources are available), employment opportunities increase and personal incomes rise. The degree of magnitude of these so-called *indirect effects* is governed by the extent to which business firms in the area supply each other with goods and services (inter-industrial linkages). In general, the smaller the economy the fewer are the linkages between firms and the greater is the likelihood that replacement orders and purchases of new machinery will be given to firms outside the area. The magnitude of the impact is diminished by these 'leakages' and also by further leakages into savings.

As wages and salaries within the economy rise, so consumer expenditure increases and this provides a further impetus to economic activity. Additional business turnover occurs and this generates further income and employment opportunities. These so-called *induced effects* can be quite considerable and in some areas have been shown to generate income effects up to three times as great as the indirect effects alone.

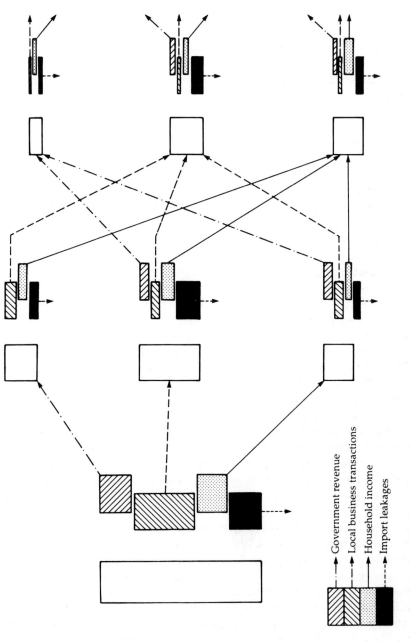

Government revenue

Local business transactions

Household income

Import leakages

Figure 2.1 The multiplier

The indirect and induced effects together are sometimes called the *secondary effects*, and the tourism multiplier is a measure of the total effects (direct plus secondary) which result from additional tourist expenditure.

The process is illustrated in Figure 2.1 where the left-hand unshaded block represents the initial revenue received from tourist spending. This revenue is shown to generate four main flows of money – government revenue, local purchases, local income and import leakages. The figure demonstrates the ripple effect of tourist spending through the economy and shows how income, government revenue and business turnover continue to be generated with decreasing effect through successive rounds of expenditure until leakages reduce the effect of the initial impact to a negligible amount. The technique used to measure such flows is called a multiplier model.

Four types of multiplier model are in common use and considerable confusion has been caused by their misuse and incorrect application in some recent studies. First, a *sales* (or *transactions*) multiplier measures the effect of an extra unit of tourist spending on economic activity within the economy. As the name implies, the multiplier relates tourism expenditure to the increase in *business turnover* which it creates.

Very similar to this model is the *output* multiplier, which relates a unit of tourist spending to the resultant increase in the level of output in the economy. The difference between the two types is that, while the sales multiplier considers only the level of sales which result from the direct and secondary effects of tourist spending, the output multiplier takes into account both the level of sales and any real changes which take place in the level of inventories (stocks) held in the economy.

Third, an *income* multiplier shows the relationship between an additional unit of tourist spending and the changes which result in the level of income in the economy. Some confusion has arisen about the nature of the income that is to be measured. In many tourism models, 'income' is defined as *disposable income*, i.e. the income which is actually received by households and is available for them to spend or save. Any income accruing to non-nationals resident in the area is usually extracted from the sum on the grounds that the incomes which they receive are not benefits to the country.

Care has to be taken, however, to include within the multiplier calculations the secondary effects which result from the respending within the economy of any part of the incomes of non-nationals. In national accounting terms some definitions of 'income' include the revenue accruing to the government. In many multiplier models this form of revenue is included within the income to be measured, while in others it is assessed separately and the household income which is generated subsequently by the respending of this revenue is included within the secondary income effects.

Lastly, *employment* multipliers describe *either* the ratio of the direct and secondary employment generated by additional tourism expenditure to the direct employment alone, *or* the amount of employment generated by a given amount of tourist spending.

The various types of multipliers are intrinsically linked. Thus, for example, additional tourist spending of, say, £1m may generate £2.5m of output within an economy and £0.5m of direct and secondary income to nationals in the area. It may create also 200 extra jobs and perhaps 180 secondary jobs. The output multiplier, therefore, is 2.5, the income multiplier 0.5 and the employment multiplier 1.9 (380/200) or 3.8 (i.e. 3.8 jobs per £10,000 of tourist spending).

Two principal techniques exist for calculating tourism multipliers and their pedigrees can be traced back in the evolution of multiplier analysis.

Origins and evolution of multipliers

The early origins and history of multipliers (from the 1880s to the early 1930s) has already been documented by several writers[1] and needs no elaboration here. The principle of the multiplier effect and the part played by leakages was already known when in 1931 R. F. Kahn[2] produced his authoritative and significant contribution to the theory. Kahn produced the first detailed model showing the direct and secondary effects of an increase in economic activity on an economy. He showed clearly how an increase in export earnings triggered off an expansion of income, employment, consumption and investment.

The main link between Kahn's work and the present-day advanced models was provided by Lord Keynes.[3] Keynes' basic model was:

$$\text{Multiplier} = \frac{1}{1 - c + m}$$

where c is the marginal propensity to consume (i.e. the proportion of any increase in income which is spent on consumption) and m is the marginal propensity to import (i.e. the proportion of any increase which is spent on imports).

Essentially, Keynes' basic model shows that the multiplier is calculated by dividing a unit of tourist (or other export) expenditure by the proportion of it which 'leaks' out of the economic system (i.e. as savings and to purchase imports).

The model is simple and clear and still forms the framework of most of the more recent advanced models.

The second major development in the evolution of multiplier models came in the 1960s with the introduction of input–output analysis, notably the work of Leontief[4] in the USA. Input–output analysis is a method of tabulating an economic system in matrix form to show as rows the sales made by each sector of the economy to each of the other sectors, and as columns the purchases made by each sector from each of the others. Tourist spending is shown as an export column and, by means of matrix algebra, the impact of this expenditure on each sector and on incomes can be measured.

Since the 1960s multiplier models have become increasingly refined and many studies have been undertaken. This surge of theoretical and practical investigation, however, has been bedevilled by the intrusion of a number of researchers whose work has obscured the true nature of multipliers and whose publications have, in some cases, brought the technique into some disrepute.

Misleading and mischievous multipliers

The theory and practice as propounded by Keynes, Leontief and many later writers are unequivocal – the multiplier measures the increase in economic activity (incomes, employment etc.) generated in an economy by a unit increase in tourist (or other export) expenditure. How then has confusion arisen and what misleading concepts and alternatives have arisen?

The first of these is the 'ratio' multiplier, which appears to date back to some research carried out in Utah during the mid-1950s by More and Petersen.[5] Basically this approach is to express the income multiplier as the ratio of the total income generated by tourism expenditure to the direct income generated. An example may help to explain this concept and show how it differs from the normal approach.

Tourism expenditure		£100
Direct income created	£25	
Secondary income created	£20	
Total income created	£45	

The Keynesian multiplier in this example is 0.45, i.e. 45/100, but the 'ratio' multiplier (total income generated to direct income) is 45/25 = 1.8.

As in the case of the Keynesian multipliers, refinements have been added to this simple approach to provide 'ratios' for each sector of the economy and to distinguish between different aspects of secondary income generation.

What use, however, are ratio multipliers as a guide for policymakers and planners? The answer is very little. What they do provide is a useful picture of the *degree of internal linkage* which exists between the various sectors of the economy concerned and between these and local consumer spending. They give no indication per se of how much tourism expenditure is needed to create a unit of direct income. In the example already quoted the 'ratio' value of 1.8 is a measure of the degree of internal linkage existing within the economy. It is not a tourism multiplier and to multiply it by tourism expenditure would be meaningless.

These two different concepts of the income multiplier are not, however, irreconcilable. The same basic data and similar modelling techniques are required for each. Where they differ is the mode used to express the multiplier value. One is useful for policymakers and planners, the other is misleading.

A second and equally misleading problem has been created by failing to differentiate between income and sales multipliers. The former measure the amount of income generated by a unit increase in tourism expenditure, whereas sales multipliers measure the value of business turnover created by the same unit increase in tourist spending. It is difficult to understand how two such different concepts can have been confused, but unfortunately several researchers have made this mistake.

An example will give some idea of the different magnitudes of the two multipliers: in Gwynedd, North Wales, when measured a few years ago, the income multiplier for the hotel sector was about 0.36, whereas the sales multiplier was 1.46. This means that an additional £1 of tourist expenditure in hotels should generate on average approximately 36p of income in Gwynedd, but business activity in the county should rise by about £1.46. Both multipliers are equally valid, but it is not difficult to imagine the effect on policymaking if such transactions and income multipliers are confused.

A third source of misunderstanding is a confusion between the multiplier and the multiplicand. We have already considered the multiplier. It is a coefficient value, i.e. a number which when multiplied by another quantity measures some property, e.g. the tourist income multiplier measures the amount of income generated by a quantity of tourist expenditure. This quantity of expenditure is basically the multiplicand, but the reality is not quite so simple. In the case of tourism, for example, not all of the expenditure is available to create income in the area: some tourist expenditure never even enters the economy at all.

Two examples may make this clearer. In many coastal areas of the UK, a large proportion of tourists use rented caravans. Many of these caravans are owned by people who themselves live outside the area. Thus, many rental charges paid by visitors (to use the caravans) go *not* to the holiday areas but to the owners of the caravans who live elsewhere in the country. The only flow of money into the holiday areas from this source, therefore, is the parking (or site) fees paid by the caravan owners to the site owner. In most cases this sum is much lower than the rental fees paid by the tourists using the caravans. Similarly in the case of package tours, especially for holidays overseas, a large proportion of the money paid by visitors accrues to the airlines, coach operators, tour companies and travel agents outside the holiday regions. Fortunately, most researchers do subtract this amount from tourism expenditure to obtain a more meaningful multiplicand, but unfortunately few researchers subtract from the multiplicand any allowances for other tourist spending, e.g. caravan rentals, which never enter the region.

This omission partly arises from uncritical acceptance of the elementary explanations of multiplier analysis given in basic economics textbooks. The naive models used in these books to illustrate, for teaching purposes, the mechanism of the multiplier are of necessity oversimplified and usually assume that the whole of the first round of expenditure is available to create income. Such models also assume that successive rounds of income generation follow a common path. In practical analysis, especially for the study of regions or small economies, such assumptions have to be removed. Input–output models can be easily adjusted to make such allowances by allocating such expenditure as a direct import. Keynesian multipliers can be adapted by showing such changes in the multiplicand in the form of direct leakages, e.g.

$$\frac{1 - L}{1 - c + m}$$

where L is the immediate leakage attributable to tourist spending not entering the economy.

A fourth source of confusion has arisen out of the negligence of some researchers, whose careless work has discredited the technique as a planning and policy tool. Rather than attempt to list the offending studies, I hope to make the point with a couple of examples. About three years ago at a conference in North America, I was informed in complete seriousness by the Director of Tourism of a large US city that the value of the tourism multiplier for his city was about 6 or 7. This figure had been obtained by marking dollar notes and then tracing them through the business community. Apparently 6.5 was the average number of times a dollar note changed hands before being lost to the system. No allowance was made for payments by credit card or by cheque and, far worse, no attempt was made to differentiate between income generation and business sales. I was unable, however, to discover what policy and planning implications the Director drew from his study.

The second example concerns a Caribbean island where a team of consultants produced a multiplier of over 2 for total tourism expenditure. If correct, this would mean that tourist spending had generated a level of income far in excess of the national income of the country concerned. Not even the most fervent advocates of tourism would wish to make such a claim.

Weaknesses and limitations of multipliers

Despite the problems caused by the intrusion of misleading and mischievous multipliers, the technique can produce valuable information for
policymakers and planners. Obviously, the accuracy of the results
depends on the adequacy of the data. The old adage of 'rubbish in,
rubbish out' applies to multiplier work as much as other forms of analysis
and the lack of good data in particular key areas often necessitates carrying out expensive field surveys.

Apart from data difficulties, the accuracy of the results depends on how
well the model has been specified and how sensitively the results are
interpreted. It is usually necessary, for example, to make assumptions
which may, to some extent, be unrealistic. Although these points are
documented in the literature,[6] the most important ones deserve mention
here.

First, multiplier models are designed to measure the impact of changes
in economies in which there are some unemployed resources, i.e. they
assume that supply is elastic in all sections of the economy and in consequence that increases in demand can be met by increases in output from
the same section which provided the previous inputs required. In practice
this may not be so if large changes in demand occur and consequently
resources may have to be diverted from other uses (with a consequent fall
in output elsewhere) or else some goods and services may have to be
imported from outside the economy with a consequent loss of currency
by the economy. The multiplier is not designed to measure the effects of
such substantial changes nor the opportunity costs which they entail to
the economy.

Second, and closely related to this latter point, multiplier analysis
assumes that no relative changes will occur between suppliers within an
economy *either* because of their inability to supply additional goods and
services *or* because of changes in technology. This problem has worried
economists for some time and many improvements have been introduced
in recent years to modify and even overcome these operational constraints. In the same manner, current research is helping to resolve other
problems, including those relating to possible changes in local consumer
spending patterns as a result of additional tourism.

Perhaps the major criticism levied at multiplier analysis is the *suitability*
of this technique for analysing the impact of tourism. As previously mentioned, multiplier analysis treats all factors of production as having zero
opportunity costs to society in terms of what they could produce
elsewhere in the economy, i.e. multiplier analysis provides little or no
information about whether or not the use of these resources in tourism is
economically efficient from the point of view of society as a whole in the

Table 2.1 Tourism income multipliers in small island economies

	Country	Tourism income multiplier
1	Dominica	1.20
2	Bermuda	1.03
3	Hong Kong	1.02
4	Indian Ocean islands	0.95–1.03
5	Hawaii	0.90–1.30
6	Antigua	0.88
7	Bahamas	0.78
8	Fiji	0.69
9	Cayman Islands	0.65
10	British Virgin Islands	0.58

Sources:
1 Bryden, J. M., *Tourism and Development*, Cambridge University Press, 1973.
2 Archer, B. H. and Wanhill, S. R. C., *Tourism in Bermuda*, a report to the Bermuda Government, 1980.
3 Archer, B. H., *Tourism in Hong Kong*, a report to the Hong Kong Tourist Association, 1976.
4 Archer, B. H., unpublished reports to the World Bank and Commonwealth Secretariat.
5 Craig, P. C., 'Future growth of Hawaiian tourism', PhD Thesis, 1963.
6 Bryden, *op. cit.*, reference 1.
7 Archer, B. H., *Tourism in the Bahamas and Bermuda*, University of Wales Press, 1977.
8 Varley, R. C. G., *Tourism in Fiji: Some Economic and Social Problems*, University of Wales Press, 1976.
9 Bryden, *op. cit.*, reference 1.
10 Bottomley, A. *et. al.*, 'Is tourist residential development worthwhile? – The Anegada Project', *Social and Economic Studies*, 25, 1976.

economy concerned. Despite claims to the contrary, multiplier analysis does not measure the *long-run* benefits gained by an economy from an expansion of tourism.

The 'value' of tourism multipliers

What value have tourism multipliers? They measure the present economic performance of the tourism industry and the short-run economic effects of changes in the level of tourism. They are designed as an aid to

Table 2.2 Tourism income multipliers in US states and counties

	State or county	Tourism income multiplier
1	Hawaii	0.90–1.30
2	Missouri	0.88
3	Walworth County, Wisconsin	0.77
4	Grand County, Colorado	0.60
5	Door County, Wisconsin	0.55
6	Sullivan County, PA	0.44
7	Southwestern Wyoming	0.39–0.53

Sources:
1 Craig, P. C., 'Future growth of Hawaiian tourism', PhD Thesis, 1963.
2 Harmston, F. K., 'The importance of 1976 tourism to Missouri', *Business and Government Review*, X (3), May–June 1969, pp. 5–12.
3 Kalter, R. J. and Lord, W. B., 'Measurement of the impact of recreation investments on a local economy', *American Journal of Agricultural Economics, 50* (2), 1968, pp. 243–56.
4 Lovegrove, R. E. and Rodhy, D. D., 'Effects of fishing and hunting expenditures on a local Colorado economy', *Annals of Regional Science, 6* (2), 1972, pp. 108–16.
5 Strang, W. A., *Recreation and the Local Economy: An Input–Output Model of a Recreation–Orientated Economy*, Technical Report No. 4, The University of Wisconsin Sea Grant Program, Madison, October 1970.
6 Gamble, H. B., 'Community income from outdoor recreation', a paper presented to the Governor's Conference on Recreation and Parks, Ocean City, Maryland, 19 May 1965.
7 Harmston, F. K., 'Indirect effect of traveller expenditures in a western community', in the *Dude Rancher*, 1960.

study the economic impact of tourism expenditure on business turnover, incomes, employment, public sector revenue and imports and, in some cases, in the light of policy objectives how this effect compares with an equivalent increase in demand for the output of other sectors. They are concerned with the effects of short-run adjustments to a change in tourism expenditure and can provide a wealth of information of value to policymakers and planners. The number of impact studies has increased considerably in recent years and the quantity of data available now permits some generalizations to be made about the size (or value) of multipliers under varying conditions.

The value of a multiplier depends on the nature of the economy concerned and on the degree to which the sectors which supply tourists trade with other sectors in the economy. Table 2.1 shows the tourism income

Table 2.3 Tourism income multipliers in UK counties and regions

Area	Tourism income multiplier
Counties and regions	
1 Gwynedd, North Wales	0.37
2 Cumbria	0.35–0.44
3 South West England	0.33–0.47
4 Greater Tayside	0.32
5 East Anglian Coast	0.32
6 Lothian Region	0.29
7 Isle of Skye	0.25–0.41
(cf. US states and counties)	0.39–0.90

Sources:
1 Archer, B. H., Shea, Sheila and de Vane, R., *Tourism in Gwynedd: An Economic Study*, Cardiff: Wales Tourist Board, 1974.
2 Archer, B. H., *Tourism in Carlisle and Kendal*, Cumbria County Council, March 1979, and Archer, B. H. and Jones, D. R., *Tourism in Appleby, Keswick and Sedbergh*, Cumbria County Council, February 1977.
3 Edwards, S. L., Jackson, B. G., Ankers, M. G. and Dennis, S. J., *Tourism in the South West Region: Methodological report*, London: Department of the Environment, 1976.
4 Tourism and Recreation Research Unit, *The Economic Impact of Tourism: A Case of Study in Great Tayside*, University of Edinburgh, 1975.
5 Archer, B. H., de Vane, R. and Moore, J. H., *Tourism in the Coastal Strip of East Anglia*, London: Department of the Environment, 1977.
6 Vaughan, R., *The Economic Impact of Tourism in Edinburgh and the Lothian Region 1976*, Scottish Tourist Board, 1977.
7 Brownrigg, M. and Greig, M. A., *The Economic Impact of Tourist Spending in Skye*, Special Report No. 13, Highlands and Islands Development Board, December 1974.

multipliers obtained from a number of studies carried in small island economies during recent years.

Those with values near or above unity fall into two categories: (a) countries such as Dominica, Hong Kong and some Indian Ocean islands, which have well developed linkages within the economy either to an agricultural base or, in the case of Hong Kong, to a manufacturing base; and (b) countries such as Bermuda and Bahamas, with a high value-added on the goods and service provided to tourists. Countries near the lower end of the range, such as the Cayman Islands and British Virgin Islands, have few sectoral linkages and high leakages.

Table 2.2 shows the tourist income multipliers in a number of US states and counties.

Table 2.4 Tourism income multipliers in UK towns and villages

Area	Tourism income multiplier
1 Carlisle	0.40
2 Great Yarmouth	0.33
3 Kendal	0.28
4 Appleby	0.25
5 Sedbergh	0.25
6 Keswick	0.24
7 Towns and villages in Wales	0.18–0.47

Sources:
1 and 3   Archer, B. H., *Tourism in Carlisle and Kendal*, Cumbria County Council, March 1979.
2   Archer, B. H., de Vane, R. and Moore, J. H., *Tourism in the Coastal Strip of East Anglia*, Department of the Environment, 1977.
4, 5 and 6   Archer, B. H. and Jones, D. R., *Tourism in Appleby, Keswick and Sedbergh*, Cumbria County Council, February 1977.
7   Archer, B. H. and Shea, Sheila, *Grant Assisted Tourism Projects in Wales: An Evaluation*, Wales Tourist Board, 1980.

As in the case of small countries, the range reflects the extent to which the sectors of the economy are linked together, and the smaller economies are found near the bottom of the scale. It is interesting to compare the US figures with those for counties, regions and towns in the UK (Tables 2.3 and 2.4).

The UK areas have lower multiplier values than US states and counties, and this is largely a reflection of the extent to which these regions and counties trade with the rest of the country. In every case the impact of tourism expenditure is diminished by the high leakages of business payments to firms located outside the region.

Perhaps the most important conclusions that can be drawn from this paper are that, despite its weaknesses and limitations, multiplier analysis is a powerful and valuable tool for analysing the impact of tourism. Many criticisms levelled at the technique apply equally well to other forms of economic analysis and, if the methodology is not abused, multiplier analysis can provide a wealth of useful data for policymakers. Most of the misleading and, I hope, all the mischievous applications have been carried out by non-specialists. The increasing number of rigorous multiplier studies in recent years provides sufficient evidence to refute the erroneous nature of much of this earlier work and illustrates the range and depth of information which the technique can yield. Much research remains to be done in both methodology and application, and I hope that some of the younger researchers especially will take the opportunity to advance the study of multipliers still further.

References

1   See, for example, Archer, B. H., *Tourism Multipliers: The State of the Art*, University of Wales Press, 1977.
2   Kahn, R. F. 'The relation of home investment to unemployment', *Economic Journal*, 41, 1931, pp. 173–98.
3   Keynes, J. M., 'The Multiplier', *The New Statesman and Nation*, 1 April 1933, pp. 405–7.
4   Leontief, W., *Input–Output Economics*, New York: Oxford University Press, 1966.
5   More, F. T. and Petersen, K. W., 'Regional analysis: an inter-industry model of Utah', *The Review of Economics and Statistics*, 37, 1955, pp. 368–83.
6   See, for example, Archer, B. H., *op. cit.*, reference 1, pp. 35–44.

Acknowledgement

This paper was originally presented to an international conference on trends in tourism planning and development at the University of Surrey in September 1982.

Postscript

Since this paper was written in 1982 there have been many articles and study reports based upon the use of multiplier analysis. Whereas the majority of these publications relied upon existing modelling techniques and made no new contributions to either methodology or the underlying conceptual framework, a small number of papers contained new ideas and developments of methodology. These new contributions are described in the context of previous developments in a recent state of the art paper by Archer and Fletcher.[1]

Most of the recent developments in multiplier analysis have been concerned with improving the efficiency of the models and overcoming some of the inherent weaknesses and limitations of the various techniques. Of particular importance in this context is the work of Wanhill[2] in constructing a matrix of sectoral capacity constraints to channel the effects of additional demand into the import sectors when the full capacity of each relevant sector was reached. The imposition of capacity constraints can significantly alter the size of multipliers. For a recent review of the application of input–output analysis for studying the impact of tourism see Fletcher.[3]

Multiplier models have become increasingly disaggregated. Indeed, the amount of disaggregation possible seems to depend only upon the amount of data available. Similarly the range of information which can be obtained from the model about the impact of tourism depends upon the range of sectors used in the model and the number of different tourist expenditure categories available. A study of Jamaica in 1984, for example, used twenty-seven different categories of tourist arrivals in order to assess the economic importance of each type.[4] In most cases, however, changing the number of categories or the number of sectors in the economy will not significantly affect the magnitude of the multiplier. However, research by S. S. Milne[5] has shown that disaggregating the model down to the level of individual establishments does affect the size of sectoral multipliers and provide a more accurate assessment of the value of the multiplier. Disaggregating the model to this extent, however, may breach the confidentiality of the data.

The large number of new studies undertaken since 1982 has enabled a reassessment to be made of some earlier conclusions. In particular the relative effects of factors affecting the first round impact has been re-examined by Archer.[6] Analysis of existing studies showed that the principal factor influencing the overall value-added in the first round was the magnitude of the linkages in the economy. Surprisingly, insufficient evidence exists at this stage to generalize about the part played by the size of the economy or by leakages out of the system. Many new studies in various parts of the world are currently in progress and it is hoped that the results of these projects will help to resolve some of the remaining uncertainties and perhaps improve still further the methodological framework.

Further References

1   Archer, B. H. and Fletcher, J. E., 'Multiplier analysis in tourism', *Cahiers du Tourisme*, Serie C, no. 103, April 1990.
2   Wanhill, S. R. C., 'Tourism multipliers under capacity constraints', *Service Industries Journal*, 8, 1988, pp. 136–42.
3   Fletcher, J. E., 'Input–output analysis and tourism impact studies', *Annals of Tourism Research*, 16, 1989, pp. 541–56.

4 Fletcher, J. E., *The Economic Impact of International Tourism on the Economy of Jamaica*, Report to the Government of Jamaica, USAID, UNDP/WTO, 1985.
5 Milne, S. S., 'Differential multipliers', *Annals of Tourism Research*, 14, 1987, pp. 499–515.
6 Archer, B. H., 'Tourism and Island Economies', in Cooper, C. P. (ed), *Progress in Tourism, Recreation and Hospitality Management* (London: Belhaven Press), 1989, pp. 125–34.

3 Can the tourist-area life cycle be made operational?

K. Michael Haywood

Considerable attention has been given in the tourism literature to the belief that tourist areas not only change over time but change for the worse.[1] Conceptualizers of this inevitable change characterize tourist areas as passing through life stages that progress from birth to death.[2] Represented by the S-shaped logistic curve, which has its basis and acceptance in biological studies, Butler has suggested that the life cycle is comprised of the following stages – an exploration stage, an involvement stage, a development stage, a consolidation stage, a stagnation stage and either a decline stage or rejuvenation stage.[3] Figure 3.1 illustrates this typical cycle.

Currently the life-cycle concept seems to be enjoying a high degree of acceptance. Researchers such as Hovinen and Mayer-Arendt have employed the concept to explain the rise and fall of a variety of tourist destinations.[4] The overall simplicity of the concept and its life-to-death

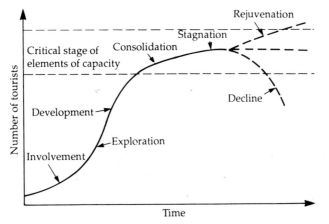

Figure 3.1 Stages in the tourist area life cycle
Source: Butler, *op. cit.*, reference 2

analogy have also helped reorientate thinking about tourist areas by suggesting new relationships that otherwise may not have been obvious. For example, Cohen's classification of tourists suggests that a destination will be initially visited by a few 'drifters' and 'explorers' followed by large numbers of 'individual mass tourists' and 'organized mass tourists'.[5] As such the tourist-area life cycle serves as a descriptive model of the stages of market acceptance, and represents the 'supply' view of the diffusion model. However, the true test of the importance of the life cycle must be based on its possible use as a tool for the planning and management of tourist areas. As Butler emphasizes:

> Tourist attractions are not infinite and timeless but should be viewed and treated as finite and possibly non-renewable resources. They could then be more carefully protected and preserved. The development of the tourist area could be kept within predetermined capacity limits, and its potential competitiveness maintained over a longer period.[6]

If the tourist-area life cycle is to be used as a management or planning tool, however, it must first be made operational. In other words, is it possible to determine or predict unambiguously the exact position or stage of a tourist area? Does knowledge of the life-cycle stage help in determining specific management actions? In an attempt to answer these questions this paper identifies six major conceptual and measurement decisions necessary for making the tourist-area life cycle operational. The paper concludes with some thoughts on the evolution of tourist areas as related to the need for tourism planning and management.

Concept and measurement

Six operational decisions

In order to make the tourist-area life cycle operational six major conceptual and measurement decisions need to be considered:

- unit of analysis;
- relevant market;
- pattern and stages of the tourist area of life cycle;
- identification of the area's stage in the life cycle;
- determination of the unit of measurement; and
- determination of the relevant time unit.

1   Unit of analysis

What is the definition of a tourist area and how can it be clearly delineated? Should the tourist-area life cycle be undertaken for a specific region, a city or town, a designated area within the city or town, hotels or other specific tourist facilities? It is surprising that little attention in the tourism literature has been given to the identification of the most appropriate unit or units of analysis. Defining and delineating the unit of analysis for a resort area is the first and most crucial step in attempting to make the life cycle operational. While a life-cycle analysis could possibly be undertaken at any level, relationships among the life cycles of these various levels should also be considered. While no a priori rule can be established as to the 'correct' unit of analysis, selection of the unit(s) of analysis should be based on need and intended use of the information.

2 Relevant market

Most applications of the tourist-area life cycle assume implicitly that the tourist market is homogeneous. This assumption ignores the possibility of sequential entry into distinctly different market segments, each of which can be further segmented according to tourists' degree of innovativeness or other relevant tourist characteristics.

While most tourist-area life cycle studies have focused on visitation at the total market level, there are occasions in which it may be appropriate and important to consider the resort-area life cycle by market type (e.g. domestic versus international tourists), distribution method (e.g. travel agent versus independent booking) or market segment (e.g. family versus corporate group).

3 Pattern and stages of tourist-area life cycle

The most common pattern of the life cycle is the S-shaped logistic function, although this is only one of many possible empirical patterns.[7] Even Butler suggests that the 'exploration' and 'involvement' stages may be of minor significance for an instant resort such as Cancun, Mexico.[8] Hovinen indicates that 'Lancaster County (Pennsylvania) shows significant departures from Butler's postulated "exploration", "consolidation" and "stagnation" stages as well as from the shape of his postulated curve of growth of numbers of tourists through time.'[9]

4 Identifying tourist area's stage in the life cycle

Two key questions face those who attempt to use the tourist-area life cycle concept:

- how to determine the stage of a tourist area; and
- how to determine when a tourist area moves from one stage to another.

Given that time-series data rarely obey the theoretical pattern of a smooth curve, and that the S-shaped curve is only one of a number of possible life-cycle patterns, it is not at all clear whether a tourist area's position in its cycle and its shift from one stage to another can be identified simply by observing the historical pattern of the number of tourists.

5 Determining the unit of measurement

While the tourist-area life cycle is based on the size of the tourist population, there are still a number of unresolved issues. The first revolves around the issue of carrying capacity or saturation level. As Hovinen says:

> A single carrying capacity threshold clearly does not exist; instead an area's capacity consists of different cultural and natural elements which vary both spatially within the county and temporally throughout the year.[10]

Furthermore, carrying capacity may be more a perceptual issue. Residents may believe that the number of tourists may be exceeded before the end of the development stage whereas some economic planners may believe that the carrying capacity may far exceed the numbers of tourists reached during either a consolidation or a stagnation stage. This suggests that if the number of tourists is to be used as a measure, consideration should be given to such ameliorating variables as:

- the length of stay;
- dispersion of tourists within and throughout the tourist area;
- characteristics of the tourist; and
- the time of year in which the visit is made.

The second issue concerns the appropriateness of using a tourist-expenditure model instead of tourist population to determine the shape, pattern and stage of the life cycle. If such a measure were used a subsequent question would be whether this expenditure should measure unit sales (e.g. number of visits to a park or a museum) or dollar values. Then, of course, there is the question as to whether the analysis of this expenditure should be based on actual expenditure or adjusted expenditure. For example, should they be adjusted to per capita expenditure? Corrected for seasonal or cyclical periods? Adjusted for general economic conditions (current versus real prices), etc?

Measurement could go beyond the typical visitation and expenditure measures and include such measures as market-share figures or profitability. For example, individual businesses that reach maturity or find themselves in a stagnation stage tend to experience a serious decline in profitability, even before reaching this stage. It is very difficult for a company or even a tourist area to rejuvenate unless the necessary resources, particularly financial resources, are available. The inevitability of the decline stage is in large part due to a lack of resources and resourcefulness.

6 Determining the relevant time unit

Most tourist-area cycles are based on annual data. Yet it is not clear why the analysis should be limited to this unit of time. In many instances, it may be appropriate to develop a tourist-area cycle based on quarterly or monthly data. Given that the shorter the time period the higher the likelihood of seasonal and other fluctuation, it may be appropriate to use some form of moving average. However, this in no way denies the need for more longitudinal data. If the tourist-area cycle-of-evolution has a major shortcoming it is the lack of empirical data over the long term.

Evolution of tourist areas

Tourism planning and management

Evolution of tourism areas is of critical importance for tourism planners and managers. The evolution process has a positive or negative effect not only on the basic attractiveness of the area and its tourism resources, but on the people who live and work in the community, on the visitors who come into the area, and on the tourism industry as a continued investment opportunity. Consequently, it is often necessary to make adjustments to ensure that the industry serves the needs of all groups and publics.[11] Understanding the process of tourist area evolution and being able to predict change are also important because the cost of reacting usually increases as the need for change becomes more obvious. Moreover, the benefit from tourist area planning is the highest for the tourist area that utilizes it.

The starting point for analysing tourist-area evolution should be a framework of structured analysis. The reason for this is that tourism, like any industry, is deeply rooted in an underlying economic and political structure which is comprised of seven major economic and social forces. The collective strength of these forces determines the ultimate success of any tourist area, and hence its evolution.

1   *Rivalry among existing tourist areas.*   Tourist areas are in competition for the prized possession and scarcest resource of all – the tourist. This is accomplished by competing for top-of-mind-awareness among

selected market segments through advertising and creation of images, pricing, new attractions, promises of increased service and hospitality.

2   *Developers and development of new tourist areas.*   New entrants to the tourism industry introduce new and novel attractions and amenities. Coupled with sufficient marketing clout to attract visitors, visitation rates and profitability in existing tourist areas could suffer.

3   *Substitutes for the tourism/travel experience.*   The tourism industry competes in a broad sense, within the leisure industry. For example, people can opt to travel vicariously at home by using their VCR and renting movies; or, they can install their own swimming pool in their backyard. Products or services that provide virtually the same function as travel and are perceived as having a better price/value relationship are candidates for substitution.

4   *Environmentalists and concerned publics who oppose tourism or tourism development.*   Tourism is a phenomenon that takes place, is produced or is performed within people's communities or home surroundings. Moreover, tourism utilizes resources which many people deem scarce, fragile and precious. Consequently, there exists a desire to protect and save these resources either from developers who might greedily and uncaringly exploit them, or from visitors who may not fully appreciate their symbolism and importance. These protectionist forces can curtail development and change; or, at the very least, encourage the aesthetic sensibilities of developers and visitors.

5   *Transportation companies, tour operators, travel intermediaries, accommodation and suppliers – their bargaining power.*   The tourism industry consists of a wide variety of interrelated and interdependent businesses that facilitate and direct visitors to specific destinations. These businesses can either increase or decrease the cost of travel to and within particular tourist areas. Some of these intermediaries are large companies with considerable bargaining power. As a result they can either encourage or discourage travel to a particular area; and they can squeeze profitability out of an industry, e.g. tour operators bargain with hotels for reduced room rates by trading off large blocks of guaranteed room nights.

6   *Tourists – their needs, wants, perceptions, expectations and price sensitivity.* The travelling public is large, diverse and demanding. No tourist area can compete successfully without carefully considering who its visitors are or who it wants its visitors to be. Whatever the situation a tourist area must offer and be able to deliver a 'tourist experience' that is unique and intensely satisfying. Experiences that are second rate quickly result in a declining tourist base.

7   *Governmental, political and regulatory bodies and forces.*   Depending on economic and social priorities, governments have a profound impact

on the success of the industry. Policies and regulations with regard to taxation, education, immigration and customs, transport, marketing, culture, environment, development, financial assistance, and industry–government cooperation can either assist industry growth and development or strangle it.

Discussion

Any significant change in these seven underlying forces will have considerable impact on a tourist area. For this reason, it can be argued that the tourist-area life-cycle model, as it is currently viewed, i.e. as a biological life cycle, provides insufficient insight into the development of policy and planning for tourism areas. It does not consider how the tourist area or competing areas can affect the shape of the curve; and if the life cycle is taken as given, whether an undesirable self-fulfilling prophecy is likely to occur.

An intriguing alternative to the tourist-area life cycle was proposed by Gross, who suggested the evolution of species as described by the theory of natural selection as a model of the evolution of products in a free market economy.[12] The basic concepts of the Darwinian natural selection theory and tourism development are strikingly similar. The individual organism in the evolution theory is analogous to a tourist area. The concept of 'variation' of species is analogous to the differences among tourist areas. The concept of 'overpopulation' relates to the tremendous number and explosion of tourist-area choices. The 'struggles for existence' and the 'survival of the fittest' are quite descriptive of the tourism marketplace in which only a few tourist areas are ever successful.

The result of too many tourist areas (overcapacity) is competition among species (tourist areas). In this competition, those best suited to the 'environment' (the marketplace) have the best chance for success (survival and growth). The important lessons from this analogy to 'tourist area evolution' are in some of the survival strategies proposed by the biologists:

- 'Whenever there is strong competition, specialization undoubtedly gives an advantage.'[13] This specialization is an important rationale for tourist-area specialization.
- As the environment changes, the characteristics that determine suitability also change, causing evolutionary development. This statement emphasizes, more than anything else, the need for long-range planning of tourist area strategy.
- Highly specialized species that are adopted for one specific set of environmental conditions are less capable of adjusting themselves to sudden or drastic changes of environment than are unspecialized forms.[14] This conclusion suggests the intriguing hypothesis that

tourist areas aimed at narrow market segments or specialized applications have shorter 'life cycles' than more broadly based tourist areas.

In conclusion, if tourist area planners and managers are to be more effective they must broaden their thinking about tourist-area evolution, and how it can best be managed given the economic, political and other forces that shape it.

References

1   Rosenow, John E. and Pulsipher, Gerreld L., *Tourism: The Good, the Bad, and the Ugly*, Lincoln, Nebraska: Century Three Press, 1979; Turner, Louis and Ash, John, *The Golden Hordes*, London: Constable, 1975; and Young, G., *Tourism, Blessing or Blight?* Harmondsworth: Penguin, 1973.
2   Butler, R. W., 'The concept of a tourist area cycle of evolution: implications for management of resources', *Canadian Geographer*, vol. 24, 1980, pp. 5–12; Christaller, W., 'Some considerations of tourism location in Europe: the peripheral regions – underdeveloped countries – recreation areas', *Papers of the Regional Science Association*, vol. 12, 1963, pp. 95–105; and Stansfield, C., 'Atlantic City and the resort cycle', *Annals of Tourism Research*, vol. 5, no. 2, 1978, pp. 238–51.
3   *Ibid*, Butler.
4   Hovinen, G. V. 'A tourist cycle in Lancaster County, Pennsylvania', *Canadian Geographer*, vol. 25, no. 3, 1981, pp. 283–6; and Meyer-Arendt, K., 'The Grand Isle, Louisiana Resort Cycle', *Annals of Tourism Research*, vol. 12, 1985, pp. 449–65.
5   Cohen, E., 'Towards a sociology of international tourism', *Social Research*, vol. 39, 1972, pp. 164–82.
6   Butler, *op. cit.*, reference 2.
7   Rogers, E. M., 'New product adoption and diffusion', *Journal of Consumer Research*, vol. 2, March 1976, pp. 290–330.
8   Butler, *op. cit.*, reference 2.
9   Hovinen, *op. cit.*, reference 4.
10   Hovinen, *op. cit.*, reference 4.
11   Haywood, K. M., 'Criteria for evaluating the social performance of tourism development projects', *Tourism as a Factor on National and Regional Development*, Department of Geography, Trent University, Peterborough, pp. 74–9.
12   Gross, I., 'Toward a general theory of product evolution: a rejection of the "product life cycle" concept', *MSI Working Paper*, no. P43–10, September 1968.
13   Mayr, E., *Systematics and the Origin of Species*, New York: Dover, 1964.
14   *Ibid*.

Further reading

Further reading on forecasting the future of tourism in *Tourism Management* 1980–9

Archer, B.A., 'Forecasting demand: quantitative and intuitive techniques', vol. 1, no. 1, March 1980, pp. 5–12.

Choy, D. J. L., 'Forecasting tourism revisited', vol. 5, no. 3, September 1984, pp. 171–6.

Emery, F., 'Alternative futures in tourism', vol. 2, no. 1, March 1981, pp. 49–67.

Liu, J. C. 'Hawaii tourism to the year 2000 – a Delphi forecast', vol. 9, no. 4, December 1988, pp. 279–90.

Martin, C. A. and Witt, S. F., 'Forecasting performance', vol. 9, no. 4, December 1988, pp. 326–9.

Martin, W. H. and Mason, S., 'Social trends and tourism futures', vol. 8, no. 2, June 1987, pp. 166–8.

Schwaninger, M., 'Forecasting leisure and tourism – scenario projections for 2000–2010', vol. 5, no. 4, December 1984, pp. 250–7.

van Doorn, J. W. M., 'Tourism forecasting and the policymaker', vol. 5, no. 1, March 1984, pp. 24–39.

van Doorn, J. W. M., 'Scenario writing – a method for long-term tourism forecasting', vol. 7, no. 1, March 1986, pp. 33–49.

Veal, A. J., 'The future of leisure', vol. 1, no. 1, March 1980, pp. 42–55.

Further reading on tourism impacts and significance in *Tourism Management* 1980–9

Cooper, M. J. and Pigram, J., 'Tourism and the Australian economy', vol. 5, no. 1, March 1980, pp. 2–12.

Coppock, J. T., 'Tourism and conservation', vol. 3, no. 4, December 1982, pp. 270–6.

Duffield, B. S., 'Tourism: the measurement of economic and social impact', vol. 3, no. 4, December 1982, pp. 248–55.

Duffield, B. S. and Long, J., 'Role of tourism in the economy of Scotland', vol. 5, no. 4, December 1984, pp. 258–68.

Haukeland, J. V., 'Sociocultural impacts of tourism in Scandinavia', vol. 5, no. 3, September 1984, pp. 207–14.

Latimer, H., 'Developing-island economies – tourism v. agriculture', vol. 6, no. 1, March 1985, pp. 32–42.

Pearce, D. G., 'Estimating visitor expenditure: a review and a New Zealand case study', vol. 2, no. 4, December 1981, pp. 240–52.

Travis, A. S., 'Managing the environmental and cultural impacts of tourism and leisure development', vol. 3, no. 4, December 1982, pp. 256–62.

Vanhove, N., 'Tourism and employment', vol. 2, no. 3, September 1981, pp. 162–75.

Witt, S. F., 'Economic impact of tourism on Wales', vol. 8, no. 4, December 1987, pp. 306–16.

Further reading on tourism planning and development in *Tourism Management* 1980–9

Baud-Bovy, M., 'New concepts in planning for tourism and recreation', vol. 3, no. 4, December 1982, pp. 308–13.

Curry, N. R., 'Economics in leisure planning: limitations in English practice', vol. 1, no. 4, December 1980, pp. 219–30.

Getz, D., 'Models in tourism planning – towards integration of theory and practice', vol. 7, no. 1, March 1986, pp. 21–32.

Haywood, K. M., 'Responsible and responsive tourism planning in the community', vol. 9, no. 2, June 1988, pp. 105–18.

Kobasic, A., 'Lessons from planning in Yugoslavia's tourist industry', vol. 2, no. 4, December 1980, pp. 233–9.

Latimer H., 'Project evaluation: the need for a rigorous approach', vol. 1, no. 1, March 1980, pp. 30–41.

Murphy, P. E., 'Tourism as a community industry – an ecological model of tourism development', vol. 4, no. 3, September 1983, pp. 180–93.

Pearce, D. G., 'Tourism and regional development in the European Community', vol. 9, no. 1, March 1988, pp. 13–22.

Ritchie, J. R. B., 'Consensus policy formulation in tourism', vol. 9, no. 3, September 1988, pp. 192–212.

Travis, A. S., 'Tourism development and regional planning in East Mediterranean countries', vol. 1, no. 4, December 1980, pp. 207–18.

Part Two

Business Growth and Development

Three case histories published in *Tourism Management* in the early 1980s have been brought together in this part of the book with short postscripts, which take the stories to the end of the decade. Two of them portray commercial firms, one a cooperative non-profit making organization. While strategic decisions in two of them led to continued expansion of their involvement in travel and tourism, in one they resulted in a much reduced presence in the market.

Derek Kartun, at the time of writing a travel writer in London, recorded the first three decades of a remarkable French enterprise in 'Club Méditerranée's growth and policies'. Many of the original features of the Club have remained, as it grew further and diversified in the 1980s, and in 1990 it celebrated forty years in business.

A contrasting story is told by Donald Stewart of Queen's College, Glasgow, in 'The growth and development of Grand Metropolitan'. A leading innovator in the UK hotel business and at various times a major operator in London, the UK and worldwide, by the end of the decade the company retained only a minor interest in its original business.

In 'Swiss Travel Saving Fund', Hans Teuscher, now Director of the Fund, outlines the history of a unique institution of social tourism in Europe. Located in the most prosperous country in the world, the organization continues to grow and develop, in spite of Switzerland's changing socioeconomic structure, and in 1989 celebrated its fiftieth anniversary.

Further cases of travel and tourism organizations published in *Tourism Management* from 1980–9 are listed on page 67.

4 Club Méditerranée's growth and policies

Derek Kartun

Viewed as a hotel chain (a not altogether adequate description), the Club Méditerranée is the largest in France, the second largest outside the USA, and the thirteenth worldwide. Its origins thirty-one years ago were modest, romantic, and suffused in ideology and a peculiarly French improvisatory style. No other major organization in the tourist industry can have started in such a manner, for such a purpose, or with such ideas.

The Club – which is not a club in any meaningful sense of the term – goes back to 1950, when Gerard Blitz and a few friends set it up as a non-profit making organization under a French law of 1901, and took off for a holiday in tents at Alcudia on the coast of Majorca. In the first full year of operation, 2300 people were accommodated. The atmosphere was left-wing, democratic, even populist. There were no frills. The emphasis was on comradeship and sport (as it still is). Comfort was not on the agenda. In 1954, the tents began to give way to straw huts. In 1956, the first mountain location was established at Leysin, in Switzerland. It was not until 1965 that the Club opened its first purpose-built and permanent bungalow village, at Agadir in Morocco, with something approaching (but not reaching) modern standards of comfort. Agadir has been the model for the majority of the Club's developments since then – all of them based on the proposition that clients appreciate the simple life with minimal accommodation (in the sense that there are no fitted carpets, quality furniture, indirect lighting, or TV in the bedrooms).

Back in 1954, Gilbert Trigano, who had supplied Blitz's tents, joined the organization as Managing Director. Since then, he has been the principal architect, motive force and ideologist of the Club Méditerranée Group, of which he is now Chairman and Managing Director. His personal background is not without relevance. Born in 1920 and starting as a comedy writer for radio and an apprentice comedian, he played an active part in the French Resistance, and later joined the Communist *l'Humanité*. He then entered his father's tarpaulin manufacturing business and converted it to the making of camping equipment. This led him eventually into the Club Méditerranée organization.

Size and sales structure

In 1981, the Club Méditerranée owns or controls 191 holiday establishments in thirty countries, and has sales organizations or agents in twenty-nine countries. Most of the Club's facilities are referred to as 'villages' and consist of straw huts or bungalows in traditional building materials, each sleeping two people and grouped round the public facilities: pools, entertainment area and bar, restaurants, nightclub, sports facilities, administration, etc. Generally, the architecture is inspired by the traditions of the locality, but usually modified strongly by a clearly noticeable French sophistication of design. Most of the winter sports facilities, and a small number of others, are hotels, adapted to the Club formula. The Club hotel subsidiary, a leading company in the time-sharing field, was acquired by the Club in 1977, and offers apartments and studios for lease or sale. The Club also holds a 45 per cent interest in Valtur Servizzi, an Italian organization operating on similar lines and owning villages in ten locations in Italy, Greece and Tunisia. The total of 191 locations of these varied types offers (in March 1980) 67,830 beds.

The structure of the Club's sales network is eclectic and has been designed to meet the local traditions of the tourist industry, country by country, as well as to seize opportunities where they exist, sometimes in novel ways. Thus the Club terminated its arrangements with a Japanese agent in 1979 in order to set up its own marketing company in this potentially important market (see below). Although the Club has a New York office, in line with established American custom, direct sales account for only some 5 per cent of turnover, the balance coming through travel agents. In France, 65 per cent of sales are by direct mail or personal visits to the company's offices. For the balance, Havas is the main retailer.

In certain cases, a Club subsidiary both creates and manages local facilities, and also does the marketing. In Brazil, for instance, Club Méditerranée do Brasil (49 per cent Club Méditerranée, 51 per cent Unibanco Group) builds and manages the local villages (of which Itaparca, the first, was opened in 1979) and markets the product.

The formula

The present style of the Club reflects in certain respects the origins and ideology of its founders. Thus, efforts have been made to blur the normal relationship between staff and customers. The former are still referred to as GOs (for *Gentils Organisateurs* – to be rendered, perhaps, as Our Friends the Organizers) and the latter as GMs (for *Gentils Membres* – Our

Friends the Members of the Club). There is still a pleasing ritual whereby the entire staff is collectively presented to the guests and thanked for their efforts with a series of individual introductions, mingled with applause and cheers. There is no tipping. The populist tendency has weakened as the original ideological impetus has been lost, and the organization is exposed to new influences, including a high proportion of guests in the upper income brackets.

Traces of the Club's origins are nevertheless still to be observed. Nowadays, perhaps, they serve more to establish an *esprit de corps* among the staff than to do very much for the guests. But any observer must take note of the ideological factor in providing, at least in the early years, a stimulus and work ethic for the staff (many of whom are not professional catering and hotel workers), as well as a coherent public relations theme and general business 'personality'. It has also created within the Club villages an atmosphere which can most readily be likened to that aboard a single-class cruise ship, making for easy contact between guests and the rapid creation of holiday friendships.

The formula on offer is broadly similar at nearly all the Club's locations. The main emphasis is on sport and the pleasures of the table – a formula with a broad appeal, since the one activity can be seen as mitigating the other. Charges are inclusive of all sports (with some limited exceptions, such as horse riding in certain locations), all meals and unlimited wine. Only the bar makes charges, and since no money is handled in the villages – a romantically coloured but quite convenient attempt to escape from the pressures of capitalist society, dating from the early days – strings of beads are purchased, can be worn round the neck, and are used by guests in payment. Such details are part of the mystique and are not to be dismissed as trivialities when seeking to understand the Club's expansion.

The extent of the Club's commitment to sport, and the extensive facilities provided, is illustrated by its ownership of 431 tennis courts. Sailing is the leading sport with 1134 boats available to guests, served by over 500 instructors and assistants. Scuba diving, water skiing, and board sailing are also provided. At the twenty-two winter sports locations there are close to 600 qualified ski instructors. All this makes the Club Mediterranée probably the largest supplier of sporting facilities in the world.

Other activities provided are yoga and gymnastic classes, bridge, folk crafts, evening entertainments, discos and classical concerts. Meals are taken at 'communal' tables for eight guests, and the standards of the cuisine are very high, even in distant African or Caribbean villages. In a number of villages, there are special provisions for children.

At every village, touring facilities (for which additional charges are made) are available. Guests are encouraged and helped to get to know the country and to visit archaeological sites, local beauty spots, etc.

Table 4.1 Club Méditerranée performance, financial years 1975–80

	1975	1976	1977	1978	1979	1980
Net profit (FF '000)	40,079	51,778	61,000	71,903	83,741	106,274
No. of hotel days (000)	4,627	5,089	5,341	5,651	5,981	6,523
No. of beds	49,010	50,942	53,865	55,630	58,662	64,677
Occupancy (%)	69.05	70.64	71.19	71.65	72.87	71.80

Source: Annual Report 1979–80.

A majority of guests buy a package which (in Europe) generally involves a Club charter to the destination. In 1979, over half the clients were carried by charter and the rest either made their own way or were flown on scheduled flights or transported by rail.

The 'all-inclusive' nature of the Club's product renders it difficult to make valid price comparisons with generally available packages from the traditional type of tour operators carrying to the same destinations; any true comparison would need to evaluate such items as no-charge sports and other leisure activities, free wine, lack of tipping, etc. The Club seems to be perceived by its clients as being in the middle to upper price range, though because of the quite extensive differences in the product being offered, clients are possibly not inclined to make meaningful price comparisons with other packages.

Profitability and financing

The Club Méditerranée today is a public company whose shares are quoted on the Paris, Brussels, and Luxembourg exchanges. Slightly under 50 per cent of the equity is held by six major shareholders who are represented on the board, and the staff investment fund. The six are:

● Union des Assurances de Paris (leading insurance group);
● Crédit Lyonnais (second largest French bank);
● Banque de Paris et des Pays Bas (leading private investment and merchant bank);
● Compagnie Financière (private investment bank, Baron Edmond de Rothschild);

- CEMP Investments Ltd (Seagram Group, Montreal); and
- IFI International (Agnelli family holding company).

The Group's accounts for the year ended 31 October 1980 show a net profit (unaudited) of FF106m (£9.6m at FF11/£) on a turnover of FF1,888m (£171m). The number of hotel days recorded in 1979–80 was 6,524,000. On 13 February 1981, the Club Mediterranée FF25 shares stood at FF410 on the Paris Bourse, valuing the company at FF1,200m (£109m).

Regarding new projects, the Club states:

As a general rule, the Club only takes a minority financial interest in the companies building new villages. However, it also provides its support in setting up the necessary long-term financial resources, which may come from various sources. In 1979, for example, the Club arranged for the private placing of three bond issues, on three continents:

- in the USA, an $8.5 loan;
- in Paris and Luxembourg, an $8m bond issue to finance Club Mediterranée Haiti; and
- in Malaysia, the Tourist Development Corporation made a Malaysian $10m issue with [the Club's] support, for the long-term financing of Holiday Villages of Malaysia.

The use of these loans will, of course, be spread over two and in some instances three years. The loans themselves complement the very substantial financing provided by the net cash flow of the Club and its subsidiaries.

The precise pattern of financing varies widely. In Bulgaria, state institutions have financed the Club's village 100 per cent. In Colorado, USA, financing is 100 per cent by the Club itself, primarily from the proceeds of the bond issue. At Sonora in Mexico, ownership of the facility is split between the state, private investors, and the Club. In Martinique there are no fewer than 240 local investors.

An organization such as the Club Mediterranée is a significant earner of foreign currency for many of the smaller territories where it operates. Its prestige is now such that it also operates as a magnet for further hotel investment and the creation of tourist facilities. Its foreign currency earnings for France itself amounted in 1978–9 to the equivalent of $68m.

World view and future policy

If the early expansion of the Club was marked by a mix of shrewd commercial opportunism, vaguely 'social' ideology, and sheer chance, there is nothing haphazard about its approach to its markets nowadays. The company's management has developed a clearly defined and well-articulated view of the world tourist market, its likely future development, and the Club's role within this broad perspective. Gilbert Trigano expresses it in the following way:

> We see the world as divided into three holiday 'lakes': the Mediterranean, the Caribbean, and the South China Sea. The major markets for tourism are to be found above and below these 'lakes'. They are Western Europe, North America, and Japan/Australia. The orientation of movements in the current phase is vertical – mainly from the north to south. There will also be a second phase, though we have no means of determining the precise moment when it will start – perhaps towards the turn of the century. This phase will witness major lateral movements of tourists from East to West and vice versa.

He explains that the Club has what he describes as a 'world vocation' – a commercial interest in tourism in all parts of the globe. It is reflected in the statistics: in 1974–5, 50.7 per cent of the visitors to the Club establishments were from France and 14.2 per cent from North America. By 1978–9, the French percentage had dropped to 45.6 per cent and the North American (on much larger figures) had advanced to 20.5 per cent. A similar internationalization of the Club's market can be observed within Europe.

The marketing strategy is also reflected in the Club's building programme. At the end of 1980, it was operating in sixteen locations which served mainly the western hemisphere. The building and opening programme for 1980–1 and immediately beyond includes five new projects for the western hemisphere out of a worldwide total of eleven. The eleven locations interestingly reflect the organization's global outlook: United Arab Emirates, Egypt, France, Brazil, Mexico, St Martin (West Indies), Haiti, Santo Domingo, Colorado (USA), New Caledonia, and Malaysia. A further nine locations will follow after these.

The total programme for the Far East, which started later than that in the western hemisphere, is advancing more slowly, though Trigano regards Japan as a major tourism target for the 1990s.

The Club's successful and rapidly expanding incursion into the North American tourism market renders it unique among non-American organizations, since no other non-American company has managed (if, indeed, anyone has tried) to capture a significant volume of North American business within the western hemisphere itself.

So much for the Club's 'horizontal' strategy. It has also developed a 'vertical' strategy. This consists of a broadening of the services on offer and, to a limited extent, a search for sources of revenue outside of, but related to, tourism proper.

Originally based entirely on the provision of low-cost, minimal accommodation in seaside villages, the Club has advanced in stages, as we have seen to encompass ski holidays, higher quality and further up-market seaside accommodation, and tours and 'adventure' packages. More recent developments include the running of hotels where sometimes only superficial aspects of the Club's original style can now be found. A further recent development has been the provision of time-sharing accommodation via the Club hotel subsidiary.

Since 1978, the Club has also entered the retail licensing field, granting the use of its name and logo to selected manufacturers of sun-protection products, sun glasses, and luggage, to which sport and leisure clothing and publishing will be added in the current year.

Postscript

In 1990, as the driving force behind Club Med, Gilbert Trigano, reached the age of seventy, the company celebrated forty years in business, and the annual report for the preceding year recorded a major improvement in its financial performance after some stagnation in the late 1980s.

- In 1989 the Club Mediterranée Group owned or controlled 234 establishments with more than 113,000 beds, accommodated 1.8 million guests, and employed 22,000 people worldwide.
- The Club was twelfth among the world's hotel chains but its 75,600 village beds made the Club the world's top holiday village organization, which received well over one million guests.
- In 1988–9 its turnover exceeded 7.5 billion and net income 365 million French francs, the number of hotel days passed 9 million, and the occupancy rate returned to over 70 per cent.
- Much of the original philosophy and the village as the core business have remained, but the Club has diversified its range of products significantly. The company expanded its Club Villas run on traditional hotel lines and its involvement in the time-share market through the Clubhotel; established the City Club, which combines a hotel, convention centre and a leisure time complex; moved into the incentive and corporate business markets. It is not only in the tour business, but also into sailing and cruising, through its first 'floating village', the sailing vessel Club Med 1.
- Operations and markets have been diversified geographically with a major thrust into North America, Asia and the Pacific, and no more than a third of the clientele of the villages are now French.
- Since 1982 the Club has operated in four largely autonomous geographical zones: Europe/Africa (based in Paris), North/Central America (based in New York), South America (based in Rio de Janeiro), and the Pacific/Asia/Indian Ocean (based in Tokyo).

5 The growth and development of Grand Metropolitan

Donald A. Stewart

The origins of Grand Metropolitan may be traced in three ways. Back in 1903 Grand Hotels (Mayfair) Limited was formed. In 1934 Mount Royal (Marble Arch) Limited was registered as a private company. Maxwell Joseph entered the hotel industry subsequent to the Second World War when, in 1948, he bought the Mandeville Hotel in Mandeville Place, London W1.

During the following decade additional hotels, mainly leaseholds, in the middle market range were acquired. The group was constituted as Grand Hotels (Mayfair) Limited but was operated as The Washington Group of Hotels – partly to attract transatlantic business and to create a market image. The group was run by Fred Kobler as Managing Director and Henry Edwards as General Manager.

In July 1957 Maxwell Joseph purchased Mount Royal (Marble Arch) Limited from Sir Bracewell Smith for £1.050m. At that time it was a lease-hold property with fifty-five years of the lease remaining, the ground rent being £40,000 per annum. Under the direction of Maxwell Joseph and with the help of Stanley Grinstead as Company Secretary (who had joined Mr Joseph's organization in that year), the profitability of the hotel improved to the extent that its value doubled within the space of four years.

In June 1961 Mount Royal (Marble Arch) Limited was converted to a public company. The Offer of Sale was an enormous success, being over-subscribed twenty-four times. The purchase and subsequent conversion to a public company of the Mount Royal was crucial to the career of Maxwell Joseph. As he said in a newspaper interview thirteen years later, 'It was the real turning point of my career'. He was then, in 1961, aged fifty-one.

In the same year Grand Hotels (Mayfair) Limited acquired Eglington Hotels (Scotland) Limited. In the following year the two groups were merged and the name of the company was changed to Grand Metropolitan Hotels Limited. In the three years subsequent to the merger additional hotels were acquired in London, in Scotland and in continental Europe. During this time Maxwell Joseph, by astute deployment of funds and effective systems of management, was able to build a position from which to launch a major series of acquisitions, mergers and takeovers.

Acquisitions and mergers 1966 to 1972

In July 1966 the directors of the drink and catering firm Levy & Franks approached Grand Metropolitan with a view to merger. The bid was relatively straightforward as latterly it had the unanimous backing of the Levy & Franks Board. The importance of the bid from the Grand Metropolitan view was that it marked the first stage in diversification away from hotels. The purchase of Levy & Franks brought with it the trade name of Chef and Brewer. This was an ideal vehicle to link in the public mind the twin activities of brewing and catering. In due course, subsequent to the acquisition of Truman and Watney, it became the main trading name for public house catering throughout the group.

In September 1967 the Bateman Catering Organization Limited was acquired. This represented an important move into the field of industrial catering which was to make considerable strides in the 1970s. With the acquisition, in the following year, of Midland Catering the group was well placed to increase its share of this expanding market.

In August 1969 the chance arose for Grand Metropolitan to bid for Express Dairy Limited. In a typically opportunistic move the company drew up and issued the offer documents. Control of Express was established in October of that year. Since 1945 it had been in the forefront of technological innovation in the dairy industry and it was an extremely important acquisition for Grand Metropolitan. At the time of the acquisition the net tangible assets of Express amounted to £22.7m, with pre-tax profits of £3.4m. By 1979 the sales of the milk and food division had reached £572m with trading profits of £27m.

In June 1970 the company bid for the issued share capital of the steakhouse chain Berni Inns Limited. The initial move was made by Berni who wished to acquire Chef and Brewer from Grand Metropolitan. Naturally the company did not wish to dispose of this recently acquired and profitable asset. The logic of the combination of the two catering companies each with a strong interest in the liquor trade was evident. It was thus agreed that Berni should come into the Grand Metropolitan fold.

Another firm which perceived the advantages of being connected with Grand Metropolitan was the leisure company Mecca. In the same month that negotiations were proceeding with Berni, informal discussions took place with Mecca. The outcome was that Mecca was incorporated in the group in September of that year. Within twelve months, therefore, the group had diversified considerably. The acquisitions, however, should not be perceived as part of a meticulously planned corporate strategy. Rather they were the result of opportunistic moves for companies which were on the market and saw advantage in being connected to a growing organization.

Maxwell Joseph and Stanley Grinstead had been interested in acquiring a brewery company as early as 1964 but it was not until 1971 that a suitable opportunity arose. When it did, in June 1971, it took eight weeks of protracted bidding to secure victory. The bid was hotly contested by Watney with the result that the final bid valued Truman at close to £50m compared with the opening bid of £34m. It was a crucial step in the fortunes of the company. It was by far the largest acquisition to date, it was the first which attracted a competing bid, and it gave the group entry to the hitherto tightly-knit brewing industry.

Almost immediately after the successful acquisition of Truman, Maxwell Joseph was persuaded to buy into Watney as a preliminary move to launching a full-scale bid for the third largest brewer in the UK. This he did in the following year and by July 1972 Grand Metropolitan had pulled off two brewery acquisitions within a year.

The acquisitions between 1966 and 1972 transformed the company from a medium-sized group in the hotel industry to a major industrial service group with interests in the food, drink and leisure industries backed by strong property assets. It was not until the Watney bid had been finalized that much thought was given to group corporate strategy. The first main task, which fell to Stanley Grinstead, was the reorganization of Watney. Essentially this was aimed at breaking down a highly centralized and functional management style, at the creation of a number of regional brewing companies and at decentralization wherever practicable. Although straightforward in conception the implementation of the new policies, to the point where they were clearly vindicated, took a full five years.

UK consolidation 1972 to 1980

1   *The re-structuring of IDV within the group.*   Prior to the acquisition of Watney, International Distillers and Vintners had been closely integrated with the parent company. Subsequent to the merger, however, the opportunity was taken to create a wines and spirits division in its own right, completely autonomous from the brewing company. This was achieved during the first two years subsequent to the merger –

1973 to 1975. A major contribution which IDV brought to the group was its wide exposure to world markets.

2   *The reorganization of the brewing division.*   In many ways this was the major objective of top management during the 1970s. From a position of relative weakness prior to the merger, Watney gradually achieved a significant measure of management capability and by the early 1980s achieved parity with its principal competitors.

3   *The development of the milk and food division.*   Subsequent to the acquisition of the milk and food division in 1969 substantial reorganization was implemented, in particular the splitting of manufacturing from distribution. By the end of the decade the division was operating the largest fresh cream manufacturing plant in Europe, had emerged as the largest single producer of cheese in the UK, was the market leader in fruit yoghurt and was the leader in the development of short-life dairy products.

4   *The changing role of the hotel and catering division.*   Subsequent to the mergers and acquisitions of 1966 to 1972 the hotel division was expanded to take in entertainment, catering and managed public houses. The hotel division did not enjoy the same degree of success in the 1970s as it had in the two previous decades. It is symptomatic of the comparative failure of the hotel division in the 1970s that, subsequent to the acquisition of the Intercontinental Group in the early 1980s, the company divested itself of all but two of the provincial properties in the UK and furthermore disposed of the great majority of its London hotel properties.

Rationale for international expansion

Towards the close of the 1970s it became clear to Maxwell Joseph and Stanley Grinstead that further expansion in the UK would be likely to attract the attention of the Monopolies and Mergers Commission. This view was duly vindicated in October 1980 when the group made a bid for the Coral gaming organization. The bid was referred to the Commission, and as a consequence Joseph withdrew.

The timing of the Coral bid was to prove fortuitous for Grand Metropolitan. With further expansion in their traditional areas of activity blocked within the UK the rationale for major international expansion was strong. One of the principal reasons for the success of the group to date was that it had concentrated on businesses which it knew and had not ventured into fields unknown. The combination of sound freehold or long leasehold properties linked to businesses that concentrated on the then increasing disposable income of the individual had proved a sound recipe.

The first major move towards international expansion came, not surprisingly, via IDV. In the USA the largest selling brand of Scotch whisky was J & B Rare, the product of an IDV company Justerini and Brooks. In the USA it was marketed by the Paddington corporation and this company held the exclusive rights to the distribution of J & B Rare until 1990. The parent company of Paddington, Liggett, had been under pressure for some years and in particular had seen its share of the US cigarette market dwindle to just 3 per cent. Grand Metropolitan had been apprehensive for some time lest Liggett either sell Paddington or worse be taken over, so putting at risk the marketing and distribution operation of the product. Stanley Grinstead perceived that the optimum method of dealing with the problem would be to bid for Liggett in its entirety which was duly accomplished in May 1980. Liggett had two major attractions for Grand Metropolitan; it produced healthy profits and a strong positive cash flow from widely differing business; also it provided Grand Metropolitan with a sound base, from which to penetrate the markets of the USA with their own products and those of IDV and Express in particular.

Acquisition of Intercontinental Hotels

Early in 1981 a combination of circumstances enabled the group to regain its reputation within the hotel industry, to take advantage of the recent abolition of exchange control and to further its international expansion. World airlines had been under increasing financial pressure as a result of soaring oil prices and Pan American was in such a poor position that it had to consider seriously any realistic offer for one of its major subsidiaries, the Intercontinental Hotels Corporation. The acquisition of IHC was carried out with secrecy and speed and many would-be bidders were left at the starting gate. For $500m Grand Metropolitan was able to secure a truly international hotel corporation at the top end of the market, catering for the businessman rather than the tourist and with a proven reputation for efficient and effective management.

While the rationale for the acquisition of Liggett was partially defensive, the acquisition of IHC was more of an opportunistic strike. By obtaining IHC, Grand Metropolitan was able to recoup its position in the hotel industry, increase its exposure to the markets of the USA, provide additional points of sale for IDV products, and withdraw from its middle market hotel operations in London and throughout the UK. The motivation was therefore more subtle and far reaching than the previous bids. Moreover, the bid fitted on the grounds that it allowed Grand Metropolitan to move up-market in the hotel industry, concentrating more on the business than the tourist market, and in time the expansion of IHC within the USA would neatly complement the anticipated increase in activity of Liggett, IDV and Express Dairy.

The importance of the two acquisitions to the group could be judged by the fact that, by the mid 1980s, the two divisions operating from the USA together accounted for more than 20 per cent of the group sales and more than 30 per cent of the group trading profits. Moreover, they allowed the corporate image to be portrayed worldwide and resulted in additional points of sale for Grand Metropolitan products which were manufactured, produced and marketed in the UK and in continental Europe. To a significant extent technological expertise, especially in the milk and foods division, was applied to the USA. This generated additional sales and profits at a capital cost much less than start-ups from scratch.

The stream of acquisitions, mergers and takeovers in the period 1966 to 1982 resulted in group sales moving from £10m to £3,848m and pre-tax profits from £2m to £200m. Even allowing for inflation this was a formidable achievement. The success of the group, however, lay not in the acquisitions themselves, but in the ability to accommodate these acquisitions, flexing the structure of the organization to match the unfolding strategy.

Strategic management – the Grand Metropolitan approach

It is reasonable to suggest that Grand Metropolitan did not genuinely arrive at the stage of being managed strategically until 1979 when the Liggett acquisition was planned. Until then, cognizance had been taken of competitive analysis, major environmental trends and market understanding – in addition there had been numerous examples of opportunistic decision making. Liggett represented the next stage – the move towards strategic thinking and strategic planning. IHC represented all three strands of strategy as it was the classic opportunistic strike which fitted into the corporate scheme on grounds of strategic thinking and strategic planning. Strategic management was now well advanced within the group and the composition of the main Board of Directors was such as to allow it to focus attention on long-term strategic matters, leaving the operation of the multifarious businesses in the hands of executive management.

Management style

Although the events surrounding the acquisitions, mergers and takeovers of the group were widely reported by the Press, it was not until during the successful acquisition of Truman that the management style of Maxwell Joseph and Stanley Grinstead was subjected to analysis. In an interview at that time they commented on their management approach and three quotations from Joseph are worthy of note.

1   I work on intuition and my own personal judgement. That's worth more than any calculations that can be made in any scientific way.
2   When I'm buying a business, I first of all look at the people I'm buying from, second at the balance sheet, and then at the prospects of the company.
3   We don't take over companies without management.

In the case of Joseph it is true to say that the acquisitions he made were, in all cases, the result of detailed and painstaking research (with the possible exception of Express Dairy) and were not merely intuitive hunches or whims. His modus operandi relied on an extremely small staff together with the advice and opinions of his personal friends.

The second quotation is indicative of the type of company to which he was attracted. Having previously researched into the company, he was in a position to decide whether the combination of friendly directors plus balance sheets with potential could produce a situation where, under his own direction and guidance, the company could be made to prosper. There are close links between the second and the third quotations. It was invariably the policy of Maxwell Joseph not to get involved with the management of companies that Grand Metropolitan acquired. He was a firm believer in the art of delegation. The single constraint placed upon operational management during this time was financial control administered by the joint Managing Directors, Ernest Sharp and Stanley Grinstead. Managers who measured up to the financial criteria imposed were successful, remained in their jobs and were often promoted.

It is difficult to evaluate the contribution made by Joseph to the success of the group over the years. Suffice it to say that his motivation, commitment and style allied to his judgement both of men and of property played an essential part in the emergence of the group as a truly international enterprise.

Events of the 1980s

After the death of the founding Chairman Sir Maxwell Joseph on 22 September 1982, Stanley Grinstead was appointed Chairman. On 16 December the first of the series of appointments was announced which reflected the emergence of the group as a genuine international firm. Effectively the group was reorganized along geographic lines – the UK, the USA and 'international'.

These changes had been accurately forecast in a study carried out by stockbrokers Wood Mackenzie. Their report had identified, via a series of 'activity-strength' matrices, the relative strengths and weaknesses of the operating companies of Grand Metropolitan on a UK, USA and international basis. The UK matrix perceived the UK brewing business as being under pressure as a result of a declining beer market with resultant pressures on both free and tied trade companies with the personalization of home entertainment. The milk and foods business was also seen as being under pressure partly as a result of the threat to doorstep deliveries of milk and a changing pattern of milk and milk-related consumption. The main growth areas in terms of profitability lay in gaming, retail catering and inclusive holidays.

Postscript

In order to help pay for Intercontinental, during 1982 and 1983 Grand Metropolitan realized £125m from hotel property sales within the UK. Simultaneously the UK hotels that were meshed with the Intercontinental division were refurbished to the tune of £60m.

In 1987 Sir Stanley Grinstead retired after thirty years' service with the group, the last five of which he had been Chairman. His place was taken by Allen Sheppard who, in the following year, took a strategic decision to move out of the hotel business. The reasoning behind this was twofold: with only 100 hotels worldwide the group would have had difficulty in significantly raising this number as the hotels operated at the top end of the market; furthermore as a result of the continuing increase in the value of hotel property, particularly in the period 1985 to 1988, the rate of return was substantially below company norms. Intercontinental was put on the market and sold to the Japanese group Saison for £1.35 billion net. This enabled Grand Metropolitan to make a post-tax profit, after expenses, of more than £500m – a very good return for seven years' ownership.

It may be seen, therefore, that the hotel interests of Grand Metropolitan underwent radical changes during the lifetime of the company. The 1950s and 1960s reflected the property-orientated approach to the hotel industry favoured by Sir Maxwell Joseph. The 1970s was a disappointing decade while the 1980s saw marked changes with the acquisition and subsequent disposal of Intercontinental, as a result of which the company effectively withdrew from the international hotel industry.

The success of the group in the hotel business was due primarily to the property dealing skills of Sir Maxwell Joseph, second to the strategic management skills of Sir Stanley Grinstead, and last but not least to the management skills within IHC that resulted in its worldwide reputation both for the tourist and more especially for the business traveller.

Grand Metropolitan was the leading innovator in the UK hotel industry in the 1950s and 1960s, the largest hotel group in London as well as the second largest in the UK in the 1970s, and one of the major hotel operators worldwide in the 1980s. At the threshold of the 1990s it retained only a very limited presence in the UK hotel market through properties with a small amount of accommodation which are in effect operated as public houses or restaurants.

6 Swiss Travel Saving Fund

Hans Teuscher

Social tourism caters for people who can afford holidays only with the aid of a third party. This aid can include information about low-priced holiday possibilities, financial contributions and the creation of holiday establishments for the lower socioeconomic strata. Aid can be given by mutual assistance institutions, employers, trade unions, social organizations, and others.

The first steps in holiday assistance date back to the last century. When in 1841 master turner Thomas Cook hired an entire train for attending an association's event and offered a substantially reduced fare to its participants, the foundations of social tourism were laid. Purely non-profit organizations for social tourism already existed in England at the end of the last century, due to early industrialization. The objective of one of these organizations, the Co-operative Holidays Association founded in 1893, was to provide relaxing and educationally valuable holidays. On the European continent and including Switzerland, holidays became customary for larger sections of the population only in the twentieth century and especially after employers first conceded the payment of wages during holidays, following the First World War. In 1910, only 8 per cent of the factory workers of Switzerland were entitled to holidays; by 1937 this figure had risen to 66 per cent.

The 1930s saw a strong development of holidays and travel by those with limited financial means. The improvements of working conditions through higher wages and longer holidays fought for by the trade unions were the decisive factors. Promotion of social tourism was tackled in different ways in the various European countries but three main types can be identified.

Britain and Northern Europe

In Britain, with the longest tradition of travelling, and to a lesser extent in Germany, the Netherlands and in the Scandinavian countries, institutions of social tourism were essentially holiday organizations for everybody. Applying commercial principles they catered for the holiday wishes of people with small budgets on a practical basis. Pleasing the guests was the important aim. Educational aims or public influence were not prominent in this type of social tourism.

Mediterranean Europe

France and most of the other Latin European countries developed a special structure of social tourism, which differed considerably from commercial tourism. These countries contributed to social tourism remaining a distinct tourist activity, even though the ways of life of different socio-economic classes were converging.

Contributions by the state and by social organizations allowed accommodation to be created for people with limited financial means; people are able to use them through such channels as the social services, trade unions and similar institutions.

Eastern Europe

In the Eastern European countries, much internal tourism is considered as social tourism and subjected to public planning. Holiday establishments are managed by firms, the trade unions and the state. Holiday places are allotted to citizens according to certain criteria. Prices are fixed mostly regardless of the market economy.

The Swiss Travel Saving Fund

With the introduction of paid holidays between the two World Wars, many social tourism institutions were set up in Europe. While in Italy and Germany they were conceived as mass organizations to propagate fascist ideology during leisure time, other countries, such as Belgium and France, put the emphasis on the need to aid the working population. The Swiss Travel Saving Fund (REKA) was founded in 1939 as a cooperative with the purpose of encouraging travel and holidays for those of only limited financial means. From the very start the organization took care to depend neither exclusively on the state nor on special interest groups, but to be able to operate neutrally.

Four distinctive groups helped to develop the Swiss Travel Saving Fund: the tourism and transport industries, employees' associations (trade unions), employers, and cooperative associations, particularly in the foodstuffs trade. These four groups are still represented today, on an equal basis, on the supervisory and managing board of REKA. Public authorities also participated in the early conception of the Fund and are represented on the board, but without holding a dominant position.

From the inception of REKA two areas of activities were prominent:

- providing a method of saving for holidays; and
- providing information about low-priced holidays.

By providing price reductions for holidays, and a guide to what was available, it is hoped to encourage people to organize their holidays themselves.

To begin with, REKA did not build its own holiday accommodation but used the already existing capacity in hotels, boarding houses, holiday apartments and group establishments. Only in the 1950s, when a shortage of family accommodation occurred, did REKA construct its own holiday establishments.

The 'REKA cheque'

In order to safeguard freedom in the choice of holidays, the 'REKA cheque' was created as holiday currency. The cheque is put into circulation like a bank note but in a closed circuit with permission of the Swiss National Bank. It is issued in denominations of five, ten and fifty Swiss francs. It flows from the Fund to the selling agents, from there to the consumers and via the suppliers of tourist services back to the Fund. The REKA has its cheques printed as a value attesting instrument (bond) with the security attributes of a bank note. They are passed on to the selling agents with an initial reduction of its price of 3 per cent.

The cheque-selling agents are mainly industrial firms and the service industries (banks, insurance companies) as well as public administrations, employees' associations, foodstuffs trade cooperatives, etc. They pass the cheques on to employees, members and clients with an additional reduction of 5–25 per cent. The current (1982) turnover of just under SFr150m is shared between industry (46 per cent), private and public services (28 per cent), employees' associations (12 per cent), retail trade cooperatives (11 per cent) and other agencies (3 per cent). The reduction in the cost of tourist services resulting from their discount on cheques amounted to SFr20.3m or 13.6 per cent in 1982. The sales of cheques are usually limited by quotas. The highest quotas are enjoyed by employees in industrial firms and the service industries, the lowest by clients of foodstuffs trade cooperatives.

The users of REKA cheques, approximately 600,000 Swiss households, can profit from prices reduced by an average of 16 per cent when

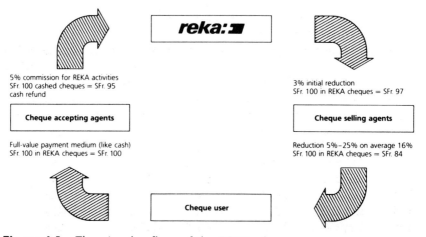

Figure 6.1   The circular flow of the REKA cheque

purchasing tourist services, thanks to the reductions granted by the Fund and the selling agents. Thus, after paying SFr84 for cheques, the users can then purchase services (excursions, holidays) to the value of SFr100.

Cheque-accepting agents are over 10,000 enterprises in tourism and transport who accept REKA cheques in payment for their services such as accommodation and travel. The highest share, 35 per cent, falls to the railways, bus lines and lake boats. Petrol stations follow with 21.6 per cent, travel agencies and coach tour operators with 19.2 per cent and cable cars and ski lifts with 12.8 per cent. The accommodation industry (hotels, holiday apartments and camping sites) and other firms cash the remaining 11.4 per cent of the cheques.

Internal tourism benefits from more than 80 per cent of the cheques used; less than 20 per cent find their way abroad through travel agencies and coach touring firms. The cheques cashed by these tourist firms are returned to REKA and thus the circle is complete. In order to compensate for the reduction of the cheques' transfer price, for the creation of additional tourist purchasing power and for information and advertising activities, REKA charges a commission of 5 per cent to most firms (see Figure 6.1).

Aims and implications of issuing cheques

Holiday expenditure is additional to daily expenses. The amount of freely-disposable income determines whether, and how much, money

Table 6.1 Use of the REKA cheque 1940–82

	Sales of REKA cheques		Savings invested in REKA cheques		Average duration of turn-round of REKA cheques in days
Year	SFr000	Index (1970=100)	SFr000	Index (1970=100)	
1940	72	0.1	50	0.1	253
1950	15,087	22.0	5,882	13.0	142
1960	39,695	58.0	18,326	41.0	169
1970	68,293	100.0	45,096	100.0	241
1975	99,031	145.0	72,039	160.0	266
1980	139,976	205.0	104,298	231.0	272
1982	149,258	219.0	116,879	259.0	286

can be spent on holidays. Only after paying for food, clothing, housing, insurance and taxes, etc., can income be spent on holidays.

Research has shown that holiday spending per person depends not only on the absolute individual income level but also to a great extent on the number of people financially dependent on the wage earner. The bigger the household, the smaller the amount per person available for holidays. Regular purchases of REKA cheques at a reduced price constitute savings, which cannot be used for another purpose, and which are ready for spending on holidays. During holidays, the largest part of the everyday expenditure of a household (rent, insurance, taxes, etc.) still has to be paid. Therefore, a holiday week for which additional costs for travel and accommodation are incurred, will amount to at least three times as much as a normal week.

Those of limited financial means can only afford to take a holiday away from home if assisted by a special measure such as the emission of REKA cheques. In today's economic system characterized by advanced division of labour, by mounting stress in jobs and long distances to work, it is especially important to regain strength by relaxing away from home.

While in most Western European countries the proportion of people taking annual holidays swings between 50 per cent and 65 per cent, the number reaches 75 per cent in Switzerland. Systematic saving for holidays may well be one of the prime reasons for the high intensity of travel in Switzerland.

REKA cheques are at the same time a stable stock of orders on hand for the tourist industry. In a country where individual tourism is predominant, holiday bookings are usually made at short notice and excursions arranged spontaneously, the industry is particularly dependent upon chance factors, such as weather. Financial resources earmarked for holidays tend to level fluctuations.

The REKA cheque, as a means of saving holiday money, does not directly bear interest; however, the substantial reduction of 16 per cent (on average) granted by REKA and the selling agents considerably exceeds the possible yield were the money to be invested in some other direct interest-bearing form.

Holiday savings tied up in REKA cheques constitute interest-bearing capital for the Fund. This has made it possible for REKA, since the 1950s, apart from undertaking information and advertising work for tourism, to invest part of these savings in the Fund's own holiday establishments for low income people. To date this aid has been concentrated on families.

As can be seen in Table 6.1 not only the sales of REKA cheques, but also the savings invested in the cheques increased steadily since the foundation of the Swiss Travel Saving Fund. Between 1970 and 1982 the sales of REKA cheques more than doubled. The amount of savings invested in REKA cheques (resulting from the difference between cheques sold and cheques cashed) grew by more than two-and-a-half times in the same period. The average length of time during which savings for holidays were tied up in cheques rose constantly from 142 to 286 days since 1950 (1940 being a war year and exceptional).

Tourist information

REKA considers that understanding the market is the prime prerequisite for optimal utilization of limited means available for holidays. For this reason it devotes considerable effort to informing people about advantageous holiday and travel possibilities. In accordance with one of the Fund's objectives to further Swiss tourism, information is largely limited to Switzerland. However, the Fund tries to inform as comprehensively as possible, from portraying the peculiarities and characteristics of the individual regions, describing towns and resorts, to listing the specific services of individual enterprises. The 290,000 member families of REKA receive tourist information free of charge after the initial modest membership fee of SFr20.

Holiday centres and apartments

After the Second World War, as increasingly larger groups of the population were able to take holidays away from home, a lack of advantageously priced accommodation catering for the needs of families soon became obvious. The traditional hotel did not meet the requirements of the family with regard to price or to amenities offered. Therefore, in the mid-1950s, REKA began to build their own holiday centres especially to suit the family. They are equipped with an indoor or heated open-air swimming pool, a mini-golf course, table-tennis and games rooms as well as numerous children's playgrounds. Two of the holiday centres offer a community building suitable for leisure activities, especially in bad weather. The guests are accommodated in individual apartments of different sizes (one to four rooms with a total of two to ten beds). They are very comfortably furnished and contain a lounge-cum-kitchen as well as modern sanitary amenities.

Two of the centres provide an individual chalet for each family, whereas in the others, five to twelve apartments are combined in one building. Today REKA owns six holiday centres with 254 family units and 1434 guest beds. Beyond these, REKA has concluded long-term leases for a further 300 holiday apartments throughout the whole country. A total of 2744 beds are offered in 550 apartments. In 1982, 36,000 guests were accommodated totalling 415,000 bednights.

In order not to exclude any families from the possibility of REKA holidays, a graded rental discount of 10 per cent to 50 per cent is granted to families with lower incomes. Also REKA annually invites 300 families to a free holiday who would otherwise have great difficulty in affording them. Whereas previously these have been mainly families with many children, today they are more and more single mothers and their children.

The future for social tourism

In addition to economic changes affecting the tourism industry, three developments specific to social tourism have recently become manifest. First, in the past, social tourism was in most countries directed towards specific groups of the population, particularly the factory workers; now however, almost all groups of the population are using institutions of social tourism at some time in their lives. Young people use them during their education (e.g. Youth Hostels) but become consumers of more expensive holidays as soon as they start to earn a living even at lower wage levels. Families with several children are in need of advantageous holiday amenities even with middle and higher range income; as soon as the children have grown up, they can again afford more expensive holidays.

Second, the fall-off in economic growth has led to stagnating or even dropping incomes, while at the same time steadily progressing rationalization of work processes increases spare time. Hence, there is less money available per day off, which especially necessitates low-priced holiday institutions.

Third, the general availability of tourism which has emerged just before, but especially after the Second World War in the highly industrialized countries, has already started in the newly industrialized countries of the Third World and is imminent in others. Especially, the workforce in the industrial and service sectors in big cities with often unfavourable environmental conditions, has an increasing need of holidays away from home. It is of special importance for these places that the planning of social tourism be encouraged.

Postscript

In 1989 the Swiss Travel Saving Fund (REKA) celebrated its fiftieth anniversary. Since this article was written in the early 1980s, REKA registered continuous growth from year to year.

● Between 1982–9 the sale of REKA cheques increased from SFr149m to SFr235m (+ 57 per cent).
● The total reduction in price of REKA cheques by REKA and more than 3500 selling agents rose from SFr23.9m to SFr38.7m.
● There was a significant increase in the use of REKA cheques over the same period from SFr144m to SFr225m, while saving with REKA cheques (cheques sold less cheques cashed) also rose from SFr117m to SFr181m.
● At the same time development continued in REKA own holidays, including improvement in the quality of holiday facilities. Two holiday villages have been renovated and expanded and another holiday centre was acquired. With seven holiday centres of its own and two holiday houses, REKA now owns 286 family units. In addition long-term leases were concluded for a further 500 holiday apartments throughout the country and 100 abroad, in France, Italy and Austria.
● In 1989 62,000 guests were accommodated in REKA holiday apartments (+ 70 per cent over 1982), totalling 615,000 bednights (+ 70 per cent over 1982). The already high average occupancy figures for available apartments rose further from 194 days occupied in 1982 to 217 days in 1989.
● More than 400 families and single mothers and fathers with their children were invited to enjoy free holidays in 1989.
● The REKA holiday service now offers a REKA Holiday Pass, a bargain short-holiday arrangement, which covers travel on all public transport plus overnight accommodation in hotels in seven attractive Swiss hiking regions.

Further reading

Further reading on business growth and development in *Tourism Management* 1980–9

Baker, P., 'Public and private cooperation in the (US) National Park Service', vol. 4, no. 1, March 1983, pp. 52–4.

Choisy, H., 'WATA – growing industrial power', vol. 7, no. 4, December 1986, p. 290.

Davies, A. H. T., 'Business planning in the Thomas Cook Group', vol. 2, no. 2, June 1981, pp. 84–98.

Elton, M. A., 'UK tour operators and retail travel agents – ABTA and the public interest', vol. 5, no. 3, September 1984, pp. 223–8.

Eser, G. O., 'The changing role of IATA', vol. 7, no. 4, December 1986, pp. 290–2.

Heape, R., 'Tour operating planning in Thomson Holidays UK', vol. 4, no. 4, December 1983, pp. 245–52.

Miller, D., 'United Nations – projects from Benin to Bali', vol. 4, no. 4, December 1983, pp. 303–8.

O'Driscoll, T. J., 'European Travel Commission', vol. 6, no. 1, March 1985, pp. 66–70.

Riley, C., 'New product development in Thomson Holidays UK', vol. 4, no. 4, December 1983, pp. 253–61.

Westwood, M., 'Warwick Castle: preparing for the future by building on the past', vol. 10, no. 3, September 1989, pp. 235–9.

Part Three

Governments, Markets and Industries

On the threshold of the 1990s, in the region of 700 million people lived in three widely separated parts of the developed world – the European Community, the United States and Japan. They received well over one-half and generated some two-thirds of the world's international tourism. In this part of the book three articles published in *Tourism Management* in the late 1980s provide tourism scenarios of these major markets.

Tourism is a major economic activity in the European Community. In 'European tourism 1992' L. J. Lickorish explains from his close involvement with the European Travel Commission and the European Tourism Action Group, the implications for the Community tourism industries of the Single Internal Market, in operation from 31 December 1992.

Until then the USA represents the largest single market for travel and tourism in the world. In 'Key issues in the US travel industry futures' Douglas Frechtling, at the time of writing Director of the US Travel Data Center, examines likely influences and developments in the US market and industry to the year 2000.

With its large population and spending power, Japan is by far the most important emerging market with a massive potential still to be realized. Ivan Polunin, who represents the British Tourist Authority in Asia, analyses the 'Japanese travel boom' with a particular focus on travel abroad against the background of the changing Japanese international outlook, life-styles and other factors.

Further articles on governments, markets and industries published in *Tourism Management* from 1980–9 are listed on page 103. See also Chapter 13 'European air transport in the 1990s'.

7 European tourism 1992

L. J. Lickorish

Member states of the European Community (EC) committed themselves to completing the Single (Internal) Market by 31 December 1992. The Single Market is defined by the EC as 'an area without internal frontiers in which the free movement of goods, persons, services and capital is ensured'. The twelve members of the EC (Belgium, Denmark, France, Greece, West Germany, Ireland, Italy, Luxembourg, Netherlands, Spain, Portugal and the UK) represent a domestic market of 320 million, almost as many as the USA and Japan combined.

Tourism is already a key trade for the twelve countries, representing 5.5 per cent of gross domestic product (GDP), 8 per cent of final private consumption, 4 per cent of foreign currency exports and 5 per cent of imports and, perhaps most important, providing jobs for 7.5m workers, or 6 per cent of the total workforce. EC receipts from international tourism account for some 60 per cent of total tourism receipts in the Organisation for Economic Co-operation and Development (OECD) member countries, which represent the industrialized countries of the world, an amount of the order of $79 billion in 1988 or over 75 per cent of all Europe's tourist income. About 46 per cent (1985) of EC receipts derive from intra-community travel, and some 56 per cent of expenditure of Community nationals on international tourism remains within the Community.

If the greater expenditure on domestic tourism within member countries is taken into account, tourism is clearly one of the largest single trades in the member countries. This part of Europe is the world's principal tourism region. All expert forecasts indicate continuing growth in tourism movement of up to 5 per cent per year, representing a massive long-term potential. The Internal Market offers prospects of substantial trading benefits, and new opportunities, but also new challenges with a number of problems or constraints to be overcome.

There is in fact much to be done before the policy and principles of a fully competitive market become a reality. A range of national restrictions affects the operation of many trades (especially public transport). Statutory controls and regulations of varying complexity (health, safety, fire, etc.), subsidies and tax regimes (especially excise duties on liquor, petrol, tobacco, etc.) vary widely.

The principal industry sectors in Europe's tourism (transport, accommodation, the travel trade, etc.) through their official bodies, welcome the advent of the Internal Market in principle, but they have some serious concerns, in their capacity as producers of the tourist services which make travel possible.[1] Governments' role is crucial but it is only part of the whole. There has to be partnership, implicit or explicit. In the free market economies the state's job is to create the conditions for economic development in a free and competitive society, to remove constraints to trade, rather than to intervene in the business or economic production process. The trade sectors seek full consultation before government intervention, full information on action proposed in the deregulation process. Changes in regulations, e.g. in airport controls and passenger handling, greatly affect the operators who will have to work the new systems. The Association of European Airlines has suggested that it might take up to five years to rearrange airport layout and control equipment to handle the new and massive 'domestic' (EC) and international (non-EC) travel flows, which in theory will also include the neighbouring European countries (Switzerland, Austria and most of Scandinavia).

To ensure success, the Brussels administration will need an open policy, with practical and flexible attitudes to the implementation of new regulations and practices.

Thus it is not the case that on 1 January 1993 the barriers will be lifted at all the frontier posts, constraints removed, and the travel world will change on one day. The truth is that liberalization in travel in Europe has been continuing for some years in favourable evolution, not revolution.

There is an important unresolved question in the relations between the twelve member countries and their European neighbours – some twenty countries. Most tourist agreements up to the present, which represented liberalizing measures (e.g. the red and green system based on minimum customs concessions) and currency allowances for travel, have been on a Western basis, or wider international basis. Similarly transport agreements (Freedom of the Road) have been made through the auspices of the OECD or United Nations agencies, covering Western or indeed all of Europe.

An examination of factors remaining to be harmonized will illustrate the substantial task ahead.

Fiscal measures

The most significant of these is the application of value added tax (VAT) at many varying rates, which in effect act as a tariff. Rates in the member countries range from as low as 6 per cent to a peak of 22 per cent. Variation on food is even greater. In the UK food is at present zero rated, but restaurant meals are charged at 15 per cent. There are wide variations in VAT on different foods in different countries, e.g. in Italy fish is taxed at 2 per cent but meat at 10 per cent, in Belgium shellfish are taxed at a high rate (28 per cent) while other foods are charged at 6 per cent and food in restaurants 17 per cent. In France the rural guest-houses (*gites-ruraux*), and effectively the small bed-and-breakfast establishments in the UK do not pay tax, but hoteliers pay up to 18 per cent in France and 15 per cent in the UK.

Many of the levies seem to have no logical rates, resulting in undoubted distortion in competition. Seven countries, with the largest share of the Community's tourism, apply reduced rates of tax to hotels and restaurants – Luxembourg, Netherlands, Greece (6 per cent), Portugal and Ireland (8 per cent and 10 per cent), and Italy and Spain, where the majority of establishments enjoy a reduced rate (6 per cent).

VAT is levied on many other tourist services, travel agents and tour packages, entertainment and recreational services, including cultural attractions and the arts. Passenger transport rates vary from zero (as in the UK) to as much as 18 per cent and more in the case of car hire (up to 28 per cent). The VAT harmonization proposals will require member countries to levy three rates – a zero rate, a standard rate (within the scale of 14–20 per cent) and a reduced rate (4–9 per cent). Goods and services have not yet been allocated to tax bands, but it has been suggested that the following goods and services may be charged at the reduced rate – food, beverages, energy for heating and lighting, water, pharmaceutical products, books, newspapers, etc., and transport of people. All other goods and services will be charged at the higher standard rate. Thus it will be seen that the majority of tourist services will suffer the higher tax, and for many countries the imposition of VAT, even at a reduced rate, on transport, including international transport (e.g. air travel), will represent a major additional cost, and affect their competitive situations.

The position is complicated further by the fact that excise duties (internal taxes), notably on liquor and petrol, present problems, so that there may continue to be varying levels of tax and prices. In any event the relatively wide bands for both standard and reduced rate will make harmonization of charges far from perfect.

Frontier controls

Frontier controls are largely already removed or considerably reduced within the Community. However, there are still some restrictions on currency exchange or availability in some of the member countries.

Passport controls have been greatly simplified, but it is still the practice to carry out inspections at most frontier crossings. The Community has introduced a Community passport and for some of the states travel is freely available with the use of the normal Citizens Identity Card. There are many problems related to the treatment of third countries, especially the availability of the multi-entry visa. Theoretically in a 'borderless' Community, once a visitor from a non-member country enters any one of the member states and crosses the new 'frontier', that visitor should be free to travel throughout the twelve member country territory without further checks. There should be no further frontier controls and no hotel or place of stay registration. There seems to be some doubt about the practical possibilities of such liberalization taking into account necessary health and security checks, and controls, e.g. against drug traffic or health hazards. There will in any case, according to the international airline organizations, be substantial changes in passenger handling at air and seaports and frontier points to segregate the Community and non-Community residents. Some destinations have large non-Community traffic flows, e.g. London as the principal arrival destination for American visitors to Europe.

At present frontier and entry checks vary considerably from country to country. Visas usually depend on bilateral arrangements, although they have been abolished for intra-Community travel by residents. Treatment by some countries of many Third World country visitors is closely controlled. Visas can be expensive and may be valid for only one entry in one country.

Port handling will be complicated, if it is decided to abolish duty free facilities for intra-Community travel. Customs allowances have been liberalized and harmonized; the allowance for importing articles bought within the Community (shopping) has been increased. It seems logical that in a 'domestic' market duty free shops would be an anomaly. But even after 1992 there will still be substantial variations and differing tax levels. Duty-free facilities will still be available in neighbouring countries, presenting opportunities for trade distortion, and placing member countries and their tourism services at a potential competitive disadvantage.

Transport

Public transport, notably air and road is still controlled, with limits on competition. Sea transport is largely free from constraint except in regard to cabotage (services by foreign operators in the national territory). Generally speaking, there are few absolute constraints on expansion of services or the entry of competitors to meet tourism demand. However, a large part of the Community's tourism movement is domestic tourism (over 50 per cent) by residents. Some 80 per cent of Community domestic holiday or private travel is by private car and much of it flows by individual or institutional arrangement, often accommodated and transported privately (friends and relatives, camping and caravanning, second homes, etc.).

There has been a substantial degree of deregulation assisted by governments. Some 50 per cent of European international air travel is by charter carriers. Furthermore, many agreements are on a wider European basis than the Community territory.

But in air transport there are many controls protecting national positions and limiting competition. On some routes fares remain at a high level. In theory by 1992 according to Article 61 all constraints on free competition must go. But in practice many aviation experts believe that further deregulation will be limited and that it will take a longer period for a more liberal policy and practice to evolve.

Coach services which are classified as regular international, occasional and shuttle operations, are relatively free in regard to the tourist services (mainly occasional and shuttle). The Commission's proposals for deregulation are broadly acceptable to the industry provided standards of safety, quality and competence are maintained. This will open up many services to competition and particularly if cabotage operation is permitted (foreign operators offering transport services within member countries). The industry has some reservations about new taxation (VAT) and the method of levy (especially if it is at the discretion of the originating country), as well as standards and regulations about drivers' hours which need to be flexible.

Fiscal and financial regulation

There are other areas in which constraints or controls limiting or distorting competition apply. In certain countries there are constraints on capital and investment is regulated, e.g. land purchase and airline investment.

Central and local taxation takes many forms, and some directly affect tourism, e.g. the taxe de sejour, port and departure taxes. Denmark levies a relatively high departure tax on charter travellers, which can distort traffic.

There are a series of subsidies or levies which can finance state intervention in tourism trading. In some countries businesses pay a compulsory contribution to the Chambers of Commerce, which can be powerful. The port of Boulogne, France, is run by the Chamber of Commerce. Conference halls and exhibition centres in many countries are owned and operated by local government involving substantial subsidy. In a domestic market it will be important to ensure that these highly competitive activities enjoy trading conditions which are fair to all and do not distort trade to the disadvantage of any member country. Governments, local authorities and other public bodies are major operators in tourism. Public purchases post-1992 should reflect fair competition, not the national interest. This could prove a major challenge.

Health, safety and consumer protection

There are necessary controls to ensure health, safety and public order. There are already directives relating to water and beaches establishing minimum standards. Although evidently desirable, such controls must be practical and flexible in administration. Standards applicable to a first-class hotel, for example, may well be unsuited to a guest-house. The industry is rightly concerned that there should be adequate consultation and cooperation in drawing up regulations and in their implementation. Some of the consumer protection measures relating to tourism have been criticized on the grounds of difficulties in implementation and practice. The recent draft directive on package tours currently under review is an example of this.

EC Commission achievements

There are already a number of positive achievements by the Commission in the tourism field. The industry benefits as do other trades in the operation of regional funds to stimulate new development, especially in the poorer regions, social funding for training, and more recently, rural incentives to supplement agricultural activities currently undergoing structural changes and reductions in output. In the poorer hill-farming regions, for example, tourism activity has been an important support (farm holidays, holiday cottages, camping, etc.).

A tourism service and a commissioner with special responsibilities for tourism have led to the elaboration of a limited tourism policy with the support of the European Parliament. The policy deals particularly with facilitation, promotion and research, establishing a framework for tourism activity and the spread of traffic geographically and seasonally. Priority is given to a number of important segments, which offer particular economic and social values, e.g. cultural, rural and social tourism activities.

A comprehensive statistical survey of holiday taking, covering 1985, was completed and plans to assist the standardization of statistical systems in tourism, a notoriously difficult task, are proceeding. Market research has been carried out over a wide field, and research activity into other important aspects of tourism has been completed, e.g. information technology.

The Commission supports promotion and market research carried out in other continents (e.g. in the USA and Japan by the European Travel Commission (ETC)) to encourage long-distance travel to Europe from other continents.

The work of the tourism service is especially important in raising the profile and status of tourism in public and government consideration. The industry does not have a high place in EC counsels and activities considering its enormous economic and social importance as the largest single trade in the community. It needs to be treated as an entity in its own right and not simply as a convenient and useful support in the implementation of policies agreed for other purposes (agricultural change, for example).

Future growth

Assuming the Single Market is created, what are the likely implications for future tourism growth? First one must take into account the problem areas. There will be an increase in taxation (VAT), notably on transport. Many tourism services (accommodation and catering) may come within the standard (higher 14–20 per cent band). The abolition of duty-free shops and the loss of considerable revenue to ports and carriers will increase cost to the travelling public. The UK and other island or fringe countries will be affected since virtually all international travel is at least in part public service carried. Some aviation and port representatives have put the likely increase in cost of air and ferry travel at more than 10 per cent. This will, of course, affect their competitive positions. Tour operators claim that the proposed consumer legislation will add further to costs.

Transport carriers, notably airlines, are concerned about problems at frontiers in dealing with third country traffic and segregation of movement into Community and non-Community travel. The absence of detailed plans and timetables for action is a threat to orderly progress.

There is concern among the trades that Community action in the field of consumer protection has in the past resulted in difficulties of a practical nature, whether it is the cleaning up of beaches, working conditions (tourist staff must work unsociable or non-factory or office hours by the nature of the trade), dimensions of coaches, classification of hotels, licensing of travel agents, or harmonization of statistics. In the first place countries are different, practices vary, change takes time and may be expensive. There is no point in harmonization for its own sake. Furthermore, sometimes regulatory action to deal with a perceived problem can be obsolescent, as the dynamics of a fast-moving industry change needs and aspirations. There is a view in some industry sectors that the Brussels bureaucracy is too interventionist pressing for new controls which act as constraints, that there is a lack of coordination, and that tourism is not given adequate priority in consultation and action.

All experts in the industry predict continued and substantial growth in tourism in the long term. If history repeats itself tourism could grow twice as fast as the increase in GDP. Clearly many of the Internal Market changes will help but some may not. The importance of a tourism policy and a greater recognition of tourism in Community action seems at least as important as the Internal Market innovations. For this reason the declaration by the Community of 1990 as European Tourism Year is to be welcomed as an opportunity for new initiatives and special efforts to deal with unbalanced seasonal flows and congestion.

Developments and trends

Air transport changes are one of the most significant potential developments. There is already a trend by charter operators, often owned by major tour operators, to go for scheduled services.

As the US experience shows, deregulation can be beneficial for the travel trade. Tour operators and travel agents are potentially the most creative element of the tourism business, but currently a weak area in new forms of tourism and domestic travel. It seems likely that the market is ahead of the trade, beginning to realize the enormous potential for leisure growth with the removal of constraints on leisure time and income, socio-economic change, notably reduction in family pressures and the power of the senior citizen market. Frequency of travel increases with a number of holidays a year and not only in the peak summer season. The main holiday for an increasing number is no longer in the summer. There are mini-mass markets in specialist activities (culture, education, health, sports and hobbies). Business travel is growing fast and increasingly taking promotable or creative forms.

But a large proportion of leisure travel is privately organized or institution led (school, church, social clubs, etc.). Major sophisticated tour operators are to be found principally in a few northern countries offering a few mass products (sun or snow) for one domestic market. It seems likely that new leisure and travel operations on a European or worldwide scale will emerge, with the development of new information and reservation systems making the product easier to buy – a necessary and desirable development in Europe.

Hotel chains have developed strongly in recent years. British and American companies (e.g. Intercontinental and Hilton originally linked to major airlines) have led the way. Expansion has been patchy, French companies (a late entry) have been growing fast. There has been an expansion in hotel marketing and reservation franchises. These are likely to expand into other leisure services. There seems room for growth in accommodation and catering services, as the chains offer important advantages in standards control, promotion and marketing (product improvement and special offers). The Internal Market does not directly remove constraints on this development. Hilton, Intercontinental, Trusthouse Forte, and fast food chains (e.g. McDonald's) have already expanded widely in Europe under present systems. That is why it is so important to stress the priority of market forces in determining change in product and market match.

Coach transport deregulation could lead to important innovation and a substantial growth in market share. While tourist package transport (similar to air charters) is relatively free, deregulation of regular international services could attract new groupings and substantial traffic growth. Coaching companies have been important creative tour operators, principally based in northern European countries with a powerful domestic market for mass travel to the south. A European approach seems likely as the coach system has not grown so rapidly in some of the European member countries.

Car hire is liberalized although the great disparity of VAT charges (up to 28 per cent) creates problems. The industry is dominated by a few large groups, notably Hertz, Avis and Eurocar, but trade is open to all and there are many smaller operators.

There is a wide field for enterprise in leisure centres, specialist and participating activity, and in the more serious area of cultural tourism learning (for all ages), health and the pursuit of sports and hobbies. The demand for such specialism is not always well catered for. Hotel groups and transport operators will use the opportunity that growing demand offers to fill space in off-peak periods. But the trends are large and serious enough to warrant major attention in their own right – not just as off-peak solutions. New partnerships by institutions, local and regional government, and the private sector are likely and, if they spread popular innovations within the new Internal Market, results could be significant.

Private car travel may offer important new potential as information and reservation systems improve. The major motoring institutions are developing new services in this field on an international and a pan-European basis. Here again market development and trends on a Western European basis will prove to be powerful market forces extending beyond both the Internal Market and its liberalized administration. It may give a sharper competitive edge to the Community members, but it will remain vital to give priority to product–market match and to ensure that relations with European and non-EC neighbours are harmonious.

Postscript

Official reports claim that major growth in Community countries' prosperity (GDP) will result from the Single Market. Although this should stimulate tourism, it should not be taken for granted. In recent years wealthier Europeans have been travelling increasingly to far distant destinations. Europe has lost market share in world travel. The massive credit balance in Europe's travel balance has been reduced by 50 per cent in four years, and may soon disappear.

The major economic and social consequences of enlarged tourism flows and their potential should persuade governments to take tourism more seriously. There is already a vast range of central and local government initiatives in the transport and leisure fields, often uncoordinated, and as the OECD has observed, poorly understood.

The European Community is reviewing its Tourism Policy as part of the European Year of Tourism Programme (1990). Higher priority, consultation with trade sectors, and coordination in government action are vital questions. The industry has warned of the danger of higher taxation of travel services in an increasingly competitive world market. Transport infrastructure is inadequate with serious congestion at times at present traffic levels, for example in air traffic controls and airport capacity. Job and social implications could be serious. Price changes due to tax and excise duty harmonization, and increases in labour costs in poorer countries as working conditions are subject to intervention, could distort traffic flows, increasingly sensitive to price.

Already the richer countries have larger tourism revenues, less congestion and better seasonality than the poorer South. In short there will be winners and losers post 1992. Tourism benefits cannot be taken for granted. However, future opportunities are vast and justify much higher priorities in EC policies.

Note

1   The following organizations meet regularly for joint consultations in the mutual task of developing Europe's tourism with the representa-

tives of the European Travel Commission and of the intergovern-
mental organizations including the EC officials through the European
Tourism Action Group (ETAG): Association of European Airlines;
Alliance Internationale de Tourisme; European Federation of Conference
Towns; *Fédération Internationale de l'Automobile*; International Air
Transport Association; International Hotel Association; International
Road Transport Union; Passenger Shipping Association; Universal
Federation of Travel Agents Associations; and International Union of
Railways.

8 Key issues in the US travel industry futures

Douglas C. Frechtling

The USA provides arguably the largest travel and tourism market in the world.[1] Nearly two thirds of our 235m residents take one or more trips to places 100 miles or more away from home each year. More than half take such a trip for a vacation or holiday. As a consequence, Americans generated more than a billion (thousand million) person-trips for all purposes in 1985, and 730m vacation person-trips.[2]

The size of this market and the character of the industry that has grown up to serve it should be of considerable interest to travel marketers around the world. One reason is that it offers considerable hope for expansion of international travel. In 1985, a banner year for US travel abroad, only 10m Americans travelled overseas. This is less than 7 per cent of all American travellers. Their trips comprised about 1 per cent of all trips taken by Americans. Even on long vacation trips, these overseas trips were a distinct minority – about 3 per cent of all trips of ten nights or more.

Our research has indicated that around 1979, the US travel market began to show distinct signs of maturity. The real growth rate of travel demand slowed down and since then has roughly matched that of US gross national product. US resident travel demand will probably continue to grow only as fast as the overall economy, there being no major new markets to open up or extraordinary cost-cutting breakthroughs in the supply side on the horizon.

While certainly not cause for celebration, the maturity of US travel demand is no reason for despair. Rather, this means that travel marketers must pay more attention to the characteristics of the market and how they change and trust less in a booming market to validate all marketing decisions. The travel market to the end of this century will be less forgiving to those who ignore the principles of effective marketing.

One of these principles must come top of the US travel marketer's agenda. This is the need to segment his market to determine what homogeneous groups are most likely to buy his product and are profitable to go after with the resources at hand.

Topics in the realm of the future must be approached warily. There is little agreement about how to approach forecasting. Britain's Edmund Burke said, 'You can never plan the future by the past,' but the American patriot, Patrick Henry, rejoined, 'I know of no way of judging the future but by the past.'[3]

There is even disagreement over whether forecasting is a respectable endeavour at all. The French author, Louis Ferdinand Celine, opined 'Those who talk about the future are scoundrels.' But the American inventor, Charles Kettering, noted 'We should all be concerned about the future because we will have to spend the rest of our lives there.'[4]

Perhaps Mark Twain made the most sensible statement about forecasting. 'Prophecy is very difficult, especially with respect to the future.'[5]

Based upon the analyses of the US Travel Data Center of travel trends over the last decade or so and the author's study of a number of works on the future of US society, industry and travel activity, certain conclusions on the major issues can be drawn that will shape the US travel market to the end of this century.

External developments and issues

We can begin with those issues that will be decided external to travel demand and the travel industry. The following are the major environmental developments that will shape US travel activity over the next fifteen years.

The economy

One major issue is how fast will the US economy expand? Economic growth provides additional personal income for consumers to spend on travel. The rate at which the economy grows also affects business travel. The following three points are of major interest to the travel industry.

The US economy will grow somewhat faster than it has in the 1980s. The US real gross national product (GNP) will grow nearly 3 per cent a year to 2000, compared to 2.3 per cent annually for the first half of this decade. The US will benefit from a maturing workforce, technological advances and the decline in government regulation of the marketplace.

Price inflation will accelerate. The beneficial effects of declining oil prices are largely behind us, and we can expect this commodity to rise at the rate of other goods and services – a bit more than 4 per cent a year. This is more rapid than our recent past but considerably better than our 9 per cent annual rate over the last decade.

The US dollar will weaken further in exchange markets. The recent US trade deficits practically guarantee that the dollar will fall further in international exchange markets. It is difficult to conceive that we can continue to pump $100 billion a year into foreign hands through US trade deficits without the market forces adjusting the value of the dollar downward in terms of other currencies. This means that travel abroad will become less competitive with domestic destinations on the basis of price.

US government policies

A variety of federal, state and local (county and municipal) government agencies have the power to affect travel demand. Four major developments are likely here.

US Federal government must redress the deterioration in transport service. 1986 is one of the worst years on record for delayed flights and outright cancellations. Summer flights were delayed an average of 2500 hours a day, and the Air Transport Association estimates delays in 1986 cost airlines, passengers and shippers more than $2 billion. The major cause is expanding airline service against limited ground service and airway control capacities.

The US federal government will increase control over airline schedules to reduce the congestion at as many as twenty-two major airports, and implement technologically superior flight control systems. While this will limit consumer advantages from competition, it will help ensure that when the traveller gets on an airplane, he has a higher probability of reaching his destination on time.

The automobile traveller is not much better off. A study by the American Association of State Highway and Transportation Officials reported several years ago that 63 per cent of US streets and roads are in fair or poor condition, and that 46 per cent of US bridges are 'structurally deficient or functionally obsolete'. The US federal government enacted an increase in the gasoline excise-tax to finance improvement of these conditions, but this was inadequate to prevent long-distance automobile travel from becoming more expensive through vehicle damage, less comfortable, slower, and more dangerous.

US state and local governments will increase tax levies on travel-related activities. Our state and local governments have been aggressive in raising revenue from travel activity. Our estimates indicate that the state/local tax receipts from domestic tourism expenditure have risen 25 per cent faster than expenditure over the last five years. Officials find it easier to tax non-residents to finance their services than residents.

All levels of US government can be expected to continue to increase their sales, use and excise taxes on travel activity in the USA. This will add to inflationary pressures and actually reduce travel to some destinations.

US states and cities will step up their travel market development programmes. The states have increased their tourism development budgets by more than 13 per cent a year over the last five years, and have allocated increasing shares of these moneys to direct advertising. The average state travel development office spends $4.7m on travel market development, and six states (Illinois, New York, Michigan, Pennsylvania, Florida, and Tennessee) now spend more than $10m a year. I expect that by the year 2000 twelve states will be in this position in 1986 dollars, and that most of these will be in the north to counterbalance the sunbelt's natural climatic advantage. Promotions to overseas markets will rise in priority.

Cities of all sizes are also becoming more active in tourism development, going beyond their traditional focus on selling venues for meetings and conventions. I expect their visitor promotion budgets will double in real terms by the end of the century, and focus on persuading convention delegates to bring their families, stay extra days, and return for pleasure visits.

The US federal government, on the other hand, will not be a serious player in tourism marketing. Since 1979, the federal budget for international tourism promotion ($11.5m in fiscal year 1987) has declined by more than one-half in real terms. Budget exigencies and disagreement over the appropriate federal role in tourism promotion will limit the US Travel and Tourism Administration's activities to technical assistance and facilitating cooperative marketing over most of the next fifteen years.

Leisure time and discretionary dollars

The critical developments in leisure time to the end of this century have little to do with the amount of it but much to do with how the consumer chooses to use it.

Leisure time will grow in small blocks rather than large ones. The average US employee's work week is projected to decline marginally, from thirty-five hours in 1986 to thirty-three hours in fifteen years. But as more women enter the workforce and spouses' work schedules do not necessarily complement one another, families have less leisure time to spend together a week rather than more.

Substantial increases in large blocks of non-work time coordinated within the household would offer more time for vacation travel, but the pressure for this leave is becoming less. The changes that John Naisbitt says will characterize work life in the future cast doubt on the concept of 'leisure time' as a distinct entity.[6] The boundaries between work and leisure become blurred through the rise in participatory management, flexitime, job-shaping in the traditional workplace, and work at home through computers. There is a declining need to get away from it all because 'it all' has become more fulfilling.

Growth in mini-vacations will characterize the working population and retired Americans will dominate long vacation travel expansion. I expect that 'mini-vacations' centred around weekends and holidays will increasingly characterize the pleasure travel of working-age households. These are easier to coordinate with conflicting work schedules and book at the last minute. Those with the largest amounts of guaranteed leisure time – the retired population – will increasingly dominate long vacation trips and cause an increase in this market.

Pleasure travel must increasingly vie with alternative uses of discretionary time and dollars. For the first two years of recovery after the 1980–1 recession, pleasure travel failed to grow because consumers turned their discretionary dollars to purchasing more goods: automobiles, housing and home-repair items, appliances and home furnishings, and home-entertainment equipment. Expenditure on these items increased by $120 billion in 1983–4. While this was a cyclical boom, over the long term these items are strong competitors for discretionary dollars, and they will compete for discretionary time as well. The American home will grow as an entertainment centre through the rest of the twentieth century. Television reception by satellite dish and cable, digital audio and video recording and playing, electronic motion picture cameras, and home computers all vie with the entertainment options away from home that tourism affords.

Even when the American family wants entertainment or recreation outside the home, a plethora of opportunities have grown up within easy driving distance. Parks and recreation sites in urban areas have blossomed, and the National Park Service hosts more visitors at its urban sites than at the better-known rural places. Enclosed shopping malls have become major entertainment centres as well.

Overall, competition for pleasure travel of the short distance and duration variety will continue to grow. These in-home and close-to-home alternatives will increase the price elasticity of demand for pleasure travel. And if the industry does not deal with the problems of delivering the tourism product to the consumer, we can expect pleasure travel to show little growth at all.

Market structures

Demographers project that the US population in 2000 will be markedly different from the population today in a number of ways.

US population is growing older. The median age of the US population is 31.4 years and will be five years older by the turn of the century. The 'baby boom' generation (born between 1946 and 1964) will occupy the 36–54 age group in 2000, increasing its numbers by 26m over today. In contrast, those adults under the age of thirty-five will decline by 10m. The 36–54 age group consistently shows higher rates of trip generation than others, so the increase in their numbers should provide a mild boost to travel demand, all other things being equal. But all things are not equal, and this growth is not guaranteed given pressures on the family's leisure time and competition for the discretionary dollar.

Retired population will be an excellent market for pleasure travel. The most dramatic changes in the leisure life of an individual occur when he enters the labour force and when he leaves it. In 2000, there will be 22 per cent more people aged sixty-five or older than there are now. In this age group 87 per cent of the men and 94 per cent of the women will not be working.

The US retired population will be increasingly better educated, with experience in travelling long distances. And the retired market is increasingly well off, both objectively and in their own eyes. The current income per person in households aged sixty-five years or more equals 90 per cent of the average for all households. Yet their financial obligations are considerably less.

Recent surveys indicate that the retired are just as satisfied with their financial situations as other households, and that lack of money to live on is not a problem.[7] The same surveys indicate more than one-half of those in the senior market view their physical health as excellent or good, and that poor health is a serious problem for only one in five. The retired do not take as many trips away from home as other age groups, but when they do, they tend to stay away 50 per cent longer and travel 10 per cent further than their younger counterparts. They are also more likely to travel to a foreign destination.

The growth of this segment to the year 2000 should boost long-distance and duration travel, travel to foreign destinations, sales of package tours, common carrier travel, travel during non-summer seasons, and travel by recreational vehicle.

Minority ethnic and racial markets are growing rapidly. Black, Hispanic and Asian Americans now comprise nearly one-quarter of our population. By 2000, we expect them to make up one-third, with Hispanics outnumbering blacks. We know relatively little about the travel patterns of our minority populations, and there seems no reason to assume they match those of the whites. This subject is worthy of a good deal more research to determine how best to satisfy their travel desires. But we do know that immigrants now comprise one-fourth of our net population growth. These new Americans may well be a lucrative market for international home travel in the decade ahead.

Geographic distribution of the US population will change dramatically. Overall, the US population is projected to grow by 12 per cent to the end of the century (0.8 per cent annually). However, this growth will not be evenly spread among our regions. The Rocky Mountain region is projected to grow faster than any other, with the southeast and far west also growing 60 per cent faster than the nation. Among states, Arizona, Alaska, California, Colorado, Nevada, and Wyoming will show the most growth. By contrast, the northeast population will grow by only 6 per cent between now and 2000, while that of the Great Lakes area will grow by only 1 per cent, according to the US Department of Commerce. This suggests changes in target marketing are in order.

US population will be better educated. The incidence of vacation travel is highly correlated with educational level. For example, those adults who have completed college tend to average twice as many trips a year as those who have only completed high school. It is encouraging then that the percentage of those attending college grows with each successive generation. Now, 36 per cent of Americans aged twenty-five years or more have attended college. By the end of the century, this proportion is expected to reach 40 per cent.

Singles market is growing stronger. The size of the average US household is projected to decline from 2.69 now to 2.48 at the end of the century. Continued high levels of divorce, increased longevity and elderly people able and willing to live alone, and a declining incidence of childbearing will combine to produce this pattern.

Non-family households, those comprised of individuals living alone or with unrelated others are projected to increase 2.5 times as fast as family households. Married couples will comprise only 53 per cent of all households – down from 58 per cent today.

Upper income households will grow fastest. Demographers project that the number of households with family incomes of $50 000 or more in 1982 dollars will rise 86 per cent to 1995, and comprise 21 per cent of all family households – up from 12 per cent now. Contributing causes are the ageing of the population and its income-earning capacities and the continued growth of multi-earner households. Of working age households (18 to 64 years old), 55 per cent now have both spouses employed. This is expected to rise as women account for two-thirds of the labour force growth to the end of the century.

Projected shifts in employment growth will benefit business travel. Employment opportunities will shift to a number of the service-producing industries. 'High-tech' employment will also grow dramatically, but will account for only a small percentage of the new jobs up until 1995. Defence production manufacturing industries will tend to outpace the overall economy in employment opportunities as long as the current defence build-up continues.

The relatively large increases in employment in services, finance, insurance, and real estate industry projected to the end of the century will boost business travel demand. All of these show trip generation rates twice the national average. Currently, business travellers include vacation activities on one-third of their trips. To the extent that this proportion holds or increases to the end of the century, pleasure travel will receive a boost as well.

The decline in communications costs from technological innovations will allow firms to locate outside major population areas to an increasing degree. This decentralization will also encourage business travel, and stimulate growth of the USA's second-tier and third-tier cities.

World political developments

US relations with other countries do affect international travel, directly through protectionist measures, and indirectly through anti-American acts such as terrorist attacks.

USA will not adopt major protectionist programmes. US international trade accelerated in the year of the strong dollar. Consumers and businesses have become accustomed to buying in world markets. This, and the proliferation of multi-national US companies will prevent extensive US protectionism. This is not to say the US government will not increase its revenue from all international travellers through higher taxes and fees.

Impact of terrorism on international travel will wane. Terrorist attacks on US travellers and companies abroad devastated travel to Europe in 1986. US travel to Europe declined from 1985 levels for every month since February. In June, this travel was down 42 per cent but this proved to be the low point. By October 1986, US travel agencies reported international sales were only 4 per cent below the 1985 level.

Terrorism will not disappear in an information society because it is an extreme form of political statement. However, government abilities to suppress it will pay off. Moreover, Americans are getting over the shock of the worst attacks. Future attacks can be expected to have less effect on their overseas travel.

Internal developments and issues

A number of changes are occurring in the US travel industry that will affect the terms on which Americans will make their travel choices over the next fifteen years.

Travel industry is consolidating. Financial difficulties born of excess capacity, economies of scale, high costs of computerization, cost of competing effectively, and corporate customer demands for discounts are working to concentrate airline, hotel and travel agency businesses in fewer, more powerful, hands. The nine major US carriers now account for more than 90 per cent of airline passenger-miles, whereas on 1 January 1986 thirteen airlines accounted for this total. Many independently-owned hotels and motels have failed, and some project the lodging chains will increase their share of the market from 60 per cent today to 75 per cent by the end of the century. Corporations are consolidating their travel accounts in single travel agencies and demanding commission sharing.

This suggests a stronger and more competitive travel industry in the years ahead, one with a recognized stake in travel market development with the ability to mount large and effective marketing programmes. The US travel industry will wield more political weight in the future as well, heading off protectionist measures and lobbying for tax and other policies to promote travel.

Industry firms will rely more on product and market segmentation. Americans are increasingly diverse, dividing into more differentiated segments with regard to life-styles and attitudes. Tourism operators are diversifying their products as well to reduce risk and approach a larger market overall. Examples today are the development of different types of lodging properties to appeal to the budget-conscious, the business traveller, the affluent and other segments. Airlines, as well, segment their service by on-board amenities, advance purchase discounts, and frequent-flier bonus programmes. The result is more competition for each market segment. Marketers of the future must understand more about what their prime segments demand, how they are changing in size and composition, and who their competition is.

Projected labour-supply squeeze will pressure prices upward. The US labour force is projected to slow from the 3 per cent annual rate of growth in the 1970s to less than 1 per cent a year in the 1990s. The number of very young and the elderly in the labour force will actually decline, producing a potential shortage of semi-skilled employees for the hospitality sector. The eating and drinking place sector is already experiencing shortages and expects a shortfall of 1.1m workers in 1995 based on current real wage and benefit levels. One hotel industry analyst has projected the US lodging sector will be limited in real growth to 1.1 per cent a year by the shortages developing.

Despite currently successful efforts to cut labour costs – two-tier compensation systems, lump-sum payments in lieu of wage increases, stock ownership, profit-sharing – labour costs may be expected to rise for the travel industry in the 1990s in response to fewer unskilled and semi-skilled workers. This will place upward pressure on prices and stimulate a search for labour-saving strategies, such as automated cooking equipment, self-service arrangements, automated check-in/check-out procedures and even robots.

US travel industry will employ technological developments to offset this price pressure. The industry has found that raising prices as if in a vacuum chokes off demand (witness the glut of hotel rooms expected to continue to 1992). Consequently, future pricing will be increasingly sophisticated, aided by computer monitoring of market conditions.

The airlines have already found that changing prices (or frequent-flier bonus points) on selected routes at certain times can maximize revenue. One analyst projects airline yields overall will rise half as fast as all consumer prices over the next decade yet still provide growing profits for the industry, e.g. propjet technology will reduce airline fuel costs by 40 per cent to 50 per cent for near-supersonic travel. Aircraft will become more comfortable, as well. The planes of the next decade or so will offer double aisles even on medium-sized aircraft, movable galleys, on-board computer terminals for passenger use, and electronic entertainment systems including seatback video screens.

Lodging firms as well will place increasing emphasis on technological solutions to guest needs and desires – automated check-in and check-out, teleconferencing, in-room entertainment, personal computer hookups, full secretarial services, and health and exercise facilities as standard. Room designs will change – larger guest rooms at expense of spacious lobbies, more residential ambience (rooms on central courtyard), and larger bathrooms with separate tubs and showers.

Conclusion

To summarize, the economic and discretionary time environment in which travel demand will develop over the next fifteen years will be favourable to travel, but not overly so. The travel consumer of 2000 will be older, better educated, more affluent, and less encumbered with dependants. By extension, he or she will be more demanding, less brand-loyal, and less willing to put up with shoddy service and exorbitant prices. With ample alternatives to the pleasure trip, tomorrow's consumer will require more of the industry's personal attention if demand is to grow even as fast as the real growth of the economy. US travel to foreign destinations has not reached maturity, and may be expected to grow at least twice as fast as domestic travel in real terms to the end of the century.

While overall travel may rise as fast as real GNP over the long term, fares, fuel prices, changing tastes, frequency of service, and trip durations can break this relationship for individual transport modes. Air travel, for example, is projected by experts to grow by 5 per cent to 7 per cent a year to 2000, about the same rate as over the last fifteen years.

Car travel will rise less rapidly than during the past decade despite declines in operating costs per mile as the quality of highways and the spread of smaller automobiles reduce the comfort of this type of travel. But travel by recreational vehicle will outpace other road-vehicle travel as the elderly segment blossoms. For the same reason, cruise travel may be expected to grow 10 per cent a year or more in passenger-nights from a small base. Travel by rail, selectively offered by Amtrak in profitable markets, will also outpace car travel over the long run. Intercity bus travel, however, will continue to decline in regular route service, but the motorcoach tour side will expand relatively rapidly as it caters to the senior travel market.

As the population ages, we can expect people to carry with them their interest in healthy diets, fitness, exercise and outdoor activities. Full-service luxury resorts that offer these amenities will grow in number and capacity.

The meetings and conventions business should grow faster than travel for other purposes as special interest associations continue to grow in number. The conclaves will become more educational to outfit their members for competing more effectively in a challenging world.

Despite increasing communication technology and declining costs, teleconferencing will not replace today's business meetings and conventions, except those periodic corporate meetings designed only to update staff. Widely heralded five years ago as the way to cut corporate travel costs, teleconferencing has been a major disappointment. Only 10 per cent of meeting planners indicate they used this technology, according to a recent survey.

In short, the future will be a challenging place to do business in and success will come to those best prepared.

Notes and references

1   I use the terms 'travel' and 'tourism' interchangeably to mean travel away from home to a place at least 100 straightline miles and return.

2   A 'person-trip' is counted each time one person goes on one qualified trip. Three people on a trip comprise three person-trips, as do three people travelling separately. These estimates of US travel activity are derived from the US Travel Data Center's National Travel Survey.
3   Edmund Burke, in a letter to a member of the National Assembly, 1791; and Patrick Henry, in 'Speech in Virginia Convention', Richmond, 23 March 1775.
4   Louis Ferdinand Celine, *Voyage au Bout de la Nuit*, 1932; and Charles F. Kettering, *Seed for Thought*, 1949.
5   Mark Twain.
6   Naisbitt, John, *Megatrends, Ten New Directions Transforming Our Lives*, New York: Warner Communications Company, 1982.
7   National Opinion Research Center *et al*, 1985.

Acknowledgement

This chapter is based on a contribution to an international conference on tourism in the 1990s, organized by *Tourism Management* and the Department of Hotel, Catering and Tourism Management, University of Surrey, in London in November 1986.

9 Japanese travel boom

Ivan Polunin

In the early 1980s Japanese overseas travel grew from 4.0m trips in 1979 to 4.9m in 1985 (see Table 9.1). In spite of Japan's economic strength and affluence the low incidence of travel by a population of 121m and modest growth were regarded as the norm. The 'Japan is different' school of thought explained that because of the strong economy the Japanese were too busy to travel. Since the 'second oil crisis' in 1980 affordability was not thought to be a hindrance to growth in overseas travel.

What caused a change in the norm? What led to the current surge in overseas travel, that now looks set to continue into the 1990s? The event which triggered off change was the Plaza Accord reached in New York in September 1985 by the monetary authorities of the UK, the USA, Japan, West Germany and France (G-5). This led to the revaluation of the yen, in particular against the US dollar.

Table 9.1 Outbound travel from Japan

Year	No.	Change (%)
1979	4,038,298	
1980	3,909,333	− 3.2
1981	4,006,388	+ 2.5
1982	4,086,138	+ 2.0
1983	4,232,246	+ 3.6
1984	4,658,833	+10.1
1985	4,948,366	+ 6.2
1986	5,516,193	+11.5
1987	6,829,338	+23.8
1988	8,426,867	+23.4
1989	9,662,752	+14.7

Source: Ministry of Justice, Japan

Arguably the root cause of the current travel boom was the huge US deficit which had reached alarming dimensions. A remedy was sought. Japan, with its huge and growing surplus with the US, its restricted markets, and dependence on exports was the scapegoat. G-5 members agreed that revaluation of the yen, would be one of the best and quickest remedies. The revaluation was indeed quick and, for Japan, traumatic. The yen went from 235 to the US dollar before the Plaza Accord to 175 within six months. However, the immediate impact was the opposite of what was hoped for. The trade imbalance worsened as the dollar value of exports soared. While import costs dropped the shelf prices of imported goods remained little changed, so there was not a sudden increase in imports. Tourism, which in developed countries usually responds quickly to significant currency changes, reflected little impact. Tour prices remained unchanged and outbound travel grew modestly, as before.

The business mood in Japan following the Plaza Accord was pessimistic. Manufacturers became increasingly concerned about their competitiveness overseas and forecast increasing losses as the yen notched its way ever upwards. Financial year 1986–7 saw several of the big manufacturers reporting huge losses for the first time in years. Unemployment reached the unknown heights of 3.8 per cent. In spite of falling costs overseas the travel industry shared in the gloom. The 'Japan is different' school now said that the Japanese would have to stay at home and work harder to keep business afloat. For a while this view was supported by fact, particularly in the Kansai Region (around Osaka) where many small businesses, that supply parts to the large manufacturers, are based. They were being squeezed by their principals who in turn were trying to keep export price rises at modest levels. Selling travel in Kansai was tough in the spring of 1986 and long-haul group airfares were significantly lower there than from Tokyo. Interestingly, during that period few talked about the benefits of the rising yen, namely the falling cost of imported raw materials, falling fuel prices and the dramatically increased spending power, notably in US dollar destinations, of the overseas traveller. The Japanese were not yet aware of how cheap it was becoming overseas. Tour operators were not reflecting this to any significant extent in their pricing or publicity. Foreign airlines were keeping quiet about the great increases in yield they were making in their local currencies. The yen appreciation (*endaka*) took time to bite.

The importance of *endaka* to the current travel boom cannot be denied. It has contributed to a confident, more aggressive and innovative travel industry based on good profits. However, it has not been just the new affordability of travel nor falling costs and prices that have caused the boom. Rather it has been the coincidence of a number of factors, many of which relate back to that American trade deficit.

'Internationalization'

The buzz-word in Japan in recent years has been 'internationalization', a 'Japlish' (Japanese–English) word which no one can clearly define but which is all the more potent because of its variable interpretation. It reflects the mood of the newly-confident Japan which is 'coming out' into the world from its former shy and reticent international position. Tourism is a price beneficiary of internationalization.

Mr Nakasone was the first Japanese prime minister who was visibly internationalist. Although generally regarded as un-Japanese in style, he reflected the spirit of internationalization to the outside world and to the Japanese. Instead of resorting to typically Japanese political vagueness, which foreigners tended to label evasive and even dishonest, he tried, on the surface, to answer American (and European) complaints directly. Thus he appeared on television buying foreign goods at a Tokyo department store and told the Japanese to do the same. He made a show of buying French helicopters instead of Japanese just before the economic summit held in Tokyo in 1986. Luggage trolleys at Narita airport bore the slogan, in English, 'import now'. Duty-free allowances for the Japanese became probably the most generous in the world. Outwardly these tactics were for foreign consumption, to show that Japan was making specific efforts to reduce its trade surplus. In Japan their main impact was cultural. The Japanese government was telling the nation that it was not unpatriotic to buy foreign – in fact it helped Japan. A side effect was that the Japanese were being exposed, in a positive way, to a wider range of foreign goods and influences.

During Nakasone's administration two major programmes influencing travel were announced. The government was concerned about the increasing number of old people and the quality of life which would face the retired in Japan, given its restricted space and rising costs. The 'Silver Columbia' programme ('Silver' for old age, 'Columbia' for discovery overseas) was a proposal to develop Japanese retirement centres overseas. The scheme was quietly shelved after target countries reacted against the thought of Japan dumping its aged. However, official support for the novel idea of retirement overseas contributed to the mood of internationalization.

The other plan, which has aroused a lot of foreign interest, is the '10 Million Programme'. It took the government some time to realize that overseas travel, competing with no local industry, was an ideal answer to the trade surplus problem. In September 1987 the Ministry of Transport announced that overseas trips by Japanese would double from five to ten million in five years (1986–91). Cynics view the programme as a PR exercise whereby the authorities are claiming an existing trend as a government initiative to which they can point in the future as a positive response to foreign criticism. Certainly details in the programme, which do not stand up to critical analysis, offer little of direct benefit to Europe and the USA which it is supposed to please. In reality travel is booming anyway. The ten million figure will be reached in 1990.

Again the importance of the programme lay in its timing and cultural impact. Japanese tend to regard government bureaucrats as well-intentioned partners in progress, even as some kind of father figures. They respond positively to being told what to do. The '10 Million Programme' said that travel was desirable and indeed expected.

Another change stimulated by Japanese government pronouncements is a changing attitude towards leisure. Working Japanese use little more than half their annual leave entitlement and, except for their honeymoon (an overseas travel market of 1.2m a year), will seldom take off more than three to four days at a stretch. In 1988 the average Japanese worker worked 2,168 hours – over 500 hours more than the average West German worker, whose economy and business style are so much admired in Japan. It has even been suggested that Japan is competing unfairly with other developed countries by working much longer hours. The Japanese government has tried to lead the way, with difficulty, towards a five-day week, and has suggested that the time has come for the Japanese to relax a bit and to enjoy the fruits of their labour. No longer should 'we Japanese' see ourselves as a nation having to work harder to catch up, sacrificing all to economic growth. It will take years before a few extra days off translates into increased overseas holidays, but at least the guilt felt about taking time off is being officially eroded.

At the same time there is a growing interest in life-styles. Overseas travel is now regarded by many as an important ingredient of a desirable life-style. It was first emphasized by the entry in 1986 of overseas travel into the annual list of top ten best-selling 'hit-products' as compiled by Dentsu, Japan's biggest advertising agency.

Thriving economy

The speed and success with which Japan adapted to the yen revaluation has been called, by some, the 'new economic miracle'. Japanese businessmen thought they were in serious trouble in 1985–6. Three years later the economy was stronger than ever and recorded the highest GNP growth rate of all OECD countries in 1988. One industry that thrived on *endaka* from the start was the financial services sector. From being a quiet inward-looking giant, Tokyo burst on to the international financial scene within a year, because of the strong yen. Japanese banks suddenly dominated the top ranks of the world's biggest banks. The Tokyo stock exchange overtook Wall Street in terms of market valuation and turnover. Activity between London, which was experiencing the 'Big Bang', New York and Tokyo increased greatly, and with it travel, not only for short business trips but also to set up new offices and to move staff and families. A greater presence overseas itself led to new opportunities and still more movement.

The greatest new investment was in offshore manufacturing, made easier by the presence of familiar financial institutions. Britain, with financial, linguistic and now air-communication advantages has become the Japanese capital of Europe, hosting an estimated 40,000 residents, many more than second-placed West Germany. They have created a need for Japanese schools, leisure facilities, services and restaurants. Their presence stimulates visiting friends and relatives (VFR), study, and business traffic. Australia, the USA and parts of Asia where Japanese investment has greatly increased, have experienced similar tourism gains. New opportunities in the Gulf, where Japan maintained relations with both sides during the war, in eastern USSR, China, in the Burma to Vietnam region, and now in Eastern Europe, will stimulate travel.

Greater confidence in, and experience of, living overseas have resulted in a greater interest in and willingness to study overseas. There is also growing interest in English language studies overseas and in learning about foreign life-styles, culture, crafts and even etiquette.

Another important stimulant to the travel boom was the start, by All Nippon Airways, Japan's huge privately-owned second airline, of international flights, first to the US mainland, from July 1986, then to Asia and in 1989 to Europe. Each new launch has been heavily promoted. The introduction of non-stop services, particularly to Europe over the USSR, has brought destinations nearer in time, cost and mind. Increased activity by competing foreign destinations has been evident. Japan's greater international visibility and wealth has attracted a flood of travel salesmen to Tokyo. There are now over eighty foreign government tourist offices based in Japan competing for Japanese traffic.

Obstacles to tourism

With the rapid growth of tourism blockages have appeared. Airline capacity is critically short on many Asian routes and between Japan and Australia. Tokyo's Narita Airport is stretched year round and is now 'full' at 360 flights a day in peak periods. Building of the second runway at Narita is meeting with resistance from environmentalists and farmers, reminiscent of that which long delayed the opening. Offshore expansion of Haneda, Tokyo's second airport, where two more runways are being added to the present two, will not be complete until 1995. The 'floating' New Kansai International Airport in Osaka Bay, which may relieve pressure, was started in 1987 and will not have its first runway operational until 1993 at the earliest. The only other definitely planned international airport is Chubu International in Nagoya which is due to start construction in the mid-1990s.

A number of cultural factors will continue to inhibit overseas travel growth during the next decade. The inability of working men to take off more than a few days at a time will hinder travel. The importance of work and sense of duty to the company will make it difficult for the Japanese to extend business trips particularly in long-haul destinations which are further away from base. Thus, for example, products like golf weekends added to a trip are only viable if they can be business related.

English language ability may be improving fast but the Japanese will continue to be particularly worried about exposure to language difficulties. Detailed pre-departure information in Japanese is critical. Many will feel too nervous to use tourist information centres on arrival unless there is a special welcome for the Japanese. In receiving countries, particularly in Europe, the shortage of Japanese speaking guides is seriously worrying Japanese tour operators.

The Japanese, by nature, are not individualists or adventurous on their own. They are nervous about doing the wrong thing and causing embarrassment. Group travel, and the security it provides, is therefore to be preferred. The Japanese are used to attentive service and high standards of presentation back home. Tour operators find it easier, therefore, working with overseas establishments, be they shops, restaurants or accommodation, which are attuned to these standards and expectations. This hinders the introduction of new products. It also explains the strong tendency of tour operators to use Japanese ground operators, or those with Japanese staff, in receiving countries. Understanding the expectations and needs of Japanese clients requires special study. For example, they save all complaints for the tour organizer back in Japan, thus avoiding any embarrassment overseas. This can mislead foreign suppliers into believing that their service is fine and to being unappreciative of client expectations.

The recent increase in Japanese ownership of hotels and leisure facilities abroad could have a marked influence on tourism flows as tour operators and ground operators are inclined to work with their own countrymen. The purchases of Intercontinental Hotels by the powerful Saison Group and Westin Hotels and Swissôtel by the Aoki Corporation, and hotel expansion by Japanese airlines are interesting in this respect.

Other trends

Several other trends which are important to the dynamics of the Japanese market are worth noting. The ending of Japan Airline's monopoly of international scheduled services in 1986 added momentum to capacity expansion. In 1989 the number of direct flights between Tokyo and London nearly doubled from nineteen services a week (October 1988) to thirty-four, operated by four airlines. In 1990 the number rose to forty-two. This should cause Europe's share of overseas travel to increase above the perennial 10 per cent to 11 per cent.

The Australia phenomenon has been the most dramatic recent destination development. Notwithstanding the hiatus and check to growth caused by the damaging pilots' strike, in five years Australia rose from a relatively unknown destination to being the most desirable honeymoon destination for the Japanese, overtaking Hawaii, which for a long time had been the favourite spot. Japanese investment in Australia has been concurrent with that boom.

The outstanding demographic trend in recent years has been the growth in travel by women, particularly those under the age of thirty who are not married. In 1977 women accounted for 25.6 per cent of visits of those aged up to thirty. In 1989 they were over half the total at 56 per cent. Almost 69 per cent of the 1.5m travellers in the 15–24 age group are now female.

Postscript

The 1990s started with the travel boom continuing, almost unchecked. The economy, buoyed up by strong domestic consumer demand, is sound and is forecast to continue robust growth at around 4 per cent per annum over the next few years. Prices in Japan are as high as ever, but now consumers are well aware of the lower prices overseas. London and Broadway musicals, a novelty in Japan in the late 1980s, are now commonly imported or home produced. Italian and South East Asian food are the rage. Beaujolais Nouveau has given rise to a new industry which might surprise the French. There is a growing penchant for imported goods and 'ethnic' is a key fashion word. Internationalization is now well entrenched.

The decade started with a few jolts and hitches. The long illness and then death of the Emperor, and the sudden disaffection with China after Tienanmen Square, were both cited as hindrances to overseas travel and reasons for the 10 million mark not being reached in 1989. It should be noted that the Ministry of Justice figures do not include departing foreign nationals resident in Japan, so 10m overseas trips probably were made. There has been concern about inflation, which coincided with the intro-duction of the unpopular 3 per cent sales tax and depreciation of the yen. But forecasters say this should be contained at below 3 per cent in the early 1990s. For two years the yen slowly depreciated against the US dollar following its very rapid appreciation, and then, in early 1990, it 'dived' to 160 yen to the dollar. After a momentary scare it started to appreciate steadily. The dive was not enough to jolt demand for overseas travel but it did confront the travel industry with a shock they had not experienced before, namely forward commitments made with a weak-ening currency.

A sudden and dramatic drop in the Tokyo stock market caused another jolt. Between 1984 and 1989 the number of individual shareholders was estimated to have risen from 10 to 28m private citizens. The drop did not appear to make much impact on consumer demand. Many investors, who had already enjoyed huge appreciations in the preceding years, were able to absorb some slippage. The drop was short lived and the share index started to climb back.

Yet another alarm was raised by the Recruit Shares and the sex scandals that rocked the Prime Minister's office. The LDP lost control of the upper house as a result, and the nation braced itself for dramatic change at the general election in February 1990. In the event the electorate played safe and the LDP was, once again, comfortably voted back into power for four more years of slow change.

The only apparent hindrances ahead to continued double digit growth rates in overseas travel are the capacity shortages on air routes and at airports. The introduction of long range 747-400s on long-haul routes has been an alleviating factor and has further contributed to the psychological reduction in distance between continents. The nagging and continuing trade surpluses with the US and the rest of Asia are key international issues, which are likely to inhibit any thoughts about correcting Japan's widening travel deficit. That said, the huge planned investment in over 320 (at the last count) major leisure projects in Japan will create strong competition from the domestic tourism industry.

1992 is not only stimulating a lot of travel related to 'Single Europe', but it will also be a key year for Spain, host of two events of world standing. The Japanese will be strongly attracted to the Olympics in Barcelona and Expo in Seville. Continuing strong investment in property, off-shore manufacturing and service industries in Asia, Europe, the US and Aus-tralia will cause business travel to increase.

The 1990s will see some new segments emerging. Travel to see friends and relatives living and studying overseas will become a significant group. Incentive/study travel, helped by new tax breaks, is being increasingly used by companies to attract and retain staff in an environment where lifetime employment with one company is less common and where there is a labour shortage. A newly identified segment is ex-OLs. These are married women with fond memories of travel when they were single Office Ladies. They are now travelling again with other women while leaving their husbands at work. The Japanese have also recently discovered the pleasures of cruising. Some 120,000 went on cruises in 1988 and 20 per cent growth per annum is forecast over the next few years. The Japanese are building their own cruise boats to meet this growing demand.

The segment getting the most attention is the 'silver' market which is composed of those aged about sixty and over. Japanese life expectancy is the highest in the world and the proportion of aged in the population is rising fast. Today's 'silver' generation grew up during years of austerity and restricted travel, but by the end of this decade there will be a new generation of 'silvers' who are confident travellers. These will be the people who were responsible for Japan's post-war economic miracle, who now have substantial savings, good health and the security of owning valuable assets. The Population Research Institute of Nihon University estimates that by 2020 one in four Japanese will be over sixty-five. In 1990 12 per cent were over sixty-five. Japan's ratio of elderly people will grow at twice the rate of other developed countries.

The Japanese travel phenomenon is all the more remarkable when one considers the great distance of Japan from many popular tourist destinations. Even Korea, its nearest neighbour, which holds limited appeal for many Japanese, is over two hours' flying time away.

In the final analysis, one of the most significant points about this boom is the fact that international travel from Japan is still in the early stages of development. That 9.7m overseas trips were made in 1989 by a nation of 121m (an 8 per cent incidence of travel) suggests a market still in its infancy when compared to travel from similarly affluent nations. In the same year 61m Germans and 57m Britons both made around 30m trips (over 40 per cent incidence). Surveys put the real potential for overseas travel in Japan at something like 90m; 20m travellers by the end of the decade seems a very conservative forecast.

Further reading

Further reading on governments, markets and industries in *Tourism Management* 1980–9

Airey, D., 'European government approaches to tourism', vol. 4, no. 4, December 1983, pp. 234–44.

Airey, D., 'Tourism administration in the USA', vol. 5, no. 4, December 1984, pp. 269–79.

Go, F., 'International hotel industry – capitalizing on change', vol. 10, no. 3, September 1989, pp. 195–200.

Guangrui, Z., 'Ten years of Chinese tourism: profile and assessment', vol. 10, no. 1, March 1989, pp. 51–62.

Kaspar, J., 'Leisure, recreation and tourism in socialist countries', vol. 2, no. 4, December 1981, pp. 224–32.

Kormoss, I. B. F., 'Future developments in North-West European tourism: impact of transport trends', vol. 10, no. 4, December 1989, pp. 301–9.

Lickorish, L. J., 'UK tourism development – a 10 year review', vol. 9, no. 4, December 1988, pp. 270–8.

Nyaruwata, S., 'European market for African destinations', vol. 7, no. 1, March 1986, pp. 56–60.

Sundelin, A., 'Tourism trends in Scandinavia', vol. 4, no. 4, December 1983, pp. 262–8.

Travis, A. S., 'Leisure, recreation and tourism in Western Europe', vol. 3, no. 1, March 1982, pp. 3–15.

Part Four

Product Concepts

For business and other organizations in travel and tourism tourists are markets and tourist experiences are marketable products. All tourist products share some attributes but they also have features, which set them apart. In the 1980s *Tourism Management* articles examined a variety of types and forms of tourism, as well as particular destination products. In this part of the book three more recent journal articles have been selected from many, which discuss important products with growing markets.

Jonathan and Grace Goodrich, respectively of Florida International University and of the Kendall Regional Medical Center, Miami, explore one concept in 'Health-care tourism'. The article defines the concept, describes a pilot survey on which the article is based, and discusses its implications.

In 'Heritage management for heritage tourism' Sue Millar of the University of Birmingham, UK, highlights heritage as a major resource for tourism and examines the relationship between heritage and tourism management. The article emphasizes management responsibilities and the importance of interpretation and presentation of heritage sites.

Donald Getz of the University of Waterloo, Canada, examines a distinct form of tourist product in 'Special events'. The article discusses different aspects of the product from a visitor's, organizer's and community development perspective, with a view to effective event planning and management.

Further articles on tourist products published in *Tourism Management* from 1980–9 are listed on page 131. See also Chapter 17 'Summer Olympic tourist market'.

10   Health-care tourism

Jonathan N. Goodrich and Grace E. Goodrich

Tourism is big business in many parts of the world, such as Hawaii, Jamaica, the Bahamas, the UK and Switzerland. In other parts of the world, such as Australia, tourism, once relatively neglected, is being developed aggressively. Other countries, such as PR China and the USSR are opening their doors to more tourists.

The purpose of this article is to explore the concept of health-care tourism. As far as we know, the term 'health-care tourism' is new, but the phenomenon we describe in this article has existed for some time. The article, based on a pilot study, is divided into five sections:

- what is health-care tourism?
- data collection;
- data analysis and results;
- discussion; and
- conclusions.

What is health-care tourism?

We define health-care tourism as the attempt on the part of a tourist facility (e.g. hotel) or destination (e.g. Baden, Switzerland) to attract tourists by deliberately promoting its health-care services and facilities, in addition to its regular tourist amenities. These health-care services may include medical examinations by qualified doctors and nurses at the resort or hotel, special diets, acupuncture, transvital injections, vitamin-complex intakes, special medical treatments for various diseases such as arthritis, and herbal remedies (see Table 10.1).

Based on this explanation, there are many countries with health-care tourism facilities – Switzerland, FR Germany, Austria, Hungary, the USA and UK and France, to name a few.

Many cities or resorts in these countries have grown up around thermal

Table 10.1 Some typical elements of health-care treatments at some hotels or resorts

---

Medical examinations in the hotel (cholesterol levels, diabetes, blood pressure, etc.)
Vegetarian or special diets
Transvital injections, and vitamin-complex treatment
Daily exercise programmes
Acupuncture
Thermal swimming pools (indoor and outdoor)
Underwater massage (balneotherapy)
Body massages
Cellulite treatments (cellutron)
Saunas
Hydrotherapy treatments
Fango packs (mud)
Special stop-smoking programmes
Various baths, e.g. eucalyptus bath, and Turkish bath
Herbal wraps, and herbal teas
Use of sun-bed under supervision
Sessions on muscle development and relaxation techniques
Beauty treatments, such as facials, cream packs, face peeling, etc.

---

springs and concomitant health facilities. Examples of such cities are Baden, Lausanne, St Moritz, and Interlaken in Switzerland; Baden-Baden and Wiesbaden in FR Germany; Vienna, Austria; and Hot Springs, Arkansas, USA. From time to time, Hollywood celebrities, statesmen, and ordinary tourists visit such resorts for rest and relaxation as well as for treatment of various ailments. The concept of health-care tourism has also spread to many cruise lines which now offer some of the services listed in Table 10.1. These services will spread as we enjoy higher incomes, devote more time to leisure/recreational activities, and seek longer, healthier lives.

Data collection

Data collection for the study consisted of four parts:

- content analysis of 284 tourism brochures on 24 countries[1];
- short, personal interviews with 206 travellers – clients of a large, well-known organization in tourism and travel;

- telephone interviews with twenty-two travel agents; and
- personal interviews with twelve medical doctors and two herbalists[2].

The purpose of the content analysis was to help to identify destinations that advertise tourist health facilities or services. Table 10.1 was compiled from this content analysis. Personal and telephone interviews were aimed at gathering information on aspects of health-care tourism such as users, destinations with such tourism, and the efficacy of the related health-care services.

Data analysis and results

Tourism brochures

Content analysis of the tourism brochures indicated that five countries stood out with respect to some emphasis on health-related services at destinations. These countries are Switzerland, Austria, FR Germany, Hungary and the USA. For example, a brochure about Switzerland entitled *Nova World Tours* in cooperation with Sante International, Ltd, Worldwide Spa and Health Specialists, presents beauty and health programmes, specifies eight major cities in Switzerland, and hotels in these cities with health and fitness programmes for tourists. Some of these cities (and hotels) in Switzerland are Baden (Staadhof Hotel, Verenahof Hotel) Lausanne (Lausanne Palace Hotel), St Moritz (Hotels Kulm, Badrutt's Palace Hotel), and Interlaken (Hotel Solbad Sigriswil, Grand Hotel Beau Rivage). Although each hotel offers different health treatments, Table 10.1 shows typical elements of health programmes at these hotels. Other brochures indicated similar programmes in other cities in Austria (e.g. Baden), FR Germany (e.g. Baden-Baden, and Wiesbaden), and in many states in the USA (e.g. California, Colorado, Arkansas). In California, for example, there is the famous Pritkin Longevity Center which offers many of the services listed in Table 10.1.

Personal interviews

Personal interviews of 206 travellers who visited many countries listed in Table 10.2 produced the following results:

Table 10.2 Profile of 206 travellers

Average age	39
Average educational level	Bachelor's degree
Average annual household income	$41,000
Average number of persons in family	4
Married	146 (71%)
Single	60 (29%)
Number who used health facilities at destinations	21 (10%)

- the average age of respondents was thirty-nine;
- average annual household income was $41,000; and
- 146 respondents (71 per cent) were married (Table 10.2).

The sample could be described as higher income and with more married couples than the average household in the USA, where $20,000 is the average household income and where about 60 per cent of adults eighteen years and older are married.

None of the respondents, however, had used the criterion of 'health-care facilities at the destination' as the main reason to select that destination for a vacation. Instead, more traditional reasons, such as cost and variety of attractions, were used. Of the respondents forty-two (20 per cent) knew beforehand of the availability of special medical services and facilities (Table 10.1) at vacation destinations they visited, and used them. These respondents were older than the other respondents, with an average age of fifty-five, and suffered from muscular and arthritic ailments for which they sought treatment. The non-US destinations they visited that had these facilities were Switzerland and FR Germany. Of the respondents, twenty-one (10 per cent) had used health spas in the USA and Switzerland for muscle toning and general relaxation.

Telephone interviews

Telephone interviews with seventeen travel agents in the USA and five in Jamaica revealed that these travel agents did not generally look at destinations as having, or not having, special health facilities, nor did they perceive health care as a possible motive for visiting a destination. Agencies, also, did not compile statistics on users of special health-care facilities at tourist destinations. We think they should, for marketing strategy purposes. Switzerland and FR Germany were the most frequently mentioned countries with advertised, touristic health-care facilities.

Personal interviews with doctors

The interviews with the twelve doctors and two herbalists revealed the following. Generally, the doctors believed that the health (wellness) programmes at resorts (and corporations) were a step in the right direction, since they involved monitored exercise, dieting, and medical examinations. They cautioned, however, that these programmes were generally ineffective against diseases in advanced stages, such as cardiac diseases where heart surgery may be more effective. They also asserted that these programmes should be viewed by consumers as part of their preventative health care, not just quick-fix remedies. The doctors also cautioned against potential fraud and quackery. Finally, the doctors and the herbalists pointed out that many pharmaceutical companies (e.g. Eli Lilly, Upjohn) and doctors are becoming more informed about the curative medicinal properties of various plants found in many parts of the world.[3] Many times, a combination of herbal medicine and modern medicine, involving herbal treatments, antibiotics, and surgery, is effective in curing some diseases or ailments.[4]

Discussion

There are other facets of the concept of health-care tourism which were not empirically studied here because of the lack of data, and which include market segmentation, competition and medical facilities at destinations. These other aspects are discussed briefly below.

Market segmentation

Market segmentation is a well-known concept and strategy. Bases for market segmentation include geographic, demographic, psychographic, price, usage and benefits. In health-care tourism, there are at least two possible approaches to segmentation of the consumer market:

● health; and
● income.

On the basis of health, advertising appeals could be directed at people with various afflictions, such as obesity. These people would form the core 'health segment'. Advertising appeals could also be directed at people who wish to maintain their youthful vigour and appearance. On the basis of income, some hotels or resorts may cater to the high-income segment who can afford the high prices for the health services at the resort. Other resorts may cater to middle-class clients, furnishing similar services and facilities as the 'high class' resorts, but with much less extravagance.

These two bases for segmenting the health-care tourism market are not mutually exclusive – they overlap. The authors believe that appealing to people on the basis of their health, i.e. preventative health care, or present affliction, would be the better focus of the two segmentation methods. Such an appeal cuts across income, age, geography, benefits, and other segmentation approaches. Furthermore, with the growing health consciousness among peoples of the world, the health-care appeal seems appropriate.

Competition

Competition would be on a micro as well as macro level. On the micro level, hotels, resorts, 'health farms' and health clinics would be competing for clients. Each unit could try to differentiate itself from others through the services offered, perceived differences in service quality, locational advantages (e.g. nearness to the sea, or historic sites), prices, and so on. On a macro level, destinations such as cities, states or countries are competitors for visitors. FR Germany, for example, competes with Switzerland for visitors who seek not only the usual touristic amenities, but also the health-care services mentioned in Table 10.1. Visitors may choose one country over another based on distance, prices, kinds of touristic experiences sought, and so on. Each country could try to emphasize its differential advantages and engage in product positioning strategies through advertising and product development.

An interesting aspect of competition is that many hotels that were built years ago, in and around health resorts, such as Hot Springs, Arkansas, USA, have lost many of their customers to more modern hotels nearby; to newer, competing resorts elsewhere; and to new attractions (e.g. gambling, horse racing). Additionally, the old health resorts can suffer 'burnout' as the health facilities, thermal springs, etc., lose their original intrigue and fascination for visitors.

Medical facilities

Traditionally, tourist destinations appeal to tourists by promoting the variety of attractions, excellent convention centres, delightful cuisine, modern and beautiful accommodation, climate, opportunities for rest and relaxation, etc. Tourist destinations may attract more visitors by mentioning their excellent medical facilities in addition to their other touristic attributes. Such mention could be made in public relations pieces and other literature mailed from the tourism department of one city to another, from chambers of commerce, offices of public officials, and in speeches of government officials to conventions. The medical staff at the health-care facilities should be first class so as to maintain high-quality services. Ideally, they should be fluent in at least two languages (e.g. English and French) since they will deal with people from different countries.

Future research

Health-care tourism has the potential for many future research studies. Some of these are:

● comparison of health-care tourism in Europe and the USA;
● large-scale study of market segmentation relative to health-care tourism;
● forecasting studies of the demand for this type of tourism at a destination; and
● a study of users versus non-users of health-care tourism facilities.

Conclusions

This paper has discussed the novel concept of health-care tourism. The idea can be described as the attempt on the part of a tourist facility or destination to attract tourists by deliberately promoting its health services/facilities (as well as its other usual touristic amenities, e.g. hotel accommodation, water sports, golfing, and scenic tours). The health services could include medical check-ups, minor surgery, special diets, vitamin-complex treatments, herbal remedies, thermal swimming pools, and so on.

Tourism's health-care component is not new. It has existed for many centuries in many countries of the world, e.g. Switzerland, FR Germany, Austria, Jamaica, Hungary, the USA and the UK. What is fairly new, however, is the concept of health-care tourism as a deliberate and growing marketing strategy. It can be a positioning strategy for some hotels or resorts in a world that is becoming more health conscious. Health-care tourism can, however, become subject to quackery, so self-regulation and careful government scrutiny are imperative.

Like many pilot studies on novel concepts, this study has a few weaknesses. First, one of the objectives of the study – to profile users of health-care tourism services – was not fully achieved. This was due largely to the novelty of the concept and general lack of information in the tourism literature, at travel agencies and other tourism organizations. But this was not sufficient reason to abort the study – it encouraged us to explore the idea further. The second weakness of the study is that, given the small sample, the external validity of the findings is limited. More studies are needed. Finally, health-care tourism may be found in countries that do not appear in this study. Review of such countries would be useful and interesting. We hope, however, that this exploratory study will stimulate further studies on the fascinating subject of health-care tourism.

Notes and references

1   The countries concerned were Canada, USA, Jamaica, Brazil, Argentina, Colombia, England, France, Italy, Switzerland, Austria, FRG, Hungary, Sweden, Spain, USSR, India, Pakistan, Japan, Egypt, Kenya, Nigeria, Israel and Australia. Some brochures and booklets with the following names covered more than one country, e.g. *Egypt and Israel, Scandinavia and Russia, Australia and New Zealand*.

2   Two each of the following: cardiologist, rheumatologist, gastrointestinal specialist, dermatologist, orthopaedic surgeon and psychiatrist. Two criteria were used to select these doctors: (a) each had to have five or more years experience in his/her field; and (b) their collective areas of specialization had to be relevant to 'health-care' tourism. The herbalists were selected to add balance and other perspectives to the topic.

3   Bricklin, Mark, *The Practical Encyclopedia of Natural Healing*, Emmanus, Pennsylvania: Rodale, 1983; Swinburne Clymer, R., *Nature's Healing Agents*, Philadelphia, Pennsylvania: Dorrance and Co, 1963; Conway, David: *The Magic of Herbs*, New York: E. P. Dutton, 1973; Coon, Nelson, *Using Plants for Healing*, Emmanus, Pennsylvania: Rodale, 1979; and Trotter, Robert T. II and Chavira, Juan Antonio, *Curandirismo: Mexico American Folk Healing*, Athens Georgia: University of Georgia, 1981.

4   Barrett, Leonard E., *The Sun and the Drum: African Roots in Jamaican Folk Tradition*, Oxford: Heinemann Educational Books, 1976; Finkler, Kaja, *Spiritualist Healers in Mexico*, New York: Praeger, 1985; and Trotter, Robert T. II and Chavira, Juan Antonio, *op. cit.*, reference 3.

11 Heritage management for heritage tourism

Sue Millar

In view of the importance of 'heritage' – defined as the natural, cultural and built environments of an area – to the development of a tourist destination the emphasis on travel, hotels and catering and the scant attention given to heritage in mainstream tourism texts gives cause for concern. This article seeks to redress the balance by exploring the specialized nature of heritage management and examining the implications for heritage tourism. The expected continued expansion of international tourism into the twenty-first century and easy access to previously remote areas brings questions of heritage management centre stage.

Heritage management is a new concept that has developed alongside the growth of a new industry – the heritage industry. Heritage and tourism are dynamic areas of development in the UK and elsewhere in the world. On the one hand, the idea of heritage is central to the critical decision-making process as to how irreplaceable resources are to be used by people of the present or conserved for future generations in a fast-changing world. On the other hand, heritage tourism is part of the switch in emphasis from manufacturing to service industry.

Heritage sites provide the tangible links between past, present and future. Heritage sites are in the centre of the struggle between the potentially conflicting aspirations of conservation and tourism. Good heritage management with a major focus on heritage interpretation and presentation ensures that one complements the other (see Figures 11.1

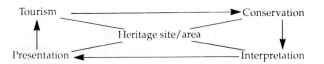

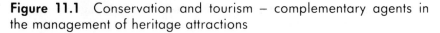

Figure 11.1 Conservation and tourism – complementary agents in the management of heritage attractions

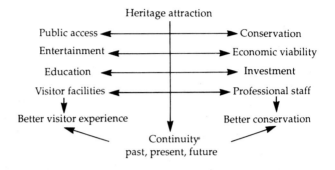

Figure 11.2 Conservation and tourism – public accountability of heritage management

and 11.2). It enables the critical balance to be maintained between the needs of the resource and the needs of the visitor. Through education and entertainment and the enjoyment of heritage attractions such as nature reserves, national parks, museums, historic houses and gardens, villages or towns by people of all ages and socioeconomic groups with different life-styles, it is possible to develop a climate of conservation awareness.

Heritage attractions cannot be put into the same category as other leisure attractions. Sports centres, leisure complexes, theme parks and even a number of heritage centres can be superseded by a new model once the current one is either worn out or out of date. Theatrical recreations with a historical basis such as the Oxford Story are short-term responses to boom times for leisure and tourism and equally disposable. But heritage resources are irreplaceable. Conservation is the critical issue in heritage management. Long-term planning and the recognition of the importance of heritage to the tourist industry are required if the increasingly sophisticated demands of the expanding, discerning tourist market are to be met. In the USA 15 per cent of bookings with travel agents are for special-interest travel where quality not price is the prime factor. In order to examine in detail the significance of heritage management for heritage tourism the following issues are addressed:

● conservation and mass tourism;
● heritage sites – the problem of uniform uniqueness;
● heritage sites – the four variables: tourist attraction, community identity, formal and informal education and economic regeneration; and
● strategic planning for heritage tourism through heritage interpretation and presentation.

Conservation and mass tourism

The conflicting demands of tourism and conservation can be seen in stark contrast in the developing countries. Either the economic benefits of tourism are promoted without a parallel investment in a conservation policy or the lack of conservation awareness merely militates against the promotion of tourism in what would otherwise be an ideal location. India is an example of a country where conservation has failed to keep pace with the explosion in tourism. Dr Narayani Gupta pointed out at the *Second World Congress on Heritage Presentation and Interpretation* at Warwick University, UK, in September 1988:

> Conservation is vitally important in India, at once an old civilization and a developing country . . . . Increased tourist traffic has led to deterioration in the fabric of some of the structures, against which corrective measures need to be taken.

Here she included such national monuments as the Red Fort, the Qutb Minar and Humayun's Tomb. In contrast, the panoramic beaches of Montevideo, Uruguay, South America remain empty because of pollution in the River Plate from the effluent produced by the chemical manufacturing industries.

In Europe, recognition of the deleterious effects of tourism on the heritage of a region has been slow to emerge. In the Balearic Islands following the dramatic changes in the landscape and way of life of the indigenous population occasioned by tourism development, the public authorities are beginning to realize that further economic development can only be justified in conjunction with a policy to promote environmental conservation. Conservation is the first stage in heritage management and heritage interpretation.

The development of commercial tourism in partnership with the conservation policy is not easy. In Autumn 1988 a skiing company from Glenshee in Scotland was prosecuted for allegedly damaging a special nature conservation area. The Glenshee Chairlift Company, it was alleged, failed to inform the Nature Conservancy Council before using a snow-smoothing piste machine on a ski-slope for which the penalty on conviction was a £1,000 fine. Clashes between the requirements for activity-based holidays and conservation in places of natural beauty are difficult to resolve. The ordering of priorities, however, can only be made by heritage managers with sensitivity to the uniqueness of the particular heritage resource combined with an awareness of economic viability.

Heritage sites

Whether recreation or conservation takes priority, the unique selling point for each heritage site is its individuality. Whereas general high standards of visitor facilities, such as clear directions to the site, car parking and toilets are required, there are dangers in greater uniformity. The provision of information boards reflecting the image of an organization such as English Heritage or gift shops selling the nationally-commissioned products of the National Trust, which makes sound sense from the retailing point of view, will nonetheless detract from the visitor's experience of the special qualities of a particular heritage site. The heritage haze of uniform uniqueness offers security to an audience unfamiliar with visiting historic sites but may ultimately have ill effects.

Similarly, the opportunity to indulge in nostalgia and reminiscence offered by actors recreating a Victorian schoolroom scene at Wigan Pier, Lancashire recreates history without the pain and anguish of human existence. The blandness of 'living history' heritage attractions that use the hook of living memory to engage the visitor is paralleled by the deadening of the atrocities of war by the re-enactment of English Civil War battles of the seventeenth century in the evocatively unreal setting of a ruined castle, despite the accuracy of the historical research. Does the future for heritage tourism lie in the gloss of superficial entertainment in the form of the special event? Or, are we underestimating the fundamental curiosity within human beings to find out more about other ways of life and other cultures both past and present in order not only to have fun and family entertainment but also to find their own identity in a fast-changing world?

Interesting work has been undertaken by Gabriel and Barbara Cherem of Eastern Michigan University, USA, looking at community interpretation and tourism. Community interpretation encourages an awareness of, and pride in, the natural and cultural heritage of the community and at the same time enables that community to be pro-active in promoting what it sees as unique in terms of developing an appropriate tourist strategy for the area. By looking into the community with the community and examining what it sees as unique about itself, there is a possibility that the heritage boom will gain in substance and variety and avoid the opprobrium of Robert Hewison's attack on the heritage industry, which he sees as pandering to 'nostalgia' and 'bogus history'.[1]

Heritage sites – the four variables

Heritage sites are multi-purpose – they provide a wide range of tourist attractions, a focus for community identity, a valuable resource for formal and informal education and in some cases, such as the inner cities, the basis for the economic regeneration of an area. The four variables under consideration are tourist attraction, community identity, formal and informal education, and economic regeneration. The emphasis a particular site gives to each of these variables will differ according to the nature of its uniqueness as a resource, the aims and objectives of the organization and its location. The dilemma for many sites is that they are resource led. Created with idealistic, often evangelical, enthusiasm for conservation and volunteer labour, personal, family, civic or national pride and government funding, nevertheless these need tourist money to survive. Ironbridge Gorge Museum, Shropshire, is one example. Formed as an educational charity to seek and foster an understanding of the Industrial Revolution in the context of the economic regeneration of the area, it is now a UNESCO World Heritage Site and a major tourist attraction. Conversely, and increasingly, sites that are mainly market-led face a different dilemma. Motivated to run a heritage attraction on a commercial basis to meet the growing demands of leisure and tourism, the operators have problems in finding spare cash for active conservation work. At Alton Towers, Staffordshire, the castle and gardens within the theme park remain merely a backdrop for funfair activities. Not far away geographically, but at the opposite end of the spectrum, the Brindley Mill Preservation Trust in Leek is run entirely by volunteers. Situated in the centre of the town it is a focus for community identity and local pride. All these sites mentioned here encourage schools and colleges to make use of their resources.

Heritage management intercepts with tourism management but the successful management of the heritage of an area or a heritage site involves a sensitivity to the requirements of both the heritage resources and the community of which they are a part as well as the demands of either short-stay or long-stay visitors.

Strategic planning

Heritage tourism is fundamental to a successful tourism policy in the UK. In 1987, tourism in England earned a record £11,150m and the importance of heritage tourism was acknowledged by Norman Fowler, Secretary of State for Employment, in his annual report entitled *Making the Most of Heritage*. Under the heading 'Heritage – developing the potential' the report states:

> The British Tourist Authority's surveys consistently show heritage as our number one strength. But it isn't enough to preserve it, although that's the

vital first step. It has to be marketed, made accessible, interpreted and woven into the wider enterprise of tourism and leisure – and all this without damaging or demeaning it.[2]

Long-term planning for heritage tourism with an integral, continuing conservation policy, is essential in ensuring a quality experience for the visitor at each heritage site, village, town, seaside resort or area of countryside.

Interpretation and presentation

Heritage interpretation provides the key to a successful management policy. Heritage interpretation and presentation are central to the management process. Interpretation not only encourages research into, and enhances, our current understanding of the existing legacy of past cultural, natural and built environments in all their manifold unique manifestations but also enables us to decide on current management priorities, thus avoiding the ill-considered, irreparable loss of heritage resources. The 'buzz' word 'heritage' – liked and loathed by participants in the heritage business – has strengths as well as weaknesses in its ambiguities. Narrowly defined, heritage is about the cultural traditions, places and values that influential groups throughout the world are proud to conserve. Broadly defined, heritage is about a special sense of belonging and of continuity that is different for each person. This can only be gained individually through a respect for, and understanding of, past roots in relation to present circumstances. The heritage site is the visible outcome of the need for continuity whether it is found under the umbrella of conservation or tourism. The presentation of heritage sites through the various media of guides, information boards and re-enactment both entertains and educates the visitor. It offers people a way of gaining a past perspective on the present, a springboard for future action and sometimes nostalgia. It fosters a climate of conservation awareness. It can also be an effective management tool in directing visitors away from sensitive areas of the site.

Interpretation and presentation provide the underpinning to management, marketing and financial decisions and strategies. Interpretation is the starting point and presentation the coherent culmination of these activities serving a disparate clientele in a variety of ways. For example, 2000 visitors tramping through the gardens of a historic house on a wet day can cause untold damage to lawns and flowerbeds, but a special event used as an interpretive management tool and held in an adjacent field retains public goodwill, attracts funds and switches the emphasis away from the house and garden. The management of interpretation and presentation is rather like juggling – done well, it is the key to conservation and commercial success, done badly, it may mean a significant part of our heritage is lost for ever. The Banff Declaration made at the First (1985) World Congress on Heritage Presentation and Interpretation rightly stated that 'Heritage Presentation and Interpretation are indispensable elements in the conservation and management of the world's natural and cultural resources.'

Conclusion

The activities of all tourists at their destinations fall within the broad remit of heritage tourism. Sunbathing on a sunsoaked beach of natural beauty, eating the local food and visiting the local town bring the visitor face to face with the heritage resources of a particular area of the world. Therefore, active support for conservation initiatives is in the long-term interest of tourism planning, research and development. Viewed in narrow focus, however, individual heritage sites such as Notre Dame Cathedral and the Eiffel Tower in Paris, or the Tower of London and Shakespeare's birthplace at Stratford-upon-Avon in England, provide the motivation for people to visit a country in the first place. In addition, the wide variety of heritage attractions from cathedrals to steam railways, historic houses to fishing boats, open-air museums to the Bank of England Museum, means that there is sufficient choice to meet the needs of different socioeconomic groups with different interests and different life-styles.

So far the marketing of heritage attractions and heritage tourism is in its infancy. Heritage sites throughout the world are able to respond to the needs of the majority of the population if heritage management is seen as an essential ingredient in successful heritage tourism. The growing sophistication of tourists, the demand for quality and increased segmentation of the tourist market into such categories as business/conference and special interest travel, highlight the importance and urgency of bringing heritage management into higher profile within tourism management.

References

1   Hewison, R., *The Heritage Industry*, London: Methuen, 1987.
2   Fowler, N., *Making the Most of Heritage*, London: HMSO, 1987.

12 Special events

Donald Getz

Special events are a unique form of tourism attraction, ranging in scale from mega-events such as the Olympics and World Fairs, through community festivals, to programmes of events at parks and facilities. Their special appeal stems from the innate uniqueness of each event, which

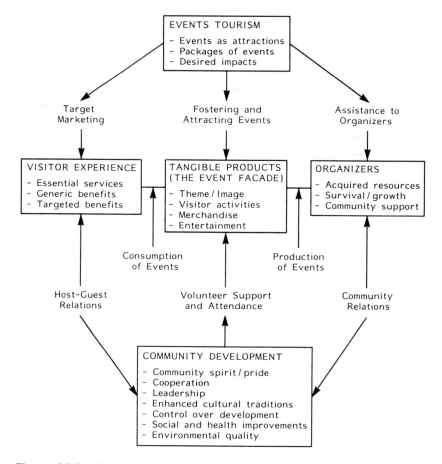

Figure 12.1 Perspectives on festivals and special events

differentiates them from fixed attractions, and their 'ambience', which elevates them above ordinary life.

Increasingly, events are being viewed as an integral part of tourism development and marketing plans. Although the majority of events have probably arisen for non-touristic reasons, such as religious holidays, competitions, community leisure, or cultural celebrations, there is clearly a trend to exploit them for tourism and to create new events deliberately as tourist attractions.

Defining the special event product, however, is subject to interpretation based on one's viewpoint. Indeed, five distinct but interdependent perspectives can be identified. Figure 12.1 presents a conceptual model of the five perspectives and the management functions which link them into a coherent structure.

The tangible product

Superficially, events are easily classified by reference to their tangible components. A number of surveys have assessed the most common themes and activities associated with festivals and special events. From these surveys a more generic categorization of tangible event products can be made.

The tangible products are really a 'façade' presented to the public. They are the mechanisms by which visitor experiences are partially created, although there must be a synergistic process involving these products and many intangibles to create the atmosphere or 'ambience' that makes events special. Furthermore, special events are usually produced as a means towards attaining broader goals. Even in cases where festivals or other celebrations are traditional and have no planned touristic orientation, tourism will often become a factor when tourism agencies begin to advertise, promote or package the event.

Visitor experiences

From the visitor's perspective, special events present the opportunity to participate in a collective experience which is distinct from everyday life. And because they occur infrequently, or are different each time, novelty is assured. It is suggested that an appropriate way to examine this perspective is to focus on benefits expected by visitors.

Generic benefits

Generic benefits are those which distinguish special events from permanent attractions. Each generic benefit is of the kind likely to be expected by the visitor regardless of the tangible event programme, although the relative importance of each will vary from event to event. A brief description of each benefit follows.

1 *Spectacle.*   While there is no doubt that spectacle, especially media-orientated events, have universal appeal, it is also true that raw spectacle can overpower the more fundamental meanings of festivity, ritual and games that events should embody. Spectacle can be an important element in any special event by focusing on visual, larger-than-life displays and performances. Events orientated towards television may achieve the greatest benefit from a tourism perspective, but run the risk of having to make sacrifices to accommodate the demands of television.
2 *Belonging/sharing.*   The sharing of experiences with others in the context of a public celebration or display is a major leisure motivator. There is usually a kind of infectious merrymaking which accompanies special events and encourages participation. This emotional 'high' might actually be the main reason why many people participate in events, either as volunteers or visitors.
3 *Authenticity.*   Authenticity has been much debated in the literature with no clear conclusions as to its significance as a motivator or as a criterion for evaluating the product. Literature on this subject has been expanding, including examination of the authenticity of folk festivals, how tourist-orientated events transform culture and history, the value of 'cultural productions' in avoiding a negative impact on tourism, and a questioning of whether or not historic recreations can be authentic. Whether or not the creation of tourist-orientated events, or the promotion of cultural events for tourism creates inauthenticity, is an issue for continued research and clarification. From a tourism perspective, the real issue is ensuring visitor satisfaction and community support. Nevertheless, tourism developers should be sensitive to the goal of protecting events which are primarily cultural and local in nature, especially in traditional societies. Not all events should be seen as resources for tourism exploitation.
4 *Ritual.*   Ritual is at the heart of most traditional festivals, but is found to some extent in most special events either in secular or religious form. Themes and symbols which invoke community or national pride and loyalty, often found in parades, are closely linked

to ritualistic activities. Even at the most basic level, opening and closing ceremonies can be enhanced through ritual.

5 *Games.* People expect to have fun at most special events. Their expectations can be met through the fostering of a general atmosphere of festivity, and through formal opportunities to participate in, or witness, games of chance, recreational activities, competitions, and humour. The most serious of ritualistic events is often counterbalanced by formal or peripheral episodes of unadulterated merrymaking.

Targeted benefits

Targeted benefits are those which differentiate events and yield competitive advantages. Visitors expect basic services to be provided and are looking for certain general benefits from all events, but their attraction to particular events in a competitive environment will require something more.

The event theme is important in conveying messages to potential visitors about the benefits they might derive from attendance. The name alone is not sufficient, nor is the tangible 'façade' in the form of activities. Rather, the theme must be presented in such a way that the unique benefits offered by the event are clear. Each element of the tangible product can provide this competitive advantage, as in these examples – entertainment, e.g. bluegrass festivals, merchandising, e.g. ethnic foods, and activities, e.g. street dances or tours.

Organizer's perspective

Once established, organizations can take on a life of their own. Over time, producing the event might become secondary to survival of the group, or original goals might be displaced by totally different ones. When assessed from this viewpoint, the 'product' takes on a completely new meaning. A model developed by this author and W. Frisby outlined three key processes requiring analysis.

1 *The organization and its environment.* The environment for events is both a physical and a community setting. The physical impact tends to be less for events than for other attractions, unless major construction occurs. However, most events have a community impact because they are dependent on community volunteer participation and attendance.

The event organizer must view the community and the physical environment as a resource, and must therefore worry about negative impact. More importantly, the organizer can deliberately employ the event as a tool in community development.

2   *Internal management processes.*   Events differ from most attractions in that their typical reliance on volunteers makes management more difficult, notably because of a lack of professional expertise, difficulty in recruiting and keeping volunteers, and diffuse goal setting and decision making. Also, to the volunteer the event might be secondary to considerations such as prestige, community involvement, or socializing. The 'product', in this light, is inward-orientated and might tend toward self-perpetuation of the organization itself, rather than production of a quality event.

3   *Transforming processes.*   Most of the organization's energies should be directed at converting resources (including the energy of volunteers) into the event and its desired outcomes. To the extent that community development or some other goal motivates the organization, the product is not the event itself but what the event can do toward achieving those broader goals. This point leads to the consideration of a whole range of possible outcomes which define the event product in terms of its effects on the host community.

Community development perspective

The term 'community development' is used here to describe the enhancement of the host population's way of life, economy, and environment. To the extent that organization of the event springs from a community it can be expected to reflect the needs of that community, but this cannot be taken for granted. Problems are particularly likely if the event is superimposed on the host population, is purely commercial in nature, or is controlled by narrow interest groups.

Little attention has been paid to the potentially positive effect of tourism on organizations, localities, and social planning programmes. However, recent interest in 'alternative tourism' has certainly awakened interest in the subject. Also, the work of sociologists and anthropologists has contributed to a better understanding of the meaning and significance of events in communities. Events create links between people and groups within a community, and between the community and the world.

Some research concerning the social and cultural impacts of events has been completed, illustrating both positive and negative forces. Clearly there is a need to weigh the costs and benefits carefully, with emphasis on the host community's perspective.

Although much work is required on the links between special events and the impact on the community, some tentative conclusions can be drawn. Special events can contribute to community development in several ways, to the extent that the following objectives are satisfied:

- the community has control over the event;
- the event is first and foremost directed at meeting community needs;
- local leadership and interorganizational networks are fostered; and
- event planning is comprehensive, taking into account the social, cultural, economic and environmental dimensions.

Events tourism

Special events are becoming established as an integral and major part of tourism development and marketing strategies. The term 'events tourism' has been employed to describe this component, and a simple definition would be the systematic development and marketing of special events as tourist attractions. Typical goals will be:

- to expand the traditional tourist season;
- to spread tourist demand more widely throughout the area;
- to attract foreign visitors; and
- to create a favourable image for a destination.

There appears to be a strong temptation for tourism organizations to think mainly in terms of mega-events, with small events being dismissed as having only local or regional significance. As well, the focus has been on economic objectives, rather than the links between events and social, cultural or ecological policies. These biases are understandable in the light of the documented benefits of hosting special events, but overemphasis on mega-events is too narrow and can be self-defeating.

The benefits of mega-events are often exaggerated. And it has been found that their attractiveness to foreign tourists can be much less than expected. Emphasizing mega-events also ignores the links between the events and the fostering of community development, the arts and culture, and more effective use of parks and facilities.

Small events also have a vital role to play in tourism development. While they might not in themselves motivate foreign travel, they can satisfy the foreign visitor's desire to experience authentic cultural ambience and to meet locals. Indeed, events could become the most common way for visitors to satisfy a variety of desires, including the sampling of local foods, witnessing costumes and traditions, participating in games or other activities, competing, or simply being entertained. The key advantage of small events is that they can make visitors believe (rightly or wrongly) that they are a part of something authentically indigenous. Local and regional events also have value in keeping the domestic market active. Finally, there is no way to predict which small events might become large attractions. Their success will depend on a host of factors, not least of which is the decision of the event to expand or remain small. A sound tourism strategy will therefore seek a balance between large, tourism-orientated events and local and regional events.

Another way to examine events tourism is by reference to the linkages between the five perspectives, as illustrated in Figure 12.1. Each of these linkages defines a planning or management task, or is subject to some control through planning.

Target marketing

Effective target marketing depends on a thorough understanding of travel motives and benefits. Each special event will have a general appeal, but specific attributes can be themed and promoted in order to attract target audiences. Marketing research must be carried out by event organizers to ensure the success of their own event, and tourist organizations at a higher level should be considering the entire range of event products and all related markets. A key planning issue will be that of developing packages of events that cater to various target groups.

Consumption of the tangible product

The actual consumption of tangible products, or participation in entertainment and other events, is a mechanism by which experiences are created. The visitor desires certain experiences which can be identified as benefits. At the same time, the visitor is engaged in activities which contribute to economic growth and community development. The activities of visitors are multi-dimensional in both meaning and impact.

Host-guest relations

To the extent that outsiders are involved, events are formalized settings for interaction between locals and visitors. It has been found that host communities tend to enjoy this relationship, as long as the perceived benefits outweigh the costs. Special events are potentially excellent means for creating host–guest contacts in non-exploitative ways, where both groups can be at leisure. Accordingly, events should be seen as important contributors to overcoming the many disadvantages of mass tourism.

Support and participation of the host community

The host population is required to organize the event, support it through volunteer labour, and attend it as a community celebration. This is the foundation upon which successful events rest, and it cannot be artificially induced from outside if the community has doubts about the costs and benefits.

Community relations

Event organizers have a responsibility to seek community support and maintain it through good community relations. This task can be facilitated in several ways: information to the community; involvement by representative elements of the local population; involvement by community leaders; and open planning and evaluation of the event and its impacts. It is a two-way process because community development depends in part on the fostering of leadership and entrepreneurial expertise through community events, and because of the profits generated for community projects.

Production of the event

The organizers produce an event which has tangible components. Rewards to the organizers (and hence to the community) are generated by attendance and consumption. But the tangible production is not the only provider of resources for the organizers, as they will probably be in part reliant on grants or sponsorships. Furthermore, the production of the tangible event is often in itself insufficient to ensure survival or success.

Assistance to organizers

Tourism agencies must determine their appropriate role with respect to special events, including types and levels of assistance. Such help can be in the form of money, expertise, promotion, or research. In return, tourism agencies will want to see events become more orientated to, and effective in attracting, tourists.

Further reading

Further reading on tourist products in *Tourism Management* 1980–9

Brissenden, C., 'Expo 86 – scenario for success', vol. 8, no. 1, March 1987, pp. 49–53.

Dernoi, L. A., 'Farm tourism in Europe', vol. 4, no. 3, September 1983, pp. 155–66.

Frater, J. M., 'Farm tourism in England – planning, funding, promotion and some lessons from Europe', vol. 4, no. 3, September 1983, pp. 167–79.

Haulot, A., 'Social tourism – current dimensions and future developments', vol. 2, no. 3, September 1981, pp. 207–12.

Hawkins, D. E., 'Tourist holiday options: timeshare versus competition', vol. 6, no. 4, December 1985, pp. 252–71.

Hughes, H. L., 'Culture as a tourist resource – a theoretical consideration', vol. 8, no. 3, September 1987, pp. 205–16.

Lawson, F. R., 'Trends in business tourism development', vol. 3, no. 4, December 1982, pp. 298–302.

Page, K., 'The future of cruise shipping', vol. 8, no. 2, June 1987, pp. 166–8.

Tighe, A. J., 'Cultural tourism in the USA', vol. 6, no. 4, December 1985, pp. 234–51.

Vandermey, A., 'Assessing the importance of urban tourism', vol. 5, no. 2, June 1984, pp. 123–35.

Part Five

Competition in Air Transport

Throughout the post-war period the growth of world tourism has been closely linked with the growth of air transport. Airline services are of major importance to tourism and trends in the industry have a major bearing on tourism development. In the 1980s deregulation and competition in the air, at airports, and in distribution channels were among the issues dominating air transport. These and other issues were reflected in *Tourism Management* during the decade and three selected articles published in the late 1980s form this part of the book.

In 'European air transport in the 1990s' Stephen Wheatcroft of Aviation and Tourism International, London, examines recent and possible future developments in the industry, drawing on UK experience, lessons from US deregulation, and European Community policies and initiatives.

As airlines are increasingly competing for connecting traffic in scheduled air transport by coordinating flights through hub airports, J. P. Hanlon of the University of Birmingham, UK, focuses on 'Hub operations and airline competition'.

The growth of inclusive tour charter (ITC) flights contributed significantly to the growth of Mediterranean tourism. In 'Mediterranean charters' Douglas Pearce of the University of Canterbury, New Zealand, provides a comparative geographic analysis of the demand over time for ITC flights from the UK, FR Germany and Sweden to Spain and Greece.

Further articles on air transport published in *Tourism Management* from 1980–9 are listed on page 176. See also Chapter 16 'Marketing of airline services in a deregulated environment'.

13 European air transport in the 1990s

Stephen Wheatcroft

The privatization of British Airways, and the subsequent merger of British Airways and British Caledonian, marked a major turning point in UK air transport history. These two developments brought to an end the 'Edwards era' in UK policy. It was the bipartisan acceptance of the Edwards Committee's recommendations[1] for the fostering of a 'second force' in the British airlines industry, and the acceptance of a mixed economy with public and private airline ownership, which were the foundation stones of UK aviation policy for almost two decades.

Both policies disappeared together. Having come to the end of the Edwards era, what new policies should be developed to serve the next two decades? The key question is the future role of airline competition, an issue on which the Edwards Report took a rather pragmatic view. The report concluded that 'competition should be regulated to the extent necessary to achieve the purposes of public policy, within the institutional and international framework'.

Lessons from US deregulation

Even the most enthusiastic of its supporters now acknowledge that US deregulation has not worked in the way its advocates thought it would and that some kind of government intervention is necessary to safeguard competition in the airline industry. Deregulation cannot automatically be equated with more competition. What the US experience has shown in particular is that large airlines enjoy enormous advantages, especially in marketing.[2]

There is little doubt that the advantages of large size explain why the US industry is now dominated by a small number of large airlines. In 1987, after the approval of the merger between USAir and Piedmont, eight airlines carried 94 per cent of all domestic traffic.

This newly-emerged concentration explains why many analysts believe that it is now almost impossible for there to be a new entrant, like People Express, able to challenge the powerfully entrenched established airlines. What seems more likely is that there will be further mergers increasing the monopolistic concentration of the industry unless the US government belatedly takes the advice offered by people like Michael Levine and uses anti-trust legislation to prevent this.[2]

Oligopolistic concentration is not necessarily a bad thing – most of our major industries are oligopolistic. But special measures are necessary in the air transport industry to ensure that the objectives of public policy are achieved and that oligopolistic concentration does not suppress competition to such an extent that the interests of users become secondary to profit maximization.

EEC policy

The central purpose of future European air transport policy must be to create a more competitive industry. There is little doubt that the past combination of government limitations on entry and capacity, together with airline agreements on pricing and pooling, produced an inadequate level of competition within Europe. The discussions and negotiations of the past few years in the European Community, and in the European Civil Aviation Conference, have been directed towards this problem.

Progress in the EEC negotiations has been painfully slow and the Gibraltar issue created an unexpectedly new obstacle to the conclusion of an agreement in June 1987. This difficulty was subsequently overcome and the Council of Transport Ministers signed an agreement in December 1987 on a package of measures which represent an important step towards a more liberal regulatory regime.[3] The package involves two regulations defining the application of the competition rules of the Treaty of Rome to the airline industry and other agreements which provide for a relaxation of pricing controls, a progressive reduction of capacity restrictions, a freer access to markets through multiple designation and the encouragement of regional services. The details of the December 1987 EEC package are admirably summarized in *The EEC's New Air Transport Package*.[4]

The objective of these new European policies is not to deregulate air transport in the region but to modify the regulatory structure in ways which will promote more airline competition. This is an objective strongly advocated in a report published by the Economist Intelligence Unit (EIU):

> Total US-style deregulation of European air services is not a practical option and no state or government body is advocating such a policy. Agreed EEC

conditions of competition are needed within the framework of an overall air transport policy. The Council of Transport Ministers must declare that the rule will not have extra-territorial application beyond the EEC; and they should take appropriate action to exempt airline technical, tariff and pool arrangements to the extent that these provide public benefits, are adequately transparent, and are subject to oversight. New conditions of competition encouraging increased efficiency and improved operating patterns will be necessary to respond to the commercial challenges from US mega-carriers, and from the low cost, highly productive airlines of South East Asia, in the years ahead.[5]

These first steps are now incorporated in the EEC package. The EIU report went further and set out the next objective for European policy. It looked towards 1992, the target year agreed by heads of state and governments for the elimination of all barriers to an internal community market, as the date for a second phase of air transport liberalization. It also stressed the importance of involving non-EEC European countries in the liberalization process and proposed a new forum for consultations between the EEC and the European Civil Aviation Commission (ECAC).

European airline industry in the 1990s

What will these changes in the regulatory regime do to the structure of the airline industry in the next decade? Relaxed regulatory controls will produce two conflicting pressures on the industry and the outcome will depend upon policy decisions of a kind not previously made on a multinational basis. On the one hand, a more liberal regime, particularly one which provides significantly more freedom for market access, will create new opportunities for the many airlines now operating inclusive tours (IT) charter services to turn their attentions towards competitive operations on scheduled service routes. This is already happening to a small extent in the UK, as illustrated by the grant of scheduled service licences to Air Europe. Similar pressures are likely to develop in other European countries.

There is considerable scope for this development because there are so many well-equipped non-scheduled airlines waiting in the wings for these new opportunities. This is a fundamental difference between the European situation and the US airline industry before deregulation. It is a unique feature of intra-European air transport that well over half of all passenger traffic – more than 60 per cent of passenger-kilometres – is carried on charter services. Even when the IT charter operations of subsidiaries of national scheduled airlines are deducted, the traffic carried by charter airlines is well over 40 per cent of the European total. This aspect of the European airline industry is a widespread characteristic of the regional industry. Of the top fifteen non-scheduled airlines in Europe, five are British and the other ten are from six other European countries.

This diversity in the European airlines industry, and the strength of the non-scheduled airlines in the large IT charter market, may continue to set the pattern of operations in the 1990s. There may still be a rigid distinction between the scheduled and non-scheduled segments of the industry but it seems more likely that this distinction will decrease. IT charter operators are already serving a substantial percentage of their capacity on a 'seat only' basis, thus combining a scheduled service product with a packaged-holiday product on many major holiday routes. The scheduled airlines are competing in the holiday market by offering part-charters.

The effectiveness of future scheduled airline competition in the holiday market will depend upon two things. First the operational ability of scheduled airlines to achieve a high degree of flexibility in the aircraft layouts, and second, on their ability to control the sale of capacity at different fare levels by computerized yield management techniques:

> Scheduled and charter services are really different types of product for different sectors of the market, which in practice overlap .... A major product distinction is seat pitch and it is that which has kept these products apart .... If seat configuration could be adjusted on turnaround, the capacity would exist for multiple-product service with precise tailoring of standards of the product/price combination on offer.[6]

This is the most probable direction in which the European market will develop in the 1990s and, with the disappearance of the dichotomy between schedule and IT charter operations, the marketing power of large airline size will emerge as the major factor in determining the structure of the industry. This is the second of the two conflicting pressures resulting from the relaxed regulatory controls agreed in the 1987 EEC package. The weight of evidence from deregulation in the USA powerfully suggests that, in the absence of anti-trust action to limit mergers, the European airline industry will similarly develop into an unregulated oligopoly in the years ahead. The pressures towards industry concentration will come from: national mergers, transnational mergers, and transnational expansion.

The BA-BCal merger

The merger between British Airways and British Caledonian represents a major step in the concentration of the UK airlines and it has profound implications for the future of the European air transport business. The UK government felt obliged to refer this merger proposal when it was announced to the Monopolies and Mergers Commission (MMC), which reported its conclusions to the Secretary of State for Trade and Industry in November 1987.[7] It its report the MMC identified several detrimental aspects of the proposed merger but saw important beneficial results:

- the strengthening of the competitive position of British Airways in the face of increasing competition from US mega-carriers;
- an increased traffic potential as a result of a greater number of connecting flights in the enlarged network; and
- financial savings of many millions of pounds annually from the merging of activities and the elimination of duplication of customer services, sales organizations, central management and other overheads.

The MMC said that its task was to balance the advantages against the disadvantages of the merger and it concluded 'that the merger situation may be expected not to operate against the public interest'. It did, however, impose certain conditions, agreed by British Airways, which offered new opportunities for other British airlines to compete on the routes previously operated by BCal. The MMC having reached this conclusion, the UK Secretary of State was obliged by the terms of the Mergers Act to accept the recommendations.

After considering the financial implications of the agreed conditions attached to the MMC recommendation, British Airways made a new offer to BCal which also reflected the fall in the value of BA shares following 'Black Monday' on the UK stock exchange.

BCal's decision whether or not to accept the revised BA offer was then complicated by the appearance of a white knight in the form of SAS which announced its willingness to buy a substantial shareholding of BCal and inject sufficient cash to meet immediate financial needs.

In the event BA determined the issue by increasing its offer for all BCal shares to £250m and this was irresistible to the major BCal shareholders. This looked like the end of the road but a further complication arose from an intervention by the Competition Directorate of the EEC Commission in Brussels. The Commissioner claimed a responsibility to ensure that airline competition in Europe was not adversely affected by the dominant market position which the merger gave to British Airways. The EEC Commission at first threatened to quash the takeover by using Article 86 of the Treaty. After some weeks of negotiations in Brussels an agreement was reached with British Airways conceding additional opportunities for other airlines. The BA concessions allow greater access to the former BCal routes in Europe and are aimed at limiting BA's domination of operations at Gatwick.

The scope for national mergers in other European countries is more limited than in the UK but there are some possibilities. A wholly or partly privatized Air France might look with interest at a takeover or merger with UTA. In West Germany Lufthansa has already taken a 10 per cent shareholding in Hapag-Lloyd. And in several other countries the major national airline may seek to take over the feeder operations which have been developed by smaller airlines in the same way that such operations have been absorbed by the major airlines in the USA in recent years.

Trans-national mergers

The SAS proposal to BCal, despite its defeat by British Airways, points the way to the radical changes which may be brought about in the structure of the European airline industry by the merging of airlines across national frontiers. Such developments will be additional to the moves to find new cooperative arrangements, short of mergers, to strengthen the position of European airlines in a more competitive worldwide environment. The long-standing cooperative arrangements of KSSU (KLM, SAS, Swissair and UTA) and ATLAS (Air France, Lufthansa, Iberia, Alitalia and Sabena) are likely to increase.

New airline groups have emerged to cooperate in the profusion of CRS facilities. One new CRS group, calling its system 'Amadeus', is led by three of the principal airline members of Atlas. They are Air France, Lufthansa and Iberia. The other CRS group, calling itself 'Galileo' is led by British Airways and two major members of the KSSU Group – KLM and Swissair. What is surprising is that there have been three major switches in the European airline allegiances. SAS and UTA have defected from the KSSU group of airlines to join the Amadeus CRS system. And Alitalia has parted from the Atlas Group to join the Amadeus CRS system. These switches in allegiances probably have something to do with technical assessments of the two systems – but they must be seen as setbacks for those who had hoped that the technical cooperation activities of Atlas and KSSU would be expanded into activities involving the coordination of marketing. Amadeus and Galileo will obviously now be better placed to develop these activities.

Beyond these prospects for increased technical and commercial cooperation lie the possibilities of full-scale mergers of airlines from different European countries. Despite the failure of the SAS/BCal negotiations there can be little doubt that trans-national mergers will produce significant changes in the European airline industry in the 1990s. A charter subsidiary jointly owned by Lufthansa and Iberia is one of several developments in train and others, based on the synergies of combined networks and hubs, are likely to emerge or, like a Swissair/Austrian merger, to re-emerge.

There may be some difficult problems in the implementation of trans-national mergers. In a trans-national merger the difficulties inherent in a national merger, like that of BA and BCal, will be greatly magnified by differences in language, culture and deeply-rooted ways of doing things. There are not just organizational problems to be resolved by efficiency experts – they are difficulties which can have profoundly adverse effects on standards of operations and service to customers. There can be little doubt that the serious decline in airline service standards in the USA, about which there was so much public and congressional complaint in 1986, must be largely attributed to the organizational disruptions which have been brought about by the tidal wave of mergers.

Trans-national expansion

The third kind of development in the structure of the European airline industry will probably produce the most radical changes of the 1990s. A policy which will allow EEC airlines to expand their operations, in their own names, into other European countries by using the 'Right of Establishment' provisions of the Treaty of Rome is recommended. This possibility was commented upon in the 1984 EEC Memorandum No 2, 'It is disappointing to note that since the first memorandum no airline has availed itself of this possibility offered by the Treaty.'[8] Almost no further consideration has been given to this subject and it is not even mentioned in the package of proposals agreed by the Council of Transport Ministers in December 1987.

The reason for this silence is, almost certainly, that most European governments are frightened by the aviation implications of the Right of Establishment provisions. More charitably, the governments may already be fully occupied working to liberalize market access and tariff agreements. But, after 1992, when all barriers to trade are removed from the internal European market, the right to establish operations in another Community country seems certain to be a major factor in reshaping the structure of the airline industry.

Articles 52 to 58 of the Treaty – 'Right of Establishment' – set out the ways in which:

> restrictions on the freedom of establishment of nationals of a member state in the territory of another member state shall be abolished by progressive stages in the course of the transition period.

Article 58 seems quite categorical when it says:

Companies or firms formed in accordance with the law of a member state and having their registered office, central administration or principal place of business within the Community shall, for the purposes of this chapter, be treated in the same way as natural persons who are nationals of member states.

This means that any EEC airline has the rights to set up a wholly-owned subsidiary in another EEC country and can expect to be treated in exactly the same way as the national airline(s) of that country. This is the view of officials of the EEC Commission in Brussels. They go further and argue that the right of establishment provisions of the Treaty mean that the 'substantial ownership and control' clauses governing the issue of licence and/or designation of airlines under bilateral air service agreements are an infringement of the Treaty when they are supplied to airline operations within the EEC.

Some governments, including the UK government, do not accept this interpretation of the Treaty. They argue, among other reasons, that the right of establishment provisions of the Treaty have to be read in conjunction with other provisions like those in the chapter dealing with 'Services'. In this chapter there are provisions, in Article 61, which read: 'Freedom to provide services in the field of transport shall be governed by the provisions of the Title relating to the transport.' This is taken to mean that the right of establishment must be dealt with in an Air Transport directive agreed by the Council.

These differences of opinion and interpretation will no doubt be tested in the course of time by cases brought to the European Court of Justice. It seems highly likely that, as with a dispute about the application of the competition rules, the EEC Commission's interpretation will eventually prevail. This may take several years, but taking a long-term view of the factors which will influence the European airline industry in the 1990s, the transformation of national airlines into Pan-European operators is an exciting prospect, provided that the appropriate policies are adopted to channel these developments in the best public interest.

Competition in the 1990s

Much of what has been said so far about the future structure of the European airline industry has looked at what may happen if we extrapolate from US precedents. But it makes more sense to consider what should happen, rather that what could happen, if there were no intervention. The most positive use which could and should be made of the trans-national expansion of airlines in the EEC is to promote competition in circumstances in which national mergers have had the effect of reducing competition. This is similar to the policy which is being advo- cated in the USA by Alfred Kahn, the midwife of deregulation.

The analogy in Europe is that airlines from other EC countries should be allowed, using the right of establishment, to provide the competition which national mergers have diminished. The Edwards notion of the second force could be replaced in the 1990s by the more effective com- petition of other major European airlines.

Another important policy to maintain effective competition in Europe is suggested by Alfred Kahn and Michael Levine who have advocated that more vigorous use should be made of the anti-trust laws to block those mergers which are essentially anti-competitive. This policy could and should be adopted within the EEC.

The powers of the Commission to regulate mergers are still an issue under discussion in the Community. At the time of writing (June 1988), the Commission does not have direct powers to disapprove a merger prior to its implementation. After a merger has taken place the Commis- sion may rule that it has resulted in an undue concentration of market power and may order divestiture. This is an illogical situation and the Commission is asking that all mergers, associations and joint ventures over a certain size should be subject to prior investigation. A merger proposal would be blocked by the Commission if the investigation con- cluded that it would threaten fair competition. If this proposal is agreed the Commission will have won its long-held argument that powers to control mergers are implicit in Articles 85 and 86 of the competition rules of the Treaty. In any event, the Commission's successful intervention in the BA/BCal merger case demonstrated that it already has effective powers to influence merger policies before they are implemented.

This development could be beneficial because the maintenance of air- line competition will necessitate the agreement of a set of rules in the EEC which define when a proposed merger is, or is not, contrary to the public interest and whether proposed airline mergers should be allowed. Some mergers will strengthen the airline system, but others, which have the elimination or reduction of competition as their primary purpose, will not. Making the EEC Commission responsible for that judgement may appear to be a large new element of airline regulation but, in essence, it is a policy strongly advocated by former leading US deregulators.

Major barriers to the promotion of a more competitive airline industry may increasingly arise from limitations of infrastructure facilities, both at airports and in the airways. New policies will be required to ensure that monopolistic control over slots and gates do not become serious con- straints on new entry and innovation. Pricing policies may help to reduce these problems but are unlikely, by themselves, to be adequate without clear policy guidelines on the relationship between competition policy and the allocation of scarce infrastructure resources.

A final point about regulation to maintain competition concerns the danger that control over the distribution system and CRS operations may create monopolistic market conditions. This may easily become a major issue for governmental intervention and, indeed, for inter-governmental dispute in the next few years. It is another issue to which the European Commission must address serious attention and, if necessary, use its powers to ensure that competition is sustained.

This is the central problem for European air transport policy in the 1990s. It must be recognized that neither deregulation nor liberalization will guarantee more effective airline competition. The prime objective of aviation policy must be to find new ways to regulate the airline industry to promote competition.

Postscript

Since this article was written aviation liberalization has continued in Europe and the world airline industry has continued to move inexorably by way of cross-border alliances towards the creation of very large trans-national companies.

In Europe the liberalization package agreed in December 1987 produced what Commissioner Karel van Miert has described as a 'modest success'. A Commission study published in October 1989[9] concluded that airline results had improved and that there had been some increase of competition on multiple designation routes. It is acknowledged, however, that there had been no substantial reduction in fares which had, in general, followed the rate of inflation.

In September 1989 the Commission produced its proposals for the second phase of liberalization for consideration by the Council of Ministers. The decisions made in June 1990 represent an important, albeit limited, progression towards reduced regulation. The Ministers agreed further reductions in the traffic levels required for multiple designation and a further relaxation of capacity controls. They agreed, in principle, that capacity controls should be abolished completely by 1993 and similarly that a system of 'double disapproval' for the regulation of fares should be adopted by that date.

To some observers these agreements seem a bit like postponing an evil day. And it must also be noted that the Ministers took no action on some of the other proposals, including one which would have recognized the right of the Commission to negotiate Community traffic rights collectively with non-EC countries.

It is in this latter area that major developments in European air transport policy will occur in the 1990s. The Commission is pressing for a recognition that traffic on all routes within the Community is cabotage and can be negotiated as such for improved rights for European airlines to, from and within other countries.

In addition to this issue of 'external competence' the Commission is also proposing an extension of joint Community action in the fields of personnel licensing, airworthiness requirements, flight time limitations, CRS regulation, denied boarding compensation, airport slot allocation and infrastructure planning.

One other major development must be noted. The Commission is becoming increasingly concerned about the anti-competitive implications of airline mergers and agreements. It is currently investigating the Air France takeover of UTA and the joint shareholding by British Airways and KLM in Sabena. It has also expressed concern about the extent of operational and marketing arrangements agreed by Air France, Lufthansa and Iberia. Competition policy is becoming more important in a less regulated industry.

References

1 The Edwards Committee, *British Air Transport in the Seventies*, Report of the Committee of Inquiry into Civil air Transport under the Chairmanship of Sir Ronald Edwards, London: HMSO, May 1969.
2 See, for example, Levine, Michael E., 'Airline competition in deregulated markets', *Yale Journal on Regulation*, Spring, 1987.
3 'EEC Air Transport Agreements', *Official Journal of the European Communities*, No: L374, December 1987.
4 EEC, *The EEC's New Air Transport Package*, London: Frere Cholmeley, February 1988.
5 Wheatcroft, Stephen and Lipman, Geoffrey, *Air transport in a competitive European market*, Economist Intelligence Unit, London, September 1986. Geoffrey Lipman is Executive Director of the International Foundation of Airline Passenger Associations.
6 Pugh, Alastair, 'Air transport at the Nouvelles Frontieres', Brancker Memorial Lecture to the Chartered Institute of Transport, *Transport*, June 1987.
7 Monopolies and Mergers Commission, *British Airways plc and the British Caledonian Group plc: A report on the proposed merger*, London: HMSO, November 1987.
8 Commission of the European Communities, 'Progress towards the development of a community air transport policy', *Memorandum No 2*, Brussels, March 1984.

9   'Report on the First Year (1988) of the Implementation of the Aviation Policy Approved in December 1987', European Commission.

Acknowledgement

1   The original article was based on a lecture first given to the Royal Aeronautical Society in London in December 1987.
2   Stephen Wheatcroft coauthored with Geoffrey Lipman a new report 'European Liberalization and World Air Transport', published by the Economist Intelligence Unit in May 1990.

14 Hub operations and airline competition

J. P. Hanlon

One of the clearest trends to emerge from airline deregulation in the USA, and from the rather more gradual liberalization of competition on international routes, is the greatly increased emphasis on hub-and-spoke networks. Many airlines have been realigning schedules at hub airports, timing services on the spokes so that they connect at the hub, arrivals preceding departures with sufficient time to permit the transfer of passengers and their baggage from inbound to outbound flights.

Hubs and schedules

Scheduling through hubs confers some important advantages on an airline. An inherent operational advantage is that it multiplies by permutation the number of city-pairs an airline can serve. From a hub with n spokes an airline can provide through connecting services for up to a theoretical maximum of $n(n-1)/2$ city-pairs. In practice of course, some city-pairs may require too great a deviation to attract traffic, and some may not be served because they are already well supplied with direct services. But a well-developed hub-and-spoke system can endow an airline with substantial competitive strengths. The additional traffic generated by connections can support higher frequencies on services to and from the hub, and through this enable the airline to achieve high market shares, not just of transfer traffic but also in local point-to-point markets. Across a network covering both large and small cities, the degree of competition may vary quite a lot, giving the airline the opportunity to charge relatively high fares in less competitive markets and relatively low fares in the more competitive city-pairs. This places the hub airline in a powerful position. Frequent connecting services between two points can inhibit the development of direct services. Unless the direct service is operated at high frequency, passengers who wish to arrive at their destinations at particular times may often prefer the connecting service, despite having to change planes *en route*.

Fortress hubs

Once an airline establishes a set of well-coordinated schedules at a particular hub, it becomes difficult for another airline to challenge it there. It will enjoy a strong position, unless a new-entrant airline can muster sufficient resources to operate a similar network of feeder services on the spokes – something that may be severely constrained by lack of runway/terminal slots at the hub. This 'fortress' effect can permit the exercise of considerable market power.

Rival airlines might seek to compete, serving just the busiest spokes or meeting passengers' normal preference for direct non-stop flights. But in either event the hub airline might respond by (temporarily) undercutting fares in all the affected markets, possibly cross-subsidizing lower revenues in the more competitive city-pairs by higher revenues elsewhere on the network.

Flight schedules

A hub will be less of a fortress if flights to and from it are not well coordinated. In this respect the essence of good scheduling is that the number of *useful* connections are maximized as far as possible. In theory, if all flights to or from a particular airport were timed so that a passenger could connect between any two, the maximum number of possible connections would equal the square of the number of flights. Not all connections are useful ones, however. Some are entirely useless connections to return flights and some involve so much backtracking as to be of little use to passengers. Some are unattractive because they entail lengthy waits at the hub.

Traditionally airline schedules were designed, either for the convenience of local point-to-point passengers, or to meet operational objectives such as maximizing aircraft/crew utilization, minimizing airport and station costs, etc. But the emphasis is now clearly changing. As markets become more competitive, more and more importance is attached to coordinating arrival and departure times to attract connecting traffic. An important part of this is to concentrate flight activity into a limited number of waves per day. Ideally, these should see a lot of inbound flights arriving within a short space of time, then departing again as soon as some minimum connecting time has elapsed. To maximize the potential benefits the amplitude of each wave should be as great as possible. The fewer the number of waves across the operating day, the greater the number of possible connections.

Competition between hubs

If, for whatever reason, flight schedules are more coordinated at some airports than at others, this would be a major factor in the relative success of different hubs. But in this there are also some other important factors:

● geographical location;
● range of destinations served:
● service frequencies;
● fare levels; and
● airport facilities.

The relevance of these factors can be seen by comparing London with other major air travel centres in Europe.

London is at a geographical disadvantage for Europe-to-Europe connections (save for city-pairs like Lisbon–Oslo). Nor is it particularly well placed to offer links between domestic points. But it is in a relatively good position for UK–Europe and also for Europe–North America, but not so well placed as its continental competitors for Europe–Africa, Europe–Middle East, Europe–Far East, etc.

Clearly, the more destinations that are served the greater the chance of an intending passenger finding a suitable connection, and the odds shorten with every additional flight. In range of destinations and service frequencies, London ranks ahead of its continental competitors, with Paris coming second, followed by Frankfurt, Amsterdam and Zurich in that order. But the lead that London and Paris enjoy in terms of range and frequency is diminished by the split of traffic between their two main airports. Heathrow is still the airport with the greatest number of destinations and frequencies, but Gatwick ranks alongside Brussels and Rome as a relatively weak hub in the international context. There is less of an imbalance in Paris, where a traditional policy of route sectorization means that as individual airports both slip below Frankfurt in scale of departures and destinations.

London and Amsterdam tend to score highly in the availability of cheap excursion and discount fares, an important factor in attracting leisure travellers in particular. Punctuality and in-flight service are often of great importance to business travellers, and the consistently high reputation with respect to punctuality earned by an airline like Swissair, plays a part in persuading businessmen to connect in places like Geneva and Zurich. Most European airports have ample facilities for duty-free shopping, etc., but perhaps Amsterdam has the competitive edge in prices and shop sites. To connecting passengers however, facilities at the transfer point are of much less importance than the quality of the transfer itself, and in this regard there can sometimes be a conflict of interest between hub airlines and profit-motivated airport authorities – for whom franchises on airport shops are an important source of non-aeronautical revenue. Good connections mean less opportunity to use airport shops.

Rank orders by size are reversed when it comes to transfer quality, a factor embracing not just the interval of time required to change from one aircraft to another but also the simplicity and convenience of the connection process. Here single-airport, single-terminal systems operating some way below full capacity (e.g. Amsterdam) are at a distinct advantage. London, however, is a multi-airport, multi-terminal system now heavily congested. A further disadvantage is that flight schedules at Heathrow and Gatwick are mostly not well coordinated.

Connecting traffic

Around four million passengers a year change planes in London. This figure excludes stopover passengers and refers only to those arriving and departing without leaving the airport. Passengers making direct connections presently represent around 20 per cent of London's scheduled passenger traffic. This compares with about 30 per cent in Amsterdam and over 50 per cent in many US hubs.

Transfers in London

In 1984 just over a quarter of total connecting traffic was intraline to BA and 6 per cent intraline to BCal. The numbers of intraline connections for the two British airlines (over a million in the case of BA and over 200,000 in the case of BCal) were about double the numbers to be expected, if the distributions of connecting passengers simply mirrored the distributions of the numbers of flights operated. So the carriers did derive significant advantages from their London hubs. But their position in London has been not nearly so dominant as that enjoyed by some foreign airlines elsewhere. For example, KLM is involved in four out of every five connec-

Table 14.1 Connections through Heathrow, 1984ᵃ

Delivering carrier	Receiving carrier					Total for delivering carrierᶜ
	BA short haul	BA long haul	Domestic UKᵇ	Foreign short haul	Foreign long haul	
BA short haul	310	297	68	153	221	1050 (32)
BA long haul	332	84	43	63	35	557 (17)
Domestic UKᵇ	95	54	13	90	75	328 (10)
Foreign short haul	165	78	74	85	170	572 (17)
Foreign long haul	257	32	67	142	236	734 (22)
Otherᵈ	14	7	5	6	7	39 (1)
Total for receiving carrierᶜ	1173 (36)	552 (17)	271 (8)	540 (16)	744 (23)	3280 (100)

Notes:
ᵃPassengers in thousands.
ᵇExcluding BA domestic (classified in short haul) but including the BCAL helicopter link between Heathrow and Gatwick (no longer operating).
ᶜFigures in parentheses are percentages.
ᵈCharters plus some survey miscodes.

Source: CAA, London Area Airport Study, CAA, 1984.

Table 14.2 Possible daily intraline connections at major European airports, summer 1986

Airline	No. of flights	Long haul to/from long haul	Long haul to/from short haul	Short haul to/from short haul	Total
BA (Heathrow)	170	23	267	969	**1259**
BCAL (Gatwick)	50	6	63	99	**168**
KLM (Schiphol)	75	10	237	514	**761**
Swissair (Zürich)	75	13	219	483	**715**
Air France (Charles de Gaulle)	80	3	101	221	**325**
Lufthansa (Frankfurt)	150[a]	16	453	1698	**2167**

Note:
[a]Including services operated by its subsidiary airline DLT.

Source: Derived from published arrival and departure schedules, allowing for MCTs specified in the *ABC World Airways Guide* and setting a maximum interval between flights of 90 min.

tions in Amsterdam, compared with the situation in London where the merged BA/BCal is involved in just half the connections. And roughly 60 per cent of Amsterdam's connecting traffic is intraline by KLM – more than twice the proportion of London transfers contributed by BA–BA connections.

A detailed examination of transfers at Heathrow (Table 14.1) reveals some striking comparisons. It is apparent that BA feeds more traffic to foreign carriers' long-haul departures than it receives in return for its own intercontinental flights – a rather unusual situation to occur at a home carrier's main base. Data derived from the CAA survey reveal that, not only was the total number of connecting passengers received by foreign carriers' long-haul services greater than the total received by BA's long-haul flights, but the number fed from BA short-haul to foreign long-haul was almost three times as great as the corresponding number fed the other way, from foreign short-haul to BA's long-haul. Of course part of the explanation for this lies in the pattern of services supplied, the preponderance of BA on short hauls and the exceptionally wide range of foreign carriers on long hauls. More than half the BA short-haul/long-haul transfers were connecting to/from domestic services.

Long-haul passengers making domestic connections were split in favour of foreign airlines, even when BA supplied the domestic leg (when the split was 53:47), and only more so when the domestic leg was supplied by another UK airline (when the split was 60:40).

Clearly, the hub airline does not dominate transfers through London to the extent that its scale of operations might initially suggest. Its schedules are far less coordinated that those of most of its competitors in Europe.

Scheduled connections

In summer 1986 BA operated some 170 daily flights from Heathrow, BCal flew around fifty from Gatwick, KLM/Swissair/Air France between seventy-five and eighty from Amsterdam/Zurich/Paris Charles de Gaulle, and Lufthansa (together with its subsidiary DLT) around 150 from Frankfurt. So just in theory, maximum possible connections for BA could have been five times those for KLM, Swissair and Air France. But in practice its intralining opportunities were nowhere near so much greater. The comparisons in Table 14.2 show the actual connections possible, allowing for the relevant MCTs and setting a maximum interval between flights of 90 min. BA did receive a large total, but the possibilities generated by its schedules at Heathrow were not much greater than those that would have existed had flight timings been uniformly distributed across the operating day – which would in effect have been almost the worst pattern for intralining.[1] Hence the potential for increasing connections by banking into waves is, at least in principle, vast.[2] Total connections achieved by KLM and Swissair were by contrast more than double the corresponding figures that would have resulted from uniform scheduling, clearly reflecting the importance these two airlines attach to intralining. Down at the bottom of the 'league table' in this respect is Air France at Charles de Gaulle, whose schedules generated virtually the same number of connection possibilities as would have a uniform distribution. At the top is Lufthansa/DLT at Frankfurt where 150 flights generated over 2000 possible intraline connections.

The importance of scheduling for hub feed can be seen in the north Atlantic market, a market in which UK airlines often do more than just hold their own in competition for point-to-point traffic, but in which they fare rather less well in competition for connecting traffic.

North Atlantic market

UK airlines carry about 40 per cent of the scheduled UK–USA traffic, a market that divides about evenly between point-to-point and connecting

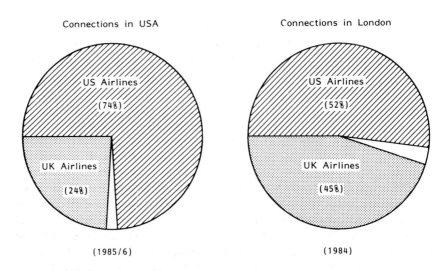

Connections in USA   Connections in London

US Airlines (74%)   US Airlines (52%)

UK Airlines (24%)   UK Airlines (45%)

(1985/6)   (1984)

Figure 14.1   Connecting traffic on London – USA routes

Sources: CAA, *London Area Airport Study*, CAA, 1984; Office of Population Censuses and Surveys, *International Passenger Survey*, OPCS, 1985–6

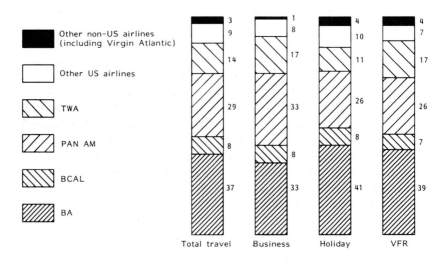

- Other non-US airlines (including Virgin Atlantic)
- Other US airlines
- TWA
- PAN AM
- BCAL
- BA

	Total travel	Business	Holiday	VFR
Other non-US airlines	3	1	4	4
Other US airlines	9	8	10	7
TWA	14	17	11	17
PAN AM	29	33	26	26
BCAL	8	8	8	7
BA	37	33	41	39

Figure 14.2   Transatlantic carriers' shares of traffic connecting in London (1984)

Source: CAA, *London Area Airport Study*, CAA 1984

passengers. In competition for point-to-point passengers, those travelling only between gateways, UK airlines do in many cases out-perform their US competitors. But in the market for passengers requiring connections, the US carriers have a substantial lead.

Survey data relating to London-USA routes (Figure 14.1) show how US airlines dominate when transfers take place in the USA and how they even have the edge for traffic connecting in London. It is difficult for UK airlines to attract passengers transferring in the USA, not only because the gateway airport is often a major hub for the US airline, but also because CRS gives advantages to intraline over interline connections – and the ability to share flight codes with domestic carriers in the USA often reinforces these advantages. In London the US airlines Pan American and TWA possess 'combination rights' which enable them to market through USA-Europe services under single flight numbers, and the shares they achieve of London transfer traffic are high in relation to the numbers of competing services they offer. In Heathrow's Terminal Three Pan American operates an effective change-of-gauge link between its 747 transatlantic services and its 737/Airbus flights to West Germany, Scandinavia, Brussels and Amsterdam. In 1984 (Figure 14.2) Pan American's overall share of transatlantic passengers in London was just eight percentage points below the shares achieved by BA and indeed the US airline tied with BA for the largest share (a third each) of the relatively high-yield business transfers. UK airlines only had the upper hand in the lower-yield leisure transfers. Thus in revenue terms the margin of advantage to US airlines in the London transfer market is greater still.

If UK airlines were to do as well in London as US airlines do in hubs on the other side of the Atlantic, they would gain a swing of some 7 per cent in UK–USA market share. At present they win less than half the traffic connecting through London. This has got less to do with the fact that two-thirds of the UK–USA passengers are US residents, and more to do with the coordination of flight schedules. One particular respect in which foreign airlines' services are often more coordinated than BA's is in the pairing of connections for round-trip journeys. Fast connections to BA's transatlantic services are quite often available in one direction but without a matching one in the reverse direction. To the extent that passengers' choice of transfer point is influenced by the ability to fly the same routing on both outbound and inbound return journeys, this is certainly one respect in which greater coordination in schedules could improve the total volume of connecting traffic passing through London.

Airline hubs in London

From the earliest days London has always been an extremely important point on the international air services map. London's role as a leading political, commercial and cultural centre generates an enormous demand for air travel, and from this strong base of local origin–destination traffic there has developed a vast set of possibilities for connecting traffic. But such possibilities are far from being maximized. Indeed, in terms of useful connections per flight, London ranks below all other major air travel centres in Europe except Paris. If there is to be any improvement, flights in and out of London will need to be better coordinated. But the scope for doing this is limited by the scarcity of runway slots and also by some problems in the utilization of terminal facilities.

Runway slots

Slots at both Heathrow and Gatwick are in short supply. The runways are in more or less continuous use. There are no longer any such things as peak periods. Peaks now last the whole of the operating day. The issues raised by capacity shortages at Heathrow and Gatwick are none too easy to resolve. This much has been amply demonstrated in various documents produced by the CAA.[3] The CAA has had difficulty in attempting to devise an appropriate set of 'traffic distribution rules' to deal with the pressure slots. The debate so far has tended to centre on what might be done – by frequency capping, displacing services with low 'interline content' from Heathrow and/or diverting charters from Gatwick, raising landing charges, introducing slot trading, etc. – merely in order to accommodate the projected secular growth in traffic. The slot allocation problems are more formidable still, if the objective is also to increase the scope for hub airlines to coordinate flights into waves.

The problem is acute at Heathrow where there is now almost no flexibility at all. Many possibilities for slot redistribution are presently precluded by international obligations and by 'grandfather rights' possessed by the airlines to whom specific slots are currently allocated. But if the hub airline is to achieve greater coordination in schedules there will have to be some reallocation. One approach might be to consider more fully the trading of aeropolitical concessions in other matters in return for greater flexibility in London, and another is to permit airlines themselves to trade slots. Some quite marginal changes in slot allocation could result in some potentially large benefits, especially if other restrictions were to be lifted at the same time.

One restriction at Heathrow is that the main parallel runways must be operated in a segregated mode, i.e. one for arrivals and one for departures. As part of a noise abatement agreement with local residents, an alternation procedure applies whenever the westerly runways are in use (about 75 per cent of the time). This requires one runway to be used for arrivals in the first half of the day (0700–1500 hours local time) and the other in the second half (1500–2300 hours), and means that one runway is used for take-offs while the other caters for landings. The capacity limit for arrivals is about thirty-four aircraft movements per hour, lower than that for departures which is about thirty-eight aircraft movements an hour. If the two runways could be used in a mixed mode – both used for arrivals in the inbound phase of a scheduled wave and then both used for departures in the outbound phase – total runway capacity could be increased. For at present capacity is constrained by the lower limit applying to arrivals, and a mixed mode of operation would enable the achievement of a higher average arrival/departure capacity level. This would require some really quite substantial changes to the present distribution of slots at Heathrow, but something along these lines may well need to be considered if there is to be much scope for realigning schedules.

Airport terminals

Another serious disadvantage at Heathrow is that ground facilities are divided between four distinct terminals, something that inconveniences connecting passengers and inflates MCTs. What is more, unlike at some multi-terminal airports, the allocation of facilities is made with little attempt to minimize the number of interterminal transfers required. This situation is without parallel at other major airports in the world and arises at Heathrow due to the preponderance of interline connections and to the sectorization of services between terminals in such a way that routes serving a similar geographical region leave from the same location. Generally passengers wish to connect between regions, not within them. There is for instance negligible demand for domestic-to-domestic or Europe-to-Europe transfers at Heathrow, and yet these are just those most likely to be accomplished within the same terminal building. A possible alternative division between terminals is by airline, a system that operates well in other places where intraline connections predominate. Such an arrangement gives the locally-based airline a useful advantage over competitors (as for example to Air France at Paris Charles de Gaulle and to TWA and Pan American at Kennedy Airport in New York).

At Gatwick the position has recently changed with the opening of a second terminal. Following the BA–BCal merger the question arises of how schedules at Gatwick can be reorganized to improve the airport's potential as a hub. Perhaps the best prospects here lie in linking major European points with secondary intercontinental points, or alternatively secondary European with major intercontinental. Major-major city pairs are often overflown, while secondary-secondary have thin demand.

Gatwick is relatively better placed for major European–secondary inter-continental, because most major intercontinental points are already served from Heathrow, and also because it would be difficult to maintain viable (jet) services between Gatwick and minor European points. But the issues involved in what might happen in the long term at Gatwick, are closely tied in with broader questions of UK government policy on airline competition.

Policy issues

In a recent review of policy the CAA stated that it will use its licensing powers to create an environment in which competition can flourish, not just between British and foreign airlines, but also among British airlines. Recognizing the concern expressed over the dominance in the UK of BA, especially following its acquisition of BCal, the CAA has based its policy on the premise that small and medium sized airlines should have the opportunity to grow and compete:

> Given the disparities in size which now exist within the UK industry, . . . the long-term interests of users will inevitably mean that the Authority will on occasion need to give a perceptible measure of preference to airlines other than British Airways, where the choice has to be made between British Airlines.[4]

This policy was reflected in the decision to award some former BCal licences for routes out of Gatwick to airlines other than BA.

The general philosophy underlying CAA policy may be summarized as follows. The CAA is aware that large airlines are better able to exploit new opportunities in the more liberalized environment, because of their extensive route networks. The Authority does not hold that large airline size is harmful *per se* but is concerned to safeguard against the possibilities of collusive, exploitative or anti-competitive behaviour. These are real possibilities because there are still some formidable barriers to entry in air transport. The trend towards liberalization is not proceeding at the same pace everywhere, creating a diversity of market conditions ranging from nearly free competition in some markets to unchallenged duopolies or oligopolies in others. Some governments will exercise close control over entry and fares, and even where they do not, airlines sometimes maintain relationships with their rivals that are as cooperative as they are competitive. And just when government policies are in general starting to become more liberal, so new entry barriers are appearing in the form of airport capacity constraints. In the CAA's view these circumstances mean that in many places competition is still largely absent, and that user choice, innovation and airline efficiency are most likely to be enhanced by giving preference in the allocation of route licences to airlines like British Midland, Air Europe, Dan-Air, Virgin Atlantic, etc., rather than to BA.

Not unnaturally this has been opposed by BA. One of the main counterarguments made by BA is that granting preference to smaller airlines weakens BA's ability to meet foreign competition. While BA is large in relation to other British airlines, it is not so large relative to many foreign airlines, and while its hub at Heathrow might be regarded as a 'fortress' by other British airlines, it does have to compete against fortress hubs in other countries.

UK airports as spokes?

The licensing of smaller British carriers on routes out of Gatwick is unlikely to do much to enhance the airport's position as a competitive airline hub. It is far more likely to emphasize its role as a spoke airport. Unless the smaller carriers can develop a useful network of long-haul services from Gatwick, the potential for developing intraline connections is going to be limited. The likelihood is, that besides carrying local traffic, the services of the newly licensed airlines will increasingly tend to supply further feed to hubs on the continent. The same might be said of European services from other airports in the London area (Luton, Stansted, and STOLport). Even Fortress Heathrow is in danger of falling behind in the race for connecting traffic – not just because of its capacity problems but also because its success hitherto as a transfer point has been in terms of interline connections and the emphasis is now switching rapidly to intraline traffic. The congested London airports system is not ready to accommodate this change, rather like the system in New York.

Foreign airlines see good opportunities in the UK. They have recently been stepping up services on spokes to UK regional airports. In the UK there is a large north–south divide in the propensity to fly, just as there is in other respects. The demand for air travel, especially scheduled air travel, is heavily concentrated in the south-east of the country. Therefore without a solid base of local traffic, it is difficult to establish a hub at a UK provincial airport.

All in all UK civil aviation is not exactly in the best possible position to respond to new and growing competition from US and European airlines operating efficient hub-and-spokes systems. The fundamental problem is lack of suitably located airport capacity. For highly complex intraline operations, airlines ideally require multi-runway sites. The only UK airport with more than one main runway is Heathrow.

If airport capacity constraints are causing lost opportunities now, they will certainly cause more in the future. Industry forecasts project a 5 per cent annual average growth in the demand for air travel between now and the end of the 1990s. But traffic through strategically located hubs could increase much faster. So is now the time to reconsider an old proposal – shelved since the early 1970s – to construct a completely new multi-runway airport for London? Or should UK airlines be looking for a possible 'green field' hub elsewhere on the continent of Europe? By 1992 the main limitations on airline operations are likely to come not so much from route licensing but from the availability of runway slots.

Postscript

The search for airport capacity on the Continent led to a proposed joint venture – between BA, KLM and Sabena – to exploit the potential for developing hub-and-spoke networks out of Brussels' relatively under-utilized Zaventem airfield. Another interesting development is the recent accord between Britain and Singapore, under which additional traffic rights for SIA on routes to/from the UK are exchanged for rights bestowed on UK airlines to use Changi airport as a hub for short-haul services in South East Asia. But perhaps more significant in the longer term are the developments occurring in France. The 'Golden Hub' scheme to expand Charles de Gaulle airport in Paris includes a proposal to increase the number of runways to five; this, together with investments in terminals and surface access would mean that early next century Charles de Gaulle would be capable of handling as many as 100m passengers a year, dwarfing London Heathrow's current capacity of about 38m. Air France's acquisition of a majority shareholding in UTA – thereby gaining effective control over the large domestic carrier Air Inter – may well see the end of the traditional policy of sectorizing routes between Charles de Gaulle and Orly, something that has in the past inhibited both airports from realizing their full potential as hubs. Thus Paris could be in a strong position to gain a large share of any future growth in connecting traffic.

Alliances between European airlines have attracted the attention of the competition authorities. Their concern here is with how competition can be maintained in the face of powerful pressures towards industry concentration. One of these pressures is the building up of dominant positions at fortress hubs. Recent evidence of US experience indicates how a dominant airline, taking advantage of differences in price-elasticities of demand, can discriminate by charging relatively high monopolistic fares to captive local traffic originating at or destined for the hub itself, and relatively low competitive fares to traffic connecting through the hub from one spoke to another. There are also some suggestions that airlines engage in predatory pricing (and/or predatory scheduling) to support this discrimination. But an increase in hubbing can also have certain pro-competitive effects, at the network level, if they increase passengers' options in major–secondary city-pair markets (or even, within the short- to medium-haul European context, in secondary–secondary city-pairs). The interesting challenge to competition authorities is how to promote such pro-competitive effects, while at the same time reducing the scope for anti-competitive behaviour.

Notes and references

1   A uniform distribution would have led to a total of 1187 possibilities, not much less than the 1259 achieved.
2   BA's total possibilities would almost double, to 2324, if all flights were to be scheduled into twelve waves, and would rise, airport capacity permitting, to 3486 with eight waves, 6972 with four waves and so on.
3   Civil Aviation Authority, *Airline Competition Policy*, CAP 500, London, July 1984; *Air Traffic Distribution in the London area – a consultation document*, CAP 510, London, October 1985; *Air Traffic Distribution in the London Area – advice to the Secretary of State*, CAP 522, London, May 1986; and *Report of the (Tugendhat) Committee on Runway Utilization at Heathrow and Gatwick*, CAP 534, London, March, 1988.
4   Civil Aviation Authority, 'Draft revised statement of air transport licensing policies', unpublished, London, January 1988, p. 1, paragraph 3.

15 Mediterranean charters

Douglas G. Pearce

The development of inclusive tour charter (ITC) flights has been a signifi-cant factor in the growth of Mediterranean tourism. During the decade 1970–80, the number of ITC passengers arriving in the region from Europe (i.e. from the member countries of the European Civil Aviation Conference (ECAC)) increased more than two-fold from 5.4m to 12.8m.

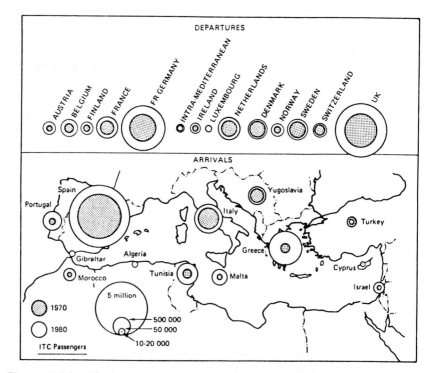

Figure 15.1 Evolution of the European non-scheduled traffic to the Mediterranean 1970–80

Source: ECAC

In this article an attempt is made to compare internal variations in the demand for charter tourism in the UK, FR Germany and Sweden, and to analyse the distribution of package tourists from these markets within the two major Mediterranean destinations, Spain and Greece. Where adequate time-series data are available, the analysis in each case is carried out over a period of years.

European-Mediterranean ITC traffic 1970–1980

Figure 15.1 shows the European-Mediterranean ITC traffic dominated by two major markets – the UK and FR Germany – and a single large destination – Spain. Expansion in these two markets accounted for about five million of the 7.4m increase in arrivals from 1970 to 1980. Their combined market share increased from 60.6 per cent to 64.8 per cent (UK, 39.3 per cent, FR Germany, 25.5 per cent). Conversely, several of the most important secondary markets – Denmark, Sweden and the Netherlands – experienced lower than average rates of growth and saw their share of the market decline. Several of the minor markets (Luxembourg, Ireland, Belgium, Norway and Austria) experienced rates of growth for the decade in excess of 300 per cent. The small intra-Mediterranean traffic had almost disappeared by the end of the decade.

But while the major markets saw their share of the ITC traffic increase, the three leading Mediterranean destinations in 1970 – Spain, Italy and Yugoslavia – all experienced slower than average rates of growth and each held less of the total regional market by the end of the decade. Greece is the major newcomer, displacing Italy in second position. A range of third tier destinations – Tunisia (5 per cent), Portugal (4.3 per cent) and Malta (3.4 per cent) – has also emerged by 1980.

A number of interrelated factors contribute to the strengths of the markets and the popularity of the destinations shown in Figure 15.1, together with the changes that have occurred over the decade. These include:

- population size;
- national vacation habits;
- the complementarity of resources;
- distance;
- the insular nature both of some markets (notably the UK) and some destinations (the Balearic and Canary Islands, and Greece);
- civil aviation policies;
- changes in aircraft technology; and
- economic and political conditions.[1]

Table 15.1   Distribution of Mediterranean charter traffic by major UK airports, 1985

Destination	No. of departures	% of departures		
		London	Luton	Manchester
Spain	6,367,481	34.5	13.2	18.0
Greece	2,324,314	52.4	5.7	23.1
Italy	1,315,265	62.5	15.7	6.9
Portugal	1,199,297	46.2	6.6	22.9
Yugoslavia	625,976	32.6	4.0	22.2
Malta	341,256	37.0	5.2	34.6
Tunisia	149,674	48.2	10.9	40.9
Morocco	98,582	64.3	7.9	17.9

Source: Civil Aviation Authority

Intranational variations in demand

Civil aviation data from the UK, FR Germany and Sweden provide information in varying degrees of detail on the distribution by airport of departures on charter flights. By examining these statistics over time it is possible to identify whether the charter traffic has been decentralized away from the major metropolitan airports to provincial centres, or whether the trend has been for increasing concentration. In a period of absolute growth, a decentralization of departures might be expected as expansion occurs through progressively tapping regional markets and as pressures increase on the metropolitan airports. This would especially be the case where a reasonable network of provincial airports existed, as is the case with the UK.

UK

In 1985 London's airports accounted for 42.8 per cent of the 12.4m charter passengers departing for the eight Mediterranean destinations shown in Table 15.1. A further 10.7 per cent of departures took place through Luton airport with the result that just over half of all charter passengers left through the London area airports. Considerable variation occurs in London's share of the charter traffic to each destination, ranging from almost two-thirds in the cases of Morocco and Italy to around a third for

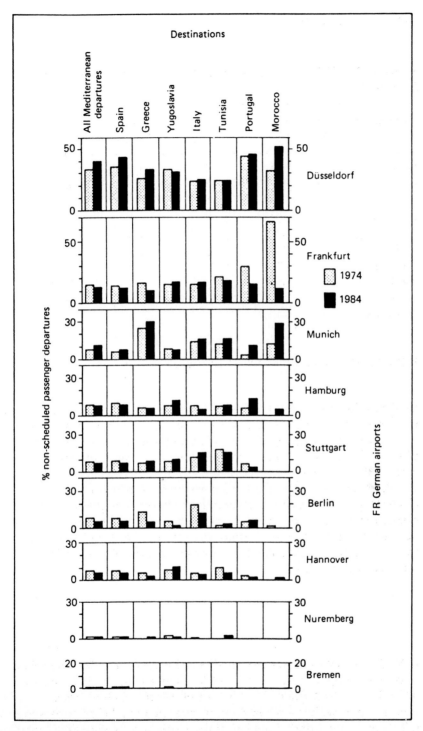

Figure 15.2 Evolution of FR German charter traffic by airport and destination 1974–84

Source: Federal Statistical Office

Malta, Spain and Yugoslavia. Manchester is the leading provincial airport, with its share of the traffic being particularly high to Tunisia and Malta, two of the newer and smaller destinations. This decentralization of charter flights stands in sharp contrast to the scheduled services which remain highly concentrated.

Analysis of the development of provincial charter departures is hampered by the statistical series for it is only recently that details are given on many of the smaller airports, and then only for the major routes. The combined share of the London area airports fell from just on 60 per cent of the charter traffic to Spain in 1972 to under half in 1985, with a consequent redistribution to the provincial airports.

The decentralization of charter flights to the provincial airports appears to reflect attempts at increasing the size of the market by broadening the market base. As each of the provincial airports serves a predominantly local clientele and as the total number of charter flights has increased, much of this expansion and decentralization would seem to be due to package holidays becoming more accessible through reductions in internal travel costs and increased direct regional promotion by tour operators.

At the same time, the existence of a large number of commercial airports in the UK and the relatively small size of the aircraft originally used in charter operations have meant that this strategy has been technically feasible.[2]

While technical infrastructural factors earlier aided decentralization, Doganis believes that subsequent changes in aircraft technology and current airline operating costs mean that the London area airports are likely to retain or even increase their position, at least in the short term.[3] The additional expenditure on airport infrastructure to handle long-haul wide-bodied aircraft would not appear to be viable in many of the regional airports.

FR Germany

Figure 15.2 depicts the share of non-scheduled passenger departures through FR German airports to the major Mediterranean countries in 1974 and 1984. Between these dates total Mediterranean departures from FR Germany grew from 2.2m to 3.7m. This growth, however, was not accompanied by a deconcentration of departures for all the airports except Dusseldorf, Munich and Nuremberg (which did not change) saw their share of the total traffic diminish.

Table 15.2 Distribution of Swedish charter departures by airport, 1973–85

Airport	% of Swedish charter departures												
	1973	1974	1975	1976	1977	1978	1979	1980	1981	1982	1983	1984	1985
Arlanda	60	65	65	61	60	57	58	57	58	59	61	66	65
Landvetter	20	20	19	19	19	19	20	21	21	21	21	20	21
Sturup	11	7	9	13	13	15	15	16	16	15	15	14	14
Jönköping	4	4	4	4	3	3	2	3	2	1	1	—	—
Other	5	4	3	3	5	6	5	3	3	4	2	—	—
Total departures	807,841	739,958	815,797	908,508	1,065,177	1,220,252	1,130,812	895,432	968,553	1,037,553	820,082	896,345	864,909

Source: Board of Civil Aviation

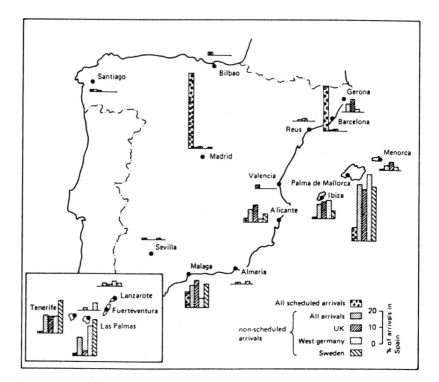

Figure 15.3   Distribution of scheduled and non-scheduled arrivals in Spain 1983

Sweden

By the early 1970s a significant decentralization of charters had occurred within Sweden, with over a third of all charter passengers leaving from airports other than Stockholm-Arlanda (Table 15.2).[4] During the late 1970s, when the Swedish charter traffic peaks, Arlanda's share drops to 57–58 per cent, with much of the dispersion involving the smaller provincial airports. The subsequent decline in departures in the early 1980s, however, is accompanied by a reassertion of Arlanda's dominance and a concentration of departures through the three main airports.

Intranational variations in destinations

Examination of country-to-country flows alone tends to mask differences in the spatial preferences shown by particular national markets within destination countries in the same way that this macro-level of analysis fails to reveal internal variations in demand. Analysis of the distribution of demand at an intranational level involves determining the extent to which all charter tourists visit the same places within a given country or whether regional biases occur from nationality to nationality. Where appropriate data exist, this analysis might usefully be extended through time to determine whether the distribution of the charter traffic holds constant or evolves across space. Where the market expands, some change through time might be anticipated as pressure develops in certain places and as other destinations are opened up to provide a greater range of choice. These questions are examined here with regard to the behaviour of UK, FR German and Swedish charter tourists in the two major Mediterranean destinations, Spain and Greece.

Spain

Figure 15.3 depicts the distribution by airport of the European scheduled and non-scheduled traffic to Spain in 1983, together with the distribution of UK, FR German and Swedish non-scheduled passengers. Marked differences occur in the structure of the scheduled and non-scheduled traffic from Europe. Scheduled arrivals in 1983 numbered 2.6m, with almost three-quarters of these bound for the two major metropolitan centres, Madrid (44.8 per cent) and Barcelona (27 per cent).

The non-scheduled traffic (9.2m arrivals in 1983) is over three times as large as the number of scheduled passengers and is directed almost exclusively to insular and coastal airports, a reflection of the demand from the tourist sector. Together the Balearic Islands accounted for 45 per cent of the non-scheduled arrivals, the Canaries, 14.8 per cent and the Mediterranean coastal airports, 38 per cent.

Significant regional biases are found in the destinations favoured by each of the three national markets depicted in Figure 15.3. The UK traffic is more widely dispersed than that of the other two countries, with the first three Spanish airports accounting for 58 per cent of UK arrivals, compared to 66 per cent of the FR Germans and 73 per cent of the Swedes.

UK charter traffic

Lack of a detailed time series limits analysis of the evolution of the UK charter traffic within Spain, particularly during the formative decade of the 1960s. However from 1977, when Spanish civil aviation figures become more specific, to 1983 little spatial change in market share is apparent. There has been some overall decline in the share held by the

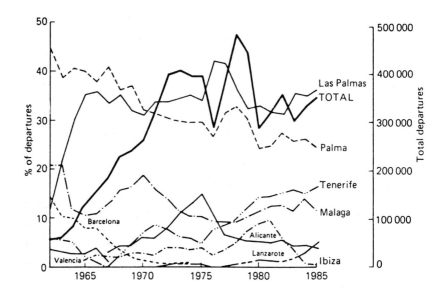

Figure 15.4   Evolution of Swedish charter traffic to Spain 1962–85
Source: Board of Civil Aviation

mainland coastal airports (41 per cent to 38 per cent) and some redistribution along the coast (Alicante 16.6 per cent to 11 per cent, Malaga 9.4 per cent to 16.4 per cent). The evolution in the demand for the various destinations reflects not only price levels but also the patterns and processes of the development of the tourist infrastructure in various regions. Bisson, for instance, cautions against explaining Mallorca's dominance in the Balearics solely in terms of the larger size and resource base of the island and the earlier development there of international air connections.[5] Rather he points to other less obvious factors such as the underlying agricultural and tenurial structures.

FR German charter traffic

FR German civil aviation figures show the major shift in the FR German charter traffic to Spain over the decade 1974–84 has been from the major Mediterranean mainland coastal airports (down from 26.7 per cent to 14 per cent) in favour of the Canary Islands (26 per cent to 37 per cent) with the Balearics continuing to attract over half of all the arrivals. It is important to note in this case that much of the mainland coastal demand is met by independent, overland travel rather than package tours by air.

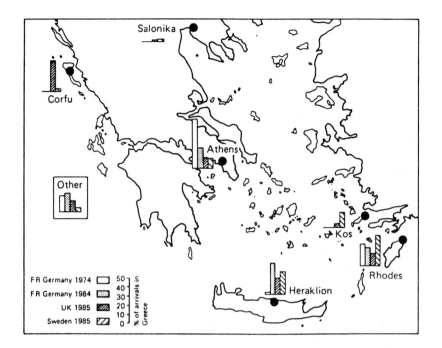

Figure 15.5 Distribution of the charter traffic to Greece by major national markets

Sources: Federal Statistical Office, Civil Aviation Authority, Board of Civil Aviation

Swedish charter traffic

Comprehensive Swedish statistics enable the development of the Swedish charter traffic to Spain to be traced almost from the beginning. Figure 15.4 depicts the distribution of Swedish charters by Spanish airport from 1962, when departures for Spain numbered only 57,000, to 1985, when charter traffic stood at 356,000. A marked redistribution of Swedish charters is apparent over this period, with important destinations in the early 1970s experiencing a significant loss of market share as other new destinations have emerged. In other instances new destinations have peaked then declined in the two decades.

The growth in the Swedish charter traffic to Spain has not been accompanied by the continuous dispersion of passengers to an ever-growing number of airports. Rather, the majority of the traffic throughout the period 1962–85 has gone to half a dozen airports. The composition of these has changed over time, however, and a marked redistribution of the traffic has occurred in favour of the Canary Islands.

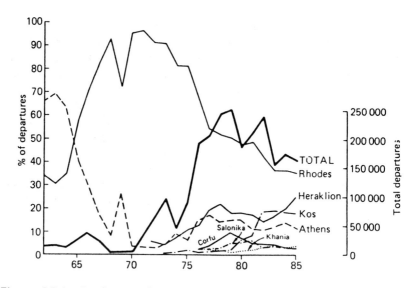

Figure 15.6   Evolution of Swedish charter traffic to Greece 1962–85
Source: Board of Civil Aviation

Greece

In Greece, as in Spain, significant regional biases occur in the regional distribution of the UK, FR German and Swedish charter traffic (Figure 15.5). In 1985 a third of the UK traffic was concentrated on Corfu with Heraklion, Rhodes and Athens being important secondary centres. Heraklion, on Crete, is the most favoured destination among the FR Germans while Rhodes attracts the largest number of Swedes. Both the FR Germans and Swedes also visit Athens but Corfu exercises little appeal. Kos, on the other hand, is a significant Swedish destination but has yet to attract a large share of the other markets. As in Spain, the UK traffic (2.3m in 1985) overall is less concentrated, with the three main airports accounting for about two-thirds of the passengers compared with about 80 per cent of West Germans (0.4m in 1984) and 78 per cent of the Swedes (163,000 in 1985).

Spill attributes the development of charters to the islands rather than to Athens to a much more liberal policy of the Greek Civil Aviation Administration towards the islands, with care being taken to protect Olympic's scheduled international traffic to the capital.[6] He also suggests the distribution of the different national flows is a function of the activities of particular tour operators.

Unfortunately, the less detailed UK statistics do not allow the spatial evolution of UK traffic within Greece to be traced. The major trend in the case of the FR German market over the decade 1974–84 has been the sharp decline in the role of Athens and the emergence of Heraklion as the principal destination, a move away to an island destination more in keeping with the pattern found in the other markets. For the Swedish market, the decline in Athens as a destination occurred much earlier and more sharply back in the 1960s (Figure 15.6). That decade saw the rise in Rhodes to a pre-eminent position, particularly during the late 1960s as the total Swedish traffic fell away markedly with the rise to power of the colonels in Greece. Throughout the 1970s and into the 1980s Rhodes' share declined as the traffic to other islands developed. Crete, with Heraklion as its chief airport, was the first of these, developing in the 1970s, followed by Kos a decade later.

Discussion

Certain parallels and contrasts exist in the evolution of the charter traffic to the Mediterranean at the two different scales examined here. In terms of origins some concentration is evident at both the national and intranational scales. Over the decade 1970–80 the two major markets, the UK and the FR Germany, strengthened their position and enlarged their share of the Mediterranean charter traffic (Figure 15.1). Increasing concentration of departures is also evident within FR Germany where Dusseldorf's share of the charter traffic to the Mediterranean increased from 33 per cent to 40 per cent over the decade 1974–84. London's share of Spanish bound departures also increased slightly from 1972 to 1985 (30.6 per cent to 34.5 per cent) although the total share of the London area airports fell through a decline in Luton's position. Within both the UK and FR Germany the share of the charter traffic held by the principal airport does, however, vary significantly from destination to destination although no overall pattern is apparent (Table 15.1 and Figure 15.2). Within Sweden some dispersion of charters occurred in the late 1970s to early 1980s but by 1985 the three major airports have reasserted their position, with Arlanda accounting for two-thirds of all departures (Table 15.2). The dispersion in Sweden occurred during a growth phase and concentration followed a decline in total departures. The same trends are not evident in the UK and FR Germany, both of which experienced some concentration during a period of absolute growth, though from a base which already represented a marked degree of decentralization to the provincial airports.

When the destinations are considered, some dispersion of the country-to-country flows is evident but at an intranational level the trends are less clear-cut. Over the decade 1970–80, the international ITC traffic throughout the Mediterranean became more dispersed, with the three leading countries seeing their share of the European market diminish as new secondary destinations emerged (Figure 15.1). Within Spain, the major destination, some redistribution of the charters has occurred, with the Canaries' share generally growing at the expense of the mainland coastal airports, while Palma de Mallorca retains its dominant position. In the case of the Swedish market the trend over the period 1962–85 was more toward a redistribution of the traffic rather than a continuing development of new routes. Redistribution was also evident within Greece, now the second Mediterranean destination, although there the tendency was more for a dispersion of the traffic away from Athens and then Rhodes to some of the other island airports and a general deconcentration of charters. This deconcentration within Greece may reflect that country's more youthful stage as a major charter destination compared to the more mature position of Spain and policies towards the operation of charters.

Within both Spain and Greece marked regional biases are also apparent in the destinations favoured by charter tourists from the three national markets considered, those of the UK, FR Germany and Sweden (Figures 15.3 and 15.5). In both cases, the charter traffic from the UK is less concentrated than that from FR Germany and Sweden – perhaps a function of the larger size of the UK market. One implication of these regional differences is that changes in the strength of any given national market will not be experienced evenly throughout any receiving country but rather they will have a greater or lesser impact on specific regions. A marked decline in the Swedish traffic, for instance, would hit the Canaries harder than a drop in the UK market while Corfu would be more affected by changes in the traffic out of the UK than any other region of Greece.

Conclusions

This comparative, geographic analysis of civil aviation data over time and at different scales has highlighted major geographical differences and changes in the structure of Mediterranean charters. In particular, it has identified significant differences in the demand for charters within national markets and in the distribution of that demand within the two main Mediterranean receiving countries. Moreover, the analysis of time-series data has shown that the geographical dimensions of the charter traffic are dynamic not constant, with a significant redistribution of flows occurring over time. The tendency in some cases and at some periods has been towards increasing concentration and at others towards a greater dispersion of the traffic.

Further work is now required in order to be able to explain more fully the patterns and trends identified so that a better appreciation can be gained of likely future developments. Of particular value would be research in a range of generating and receiving countries drawing together work on the development and organization of charter tours outlined in the introduction with this more detailed analysis of charter traffic data, particularly at the intranational level. The role of governmental airline policies, technological changes, the marketing strategies of tour operators, the attitudes of developers within the destinations and the preferences of different national and regional markets all appear to be factors influencing the patterns and trends identified but now they need to be related to each other more explicitly.

Notes and references

1 Pearce, D. G., 'Spatial patterns of package tourism in Europe', *Annals of Tourism Research*, vol. 4, no. 2, 1987, pp. 183–201.
2 'Package tours – where they have been and where they are going', *International Tourism Quarterly*, vol. 1, 1982, pp. 64–77.
3 Doganis, R., *The potential for regional diversification of air traffic from the London area*, 1981, p. 20.
4 The departure figures in Table 15.2 concern charters to all destinations. In 1985 Mediterranean charters accounted for over 80 per cent of Swedish departures.
5 Bisson, J., 'A l'origine du tourisme aux iles Baleares: vocation touristique ou receptivité du milieu d'accueil?', paper presented at the meeting of the IGU Commission of the Geography of Tourism and Leisure, Palma de Mallorca, August 1986.
6 Spill, J. M., 'L'avion et les iles: le cas de la Grèce', in *Iles de la Mediterranée*, Cahier No 4, Editions du CNRS, Marseille, 1981, pp. 49–71.

Acknowledgement

The author would like to thank Dr Damaso do Lario, Embassy of Spain, Canberra, Australia, for assistance in obtaining Spanish civil aviation data, and the Swedish Board of Civil Aviation for providing statistics on the charter traffic from Sweden.

Further reading

Further reading on air transport in *Tourism Management* 1980–9

Boberg, K. B. and Collison, F. M., 'Computer reservation systems and airline competition', vol. 6, no. 3, September 1985, pp. 174–83.

Guitart, C., 'UK charter flight holidays to the Mediterranean 1970–78 – a statistical analysis', vol. 3, no. 1, March 1982, pp. 16–39.

Hanlon J. P., 'Air fares and exchange rates', vol. 2, no. 1, March 1981, pp. 4–17.

Hanlon J. P., 'Indian air transport', vol. 7, no. 4, December 1986, pp. 259–78.

Hanlon J. P., 'Sixth freedom operations in international air transport', vol. 5, no. 3, September 1984, pp. 177–91.

Lauriac, J., 'Recent trends in international air transport regulation', vol. 5, no. 4, December 1984, pp. 298–301.

Shaw, S., 'Airline deregulation and the tourist industry', vol. 3, no. 1, March 1982, pp. 40–51.

Tye, W. B., 'Competition and subsidies in international air transport', vol. 1, no. 4, December 1980, pp. 199–206.

Wheatcroft, S., 'Current trends in aviation', vol. 10, no. 3, September 1989, pp. 213–17.

Wheatcroft, S., 'The changing economics of international air transport', vol. 3, no. 2, June 1982, pp. 71–82.

Part Six

Marketing Products and Destinations

Marketing in travel and tourism, as we understand the concept and related techniques today, is of relatively recent origin. Yet, marketing appears to have dominated the industry in the last twenty years or so, and this was also reflected in a growing volume of writings on the subject. About one-half of all articles in this book refer to marketing; two of them concerned with particular products and one with destinations form this part of the book.

Fredrick Collison of the University of Hawaii and Kevin Boberg of New Mexico State University describe in 'Marketing of airline services in a deregulated environment' the dramatic changes in marketing brought about by airline deregulation in the USA, which affected all elements of the marketing mix and most of the travel distribution system.

Sungsoo Pyo and Richard Howell of Clemson University and Raymond Cook of California State University discuss in 'Summer Olympic tourist market' the outcome of the six Games between 1964 and 1984 for the tourism of the host cities and offer some conclusions about the way future Olympic Games should be marketed.

John Yacoumis of the Tourism Council of the South Pacific describes a case study of regional cooperation in tourism in 'South Pacific tourism promotion'. The article reviews the performance, trends and prospects of the region and outlines the regional marketing and promotion objectives and strategies.

Further articles on various aspects of marketing published in *Tourism Management* from 1980–9 are listed on page 212. See also individual chapters and related further reading in Parts Three to Eight of this book.

16 Marketing of airline services in a deregulated environment

Fredrick M. Collison and Kevin B. Boberg

Changes in the operating environment of US airlines have complicated the production and sale of airline services in recent years. Forces unleashed by the Airline Deregulation Act of 1978 (ADA) are perhaps the most significant. Economic and marketing concerns have replaced regulatory considerations in selling airline services. Carriers are offering service and price options scarcely imaginable some ten years ago. Marketing strategy has become a direct determinant of an airline's success or failure.

Environmental changes

Deregulation profoundly influenced the marketing of airline services within the travel industry. Airline fare setting moved from intense regulation by the Civil Aeronautics Board (CAB) to the complete deregulation of fares as of January 1983. Entry and exit provisions allowed new entrants to initiate services, and existing airlines to enter new routes or abandon existing routes. More recently, the freedoms granted by ADA resulted in a number of mergers and acquisitions that increased the range of services and market offerings of the largest airlines.

Major changes also occurred in the economic environment concurrent with the enactment of ADA. Fuel prices and interest rates increased dramatically, boosting airline operating costs, although these costs subsequently moderated. The economic recession of the early 1980s also adversely affected the industry, with a resultant decline in both revenue passengers enplaned and actual service measured in revenue passenger-miles for 1980 and 1981.

Downward pressures on fares and rising costs intensified the need for airlines to focus substantial effort on actively marketing their services. Airlines learned to emphasize the four elements of the marketing mix:

- product – the actual transport service, plus in-flight and ground services offered to passengers;
- place – the physical network of offices and intermediaries used to sell the product;
- promotion – the means by which a passenger's awareness of, interest in, desire for, and acquisition of an airline's services are fostered; and
- price – the fares charged for the air transport and other services provided by the airline.

Airline marketing mix

Product

The diversity of transport, in-flight, and ground services offered has increased dramatically since deregulation, before which the airline product was nearly homogeneous among competitors. Deregulation has allowed airlines to experiment with different levels of service, varying from 'no-frills' transport to all-first-class service. One of the clearest examples of no-frills service was that of People Express, which provided a basic air transport service, with 'extras' such as baggage and checking and meals available for additional charges. Regent Air, at the other end of the spectrum, offered plush seating, many in-flight services, deluxe meals, and limousine service to and from the airport for the price of a first-class ticket.

In-flight services now include elements such as airborne telephone and telex services, transmission of personal computer data, current video news, on-board personal computers and computer games, and in-flight advertising (as a revenue source).[1] Innovative food service has also become a prominent component of in-flight services. At the same time, competitive pressures are forcing airlines to reduce the cost of customer service, which can result in lower levels of in-flight services than anticipated by passengers.[2]

The selection of routes is another important element of the airline product mix. Many airlines have implemented, or further refined, a hub-and-spoke routing system. Short-haul flights (spokes) connect through a limited number of airports (hubs) and long-haul flights then connect these hub airports. Airlines claim that this routing strategy increased efficiency by control of feeder traffic at the hub airports and better matching of aircraft to individual flight segment requirements. At the same time this routing strategy, in conjunction with mergers and acquisitions, resulted in the dominance of some hubs by single airlines. For example, Northwest now controls over 75 per cent of the gate space at Minneapolis-St Paul and TWA does likewise at St Louis.[3]

Hub-and-spoke systems, however, have not always benefited the traveller. In addition to reduced airline choice at some hubs, passengers may lose direct services between two points, with a resultant increase in travel times, although the frequency of service has sometimes increased on both the spoke and hub-to-hub segments. Larger airlines have entered into marketing agreements with commuter or small regional airlines to provide services on some spoke routes, often using non-jet aircraft. These agreements result in the regional airline sharing the same airline code as its large partner, making it difficult for the passenger or travel agent to determine who is actually providing the air-transport service.

Place

Managerial freedom, increased competition, and the pressing need for efficiency have caused airline management to emphasize the selling of their services through the travel-agency distribution system. In 1978, there were 14,804 travel agency locations in the USA accounting for approximately 40 per cent of ticket sales. By mid-1986, there were an estimated 28,054 locations. The continued expansion of domestic and international operations presage a growing role for travel agents, who are expected to account for 85 per cent of ticket sales by 1990.[4]

There have been some drawbacks for airlines that place a greater reliance on the travel-agency distribution system, primarily the rapid increase in the cost of travel-agent compensation. While deregulation of commission levels should theoretically give airlines the ability to reduce agent compensation, the legal freedom to reduce commissions and the ability to withstand travel-agent pressure are vastly different. Increased standard commission levels and the growing use of volume overrides to maintain agent loyalty have pushed the cost of the distribution system even higher than before deregulation. As a percent of total operating cost, travel-agent compensation doubled between 1972 and 1985.[5]

The growth of the travel-agency system has not avoided public notice. Objecting to many provisions of the travel-agency accreditation systems administered by the Air Traffic Conference (ATC) and the International Air Transport Association (IATA), the CAB withdrew the anti-trust immunity of the ATC and IATA as of January, 1985. A more liberal travel-agency appointment, operation, and compensation system has been instituted with the Airline Reporting Corporation (ARC) for US domestic carriers and the International Airline Travel Agency Network (IATAN) for international carriers.

Many aspects of the travel-sales distribution system have been unaffected by the change, e.g. full-service agencies and in-plant operations remain much the same as they were. Significant changes are, however, found in newly defined restricted-access agencies and 'other persons', which need not be accessible to the public and, in some cases, are freed from meeting ARC accreditation standards. As a result, business travel departments will be more active in buying corporate travel, a market segment accounting for about one-half of airline and agency sales.

Effective management of the burgeoning flight and fare offerings and the growth of the agency system required the development of computerized reservation systems (CRS) by a number of airlines. Although originally developed for in-house monitoring of customer reservations, the airlines enhanced their systems and began leasing them to travel agents in 1976. Only ten years later, 85 per cent of agency locations are automated – representing 90 per cent of airline revenues generated by travel agents.[6]

According to some critics, the improved marketing capabilities provided by CRS have been abused by 'host' carriers such as United and American. The magnitude of the perceived abuse is evident in anti-trust suits against host carriers and a CAB rulemaking designed to eliminate bias from CRS displays.[7] Some in the industry have criticized these rules as ineffective, and the General Accounting Office (GAO) has recently been prompted to call for a more thorough investigation of the entire CRS matter.

A most important question to be resolved is whether CRS were and are an essential part of a highly successful competitive marketing mix or part of a larger trend towards oligopolization of the US air-travel market. The fact that there are five airline-owned systems competing for agent business could be seen as prima facie evidence that the systems are nothing more than marketing tools. However, if cancellation fees realistically prohibit an agent from freely choosing or switching reservations systems, then CRS may well be one of the foundations of concentration in the airline industry.

Promotion

The increased competition fostered by airline deregulation also greatly expanded the importance of promotion. One of the most successful promotional tools in the history of the travel industry is the frequent flyer programmes developed by many airlines. These programmes are primarily orientated towards the business traveller who cannot ordinarily qualify for the deep fare discounts which contain restrictions such as advance purchase requirements. As the passenger accumulates mileage flown, he/she receives bonuses such as first-class up-grades and free coach class tickets.

Many airlines have now implemented these programmes, ranging from large airlines such as American, United and Northwest to much smaller ones such as Alaska and international carriers such as Japan Airlines. More recently, other travel-related companies such as hotels, cruise lines, and rental car firms have been added to the airline programmes as well. In addition to the benefits that may accrue to the business traveller, the airlines realize a higher level of brand loyalty. These plans, however, are not without their controversy – airlines allegedly increase fares to cover the cost of these programmes, disagreements occur over who should receive the benefits, and the Internal Revenue Service is now examining how it might tax these benefits.

Since the advent of deregulation, airline advertising expenditure and placement shifted. While total advertising expenditure increased by only about 50 per cent between 1974 and 1978, annual increases after ADA have been, with one exception, between 15 per cent and 28 per cent. Concurrently, the proportions of this expenditure devoted to various media changed, with major shifts toward television advertising and away from newspaper and magazine advertising.[8] Airlines today are using media that have a more direct impact on travellers and that can respond rapidly to environmental changes as they occur particularly in the area of pricing.

Other promotional elements have been developed by the airlines to create a greater demand for their services. An example is the introduction of comprehensive travel and tour packages, which may include air transport, hotel accommodation, and a rental car or other ground transport, as offered primarily through various tour wholesalers previously. Deregulation encouraged airlines to develop these packages to gain a greater degree of control over both the offerings and the marketplace they are serving, with the potential to generate higher revenues and profits in the process.

Airlines have also used coupon give-aways and joint promotions with other firms, in order to stimulate the demand for their services. Airlines such as United and Pan Am have, in the wake of strikes, used reduced-fare coupons to attract passengers back to that particular airline. Joint promotions have been undertaken between airlines and firms not related to the travel industry, e.g. Computerland and Kodak with Eastern, in which purchasers of computers, cameras, or film have received coupons for reduced air fares.

The success of many promotional elements seems to depend on both the formulation of the elements and also on the size of the airline offering them. Frequent-flyer programmes of the major airlines are more attractive to travellers since greater mileage can be earned and more destinations are available to those who qualify for benefits. Major airlines can also develop comprehensive tour and travel packages more successfully, particularly for prime tourism destinations such as Hawaii, Florida, and the Caribbean. The smaller airlines have difficulty in matching the resources that can be committed to promotion by the major airlines.

Pricing

The forces of costs and demand have been brought to bear on airline pricing strategies. 'Yield management' has become the key as airlines assess costs and demand on a segment-by-segment and route-by-route basis. Mileage-based fares, never fully adopted in the US, gave way to a pervasive system of discounting. In 1977, 60 per cent of all revenue passenger-miles were purchased by travellers paying the standard coach fare, but by 1986 over 90 per cent of passengers travelled on fares discounted an average of 62 per cent.[9]

The nature of these prices and their impact has varied among passengers and routes. Discretionary travellers on long-haul, high density, tourism-dominated routes have benefited most from the new discount fares. Business travellers are effectively precluded from qualifying for the largest fare reductions by the restrictions and, as a result, pay up to three times the amount being charged to those flying on super-saver fares. This differential has made super-saver fares one of the more controversial aspects of deregulation.

Two arguments can be forwarded for the explanation of the deep fare discounts. Airlines suggest that the fare differential is compensated for by the more accommodating service, increased flight frequencies, and promotional programmes discussed earlier. Second, many discount fares are a form of peak/off-peak pricing. Thus, discounting merely increases the efficiency of airline operations.

As US-style deregulation has been exported to other nations, some interesting parallels have developed. In some countries, e.g. Canada, governments have opted for some deregulation, but are careful to point out that the US model is not directly applicable or advisable. The 'Saturday night' rule has proved to be one of the more controversial deregulation issues, especially in Europe. The European Civil Aviation Commission (ECAC) recently approved a Memorandum of Understanding liberalizing fare and capacity restrictions, in which airlines are given complete freedom to set fares between 65 per cent and 90 per cent of the full economy fares.[10] Even lower fares, between 45 per cent and 65 per cent of the full economy fares, will have more restrictions, including a six-day minimum stay. The UK, Ireland, and the Netherlands have objected to the minimum stay requirement, as well as to some of the other restrictions.

Challenges and opportunities

The marketing strategies and programmes developed by airlines present opportunities and challenges to all members of the travel industry. Quite clearly, airlines are undertaking fairly revolutionary steps in marketing their services – some quite successful, others less so. But what of the rest of the travel industry? Corporate and personal travellers, both leisure and 'visiting friends and relatives' (VFR), must live within this new environment. All travel industry suppliers, such as hotels, resorts, trains, car rentals, cruises and tours are likewise affected by the new marketing orientation of the airlines. Last, the retail travel agent, the primary means of distributing travel services, is forced to cope if for no other reason than to avoid closing.

Product development

Changed products have generally acted as a spur to increased travel. Undeniably, the low-fare service offered by People Express and similar firms has stimulated airline sales and, thereby, sales of related destination services. No-frills operators have opened travel to more income-sensitive travel markets and permitted a redistribution of travel dollars among services.

There are several interesting paradoxes in product development. No-frills carriers found it necessary to move toward full service status, upgrading in-flight services and participating in the major CRS. When major airlines altered their operations to compete with no-frills airlines and still maintained product quality, People Express and other no-frills airlines experienced difficulty in successfully competing against the more established airlines. Competition has fostered a general upgrading of services by airlines across all fare classes.

No-frills airlines

No-frill, low-cost airlines also pose interesting issues for tourism planners. In some cases the markets served by these airlines somehow may be
inconsistent with a destination's attempts to cater to the high-end market.
In addition, just as some destinations are questioning the wisdom of
mass-produced tourism, the no-frills airlines, along with the low discount
fares of more traditional airlines, make long-haul travel economical to
ever greater numbers of people.

   These same airlines, and the market forces they bring with them, also
have affected the channels of distribution. To the extent that competition
drives down the average level of fares, agency commission revenues
likewise fall. Simultaneously, agency operating costs are rising. Com-
pounding the revenue-cost squeeze is the increased number of reissued
tickets precipitated by competition.

   Recent experience has shown that as more established airlines learn to
compete successfully against the no-frills airlines and new entrants in
general, it has become difficult for the no-frills airlines to achieve survival.
Many of the new entrants have faced the choice of takeover by an established carrier or bankruptcy. Many reasons can be cited for the failure of
no-frills airlines including:

● the lack of access to CRS;
● the near non-availability of gate and counter space at many airports;
● limited landing and take-off slots at major hub airports;
● restricted capital availability; and
● the susceptibility to competitive pressures from the larger, more
   established airlines on fares and levels of services.[11]

The continuing consolidation in the airline industry may tend to increase
these competitive disadvantages of the no-frills airlines.

Distribution-system trends

Several trends are emerging in the air-travel distribution system. As a
result of the increasing cost of travel-agent commissions, some airlines
have taken the first tentative steps in direct dealing. The most obvious
element in this trend is found in the corporate travel sector. Although
most airlines continue to reaffirm their commitment to the current
distribution system, direct deals between airlines and their clients are
growing.

The commission savings from bypassing agents are apparent, but the costs of direct dealing may eventually prove greater than the benefits gained. Travel agents still possess the ability to retaliate against airlines that bypass them. Many airlines can ill afford to have agents book away from them in response to direct dealing. Also, direct dealing, especially with corporate clients, often means substantial discounts from published fares.

Another trend is an increase in agency failures at highly-competitive hubs. Agency defaults in 1986 were up some four fold from 1981 levels.[12] Smaller agencies are closing down individual operations to combine with other firms. Consolidated locations seem better able to survive in the competitive marketplace. Larger agencies can exert more leverage on air carriers and are, therefore, more likely to benefit from the overrides, or volume-incentive commissions, now commonly offered by all travel industry suppliers. Alternatively, some agents are coping with declining revenues and rising costs by assessing service fees, particularly so on reissued tickets. Several risks are inherent in service fees. Unless all agents in a particular market adopt service fees under a uniform schedule, an agent will probably lose clients to agents not charging the fee. Alternatively, customers might turn to dealing directly with airline ticket offices. Since travel-agent compensation is one of the last major areas offering cost-cutting potential, airlines might welcome at least some such defection. Furthermore, the airlines are now able to handle many clients directly compared to the pre-deregulation and immediately post-deregulation periods.

Ownership of a CRS gives an airline one of the most (if not the most) powerful marketing tools in the industry. User-friendly versions of the major CRS are available to travellers via electronic mailbox or database services. This development will prove a challenge to agents and an opportunity for travel suppliers who have been participating in carrier-owned CRS with increasing frequency.

In response to customer and travel industry vendor demands, CRS are becoming more comprehensive. Information on rail service, cruise lines, tour operators, hotels and car rentals is a part of a major system. Although it was the airlines who initially offered suppliers incentives to participate to make the CRS easier to place in agency location, it is now the vendors who are providing the impetus for inclusion. For example, AMTRAK lobbied extensively to be included, and is now available in the CRS of American, United, and TWA.

A similar pattern emerges in the frequent-flier programmes. While these programmes were initiated by the airlines to overcome the apparent lack of brand loyalty in the market, vendors now seek to join, and those who do not or cannot, find themselves at a competitive disadvantage, particularly in the lucrative business sector.

Horizontal and vertical integration are major evolutionary forces in the post-deregulation airline industry. Sheer size of an airline, through horizontal integration, can confer a number of important marketing advantages on the larger carriers, while vertical integration allows the airline to offer a more complete travel service under its own aegis. Combined, these two can allow an airline to expand the scope of its market, reach segments previously untapped, and make it more difficult for other airlines to compete effectively. The advantages in terms of time and convenience for the traveller are clear. The long-term economic consequences for travellers and for those excluded from the concentration and integration are not so evident.

Conclusion

Airline operations have been affected by many factors in recent years. Statutory and economic changes have altered long-established institutional arrangements and changed a once largely non-competitive industry into a fiercely competitive one. Airline management has taken many actions in response to these new conditions, perhaps none more vigorously than those related to the marketing of airline services, in an attempt to ensure airline survival and growth. The changes in the management of the airlines marketing mix have, in turn, affected many other elements of the travel industry.

Postscript

Since the original article was written, continuing changes affected the US airline industry. A major component of these changes is the number of mergers and acquisitions that occurred since 1985. These activities on the part of larger airlines consist of the merger with/acquisition of other medium to larger airlines and the control, either direct or indirect, over regional partners that provide service on spoke routes.

Deregulation has produced more than its share of airline failures. By many estimates, at least two-thirds of the new entrants to the airline industry failed, and only very limited success has been enjoyed by either 'no-frills' or 'all-frills' airlines. Only two new entrants are successful enough to be classified as large airlines – America West and Southwest (an intra-state carrier before deregulation). Braniff is the most notable failure of a pre-deregulation airline, having now twice filed for bankruptcy. Some of the attempts at intensive integration were not very successful. United abandoned its vertical integration and is now functioning again primarily as an airline. Texas Air (Continental and Eastern) continues to suffer financially from its past horizontal integration efforts.

The US airline industry appears to be more consolidated today than pre-deregulation, particularly for the market share of the very large airlines. Because of this consolidation, CRS continues to be of concern as a potential tool for further reducing competition. The current concerns about CRS centre not only on their size/market share, but also on the contracts that CRS airline vendors have with travel agencies, which are alleged to be quite restrictive. Despite these questions about airline competition, the industry is, in many respects, more competitive today than pre-deregulation.

Some of the primary marketing activities of US airlines are found in international aviation as well. The airlines of the US and other countries are now engaging in the development of global alliances, particularly in Europe as 1992 approaches. Airlines of both the US and foreign countries have developed joint marketing programmes to increase the worldwide access of individual airlines. In a similar fashion, CRS global alliances are evolving in order to provide the economies of scale and marketing power needed to successfully compete against the major established CRS systems.

References

1   See Coker, Bill, 'In-flight services: an expanding world', *Airline Executive*, September 1984, pp. 22–4; and 'Competitive pressures spur increased variety in cabin service', *Air Transport World*, September 1984, pp. 44–8.
2   See, e.g. Lefer, Henry, 'Deregulation causes some passenger service woes', *Air Transport World*, September 1985, pp. 49–50.
3   Dempsey, Paul Stephen, 'Birth of monster airlines', *Traffic Management*, 1 December 1986, p. 77.
4   The above figures are found in Durbin, Fran, 'ARC cancels record number of agencies for defaults', *Travel Weekly*, 17 July 1986, p. 1, and in Air Traffic Conference data.
5   Feldman, Joan, 'Marketing costs pose major challenge to airline profitability', *Air Transport World*, January 1987, pp. 50 and 52–3.
6   As detailed in 'The CRT population (Louis Harris Study)', *Travel Weekly*, 9 January 1986, p. 1.
7   Civil Aeronautics Board, 'Carrier-owned computer reservations systems', Notice of Rulemaking, 49 FR 32562–32564, 15 August 1984.
8   *Trends in Travel and Tourism Advertising Expenditures in United States Measured Media 1980–1984*, Ogilvy and Mather, September 1985, p. II–3; *Trends in Travel and Tourism Advertising Expenditures in US Measured Media 1978–1982*,

Ogilvy and Mather, September 1983, p II-3; and *Trends in Travel and Tourism Advertising – 1975 Annual Review*, Harris, Kerr, Forster, 1976, p. III–3.

9   Clark, Thorton, 'Restrictions mar fares' appeal', *Travel Weekly*, 2 February 1985, p. 4, and 'Airline observer', *Aviation Week and Space Technology*, 29 September 1986, p. 33.

10 'ECAC approves liberalizing fare, capacity regulations', *Aviation Week and Space Technology*, 12 January 1987, p. 36.

11 A number of these are discussed in Levere, Jane, 'No future for no-frills', *Travel Weekly's Focus on Bargain Travel*, October 1986, pp. 61–2.

12 Durbin, *op. cit.*, reference 4.

17 Summer Olympic tourist market

Sungsoo Pyo, Raymond Cook and Richard L. Howell

The Olympic Games offer the possibility of enhancing world peace, and contributing to cultural exchange and mutual understanding among different peoples. The attendant publicity provides the Olympic host city with a unique opportunity to build a positive image in the minds of the world's people, which can be favourably extended to the city's future benefit.

Many nations want to host the Olympics for the potential honour and publicity expected, even though their capital outlay may be lost due to a number of factors, including inflation. Financial difficulties have been a problem since the first modern Olympic Games, and the financial burdens for future Games may be greater than in the past. Specifically, TV companies may be reluctant to pay a high price for the broadcasting rights. Sales of sponsorships in future Olympic Games are not expected to be successful either.

Studies to find new financial sources to lessen the monetary burden and to investigate compensatory alternatives to the financial loss of

Table 17.1 Olympic tourists for the last six summer games

Year	City	Expected	Actual
1964	Tokyo	130,000	70,000
1968	Mexico	200,000	not found
1972	Munich	1,800,000	not found
1976	Montreal	1,500,000	not found
1980	Moscow	30,000–300,000	30,000
1984	Los Angeles	625,000	400,000

Source: Organizing committees

hosting the Games are needed; the Olympic tourist, as an expenditure generator who alleviates the financial burden of the Olympic host city, should be a part of such studies.

There has been little understanding regarding Olympic tourist behaviour. For instance, only 54 per cent of the projected tourists actually visited Tokyo during the 1964 Olympic Games, while during the 1984 Games, 64 per cent of the visitors forecasted came to Los Angeles (see Table 17.1).

It is necessary to study past Olympic tourist behaviour to understand the Olympic tourist market. The focus of this article is to present an overview of the last six Olympic Games and to recommend strategies and considerations for attracting a large number of tourists to the Olympic host city. The purpose of the study is:

- to diagnose why the recent Olympic host cities were not successful in generating the expected number of tourists during the Games; and
- to recommend possible alternative strategies for attracting a large number of tourists.

In the following sections, recent Olympic tourism impact is reviewed to demonstrate the importance of the Olympic tourist market study.

Tourist impact

The Japanese recognized that preparations for their Olympic tourists were an investment for the future. Consideration for the future was also emphasized during the Los Angeles Olympic Games and the upbeat image of Los Angeles built during the Games was used to sell the city to future tourists and conventioneers.

If the primary long-term goal in the tourism sector during the Olympic Games is to build a positive image in the tourist's mind, the dominant short-term objective should be generating a large amount of tourist expenditures.

The effect of the 1976 Montreal Olympic Games upon tourism spending was assessed to be between $77m and $135m. In addition, the multiplier judged by economists was 1.6 on tourist expenditures. Therefore, the total tourist spending of about $100m during the Montreal Olympic Games would result in a contribution of $160m to the gross national product.

The economic impact of the Games was widely acclaimed during the Los Angeles Olympic Games. Total impact was estimated at $3.29 billion. The value-added, out-of-town tourist expenditures were $417m, or 38.1 per cent of the total value-added expenditures ($1.1 billion).

Arrangements and responses

In this section, covering the period from the 1964 Tokyo Games to the 1984 Los Angeles Games, arrangements made for the Olympic tourists, and the responses of the Olympic tourist markets are examined to diagnose the sluggish Olympic tourist market of the past.

Tokyo Olympic Games, 1964

Although Olympic ticket sales were successful, the tourist business was sluggish. Forecasts projected that 130,000 foreign tourists would attend the Games. 70,000 actually visited Tokyo.

For the convenience of foreign tourists, Japanese customs inspectors were sent abroad to simplify entry into Japan. A Hotel and Housing Centre was established to supply information on local housing conditions to overseas enquirers. Information Offices assisted visitors who were to be accommodated in Japanese homes. The Japanese government waived the usual 10 per cent tax on hotel bills for foreigners.

Because many tourists felt wholly illiterate and helpless in reading ideographic road signs, 80 per cent of the tourists made arrangements through travel agents for organized tours. Tourist officials expected the Olympic tourists to be young, less affluent, and a bit more energetic than general tourists. Special interest groups such as judo clubs were expected to visit Tokyo during the Games and to meet special tourist interests the Japan Tourist Bureau arranged a variety of low-cost itineraries which included touring historic sites, industrial factories, high schools, and private homes. In addition, travel officials arranged for a low-cost company-operated dormitory and economical one-week tours for special interest visitors outside the capital.

Although much accommodation was constructed, all available rooms were quickly reserved as soon as hotels began to accept reservations for the Olympic Games. Travel agencies may be blamed for panic thanks to incorrect speculation. Fears of overcrowding discouraged thousands of regular visitors. Many scheduled tours from the USA and Europe were cancelled and four cruise ships bypassed Tokyo. Consequently, some fully-booked Tokyo hotels had empty rooms, even though they had been paid for in advance by travel agencies anticipating room shortages.

Japan experienced an overall decrease in numbers of tourists in 1964 compared to 1963. The Olympic tourists had different interests from those of the usual visitors (e.g. sightseeing). Restaurant and night club receipts were below normal. However, stores selling cameras, transistor radios, and portable television sets experienced increased business.

Mexico Olympic Games, 1968

Mexico significantly expanded its tourist facilities for the Olympic Games. The Mexican National Tourist Council undertook an extensive advertising campaign to promote tourism and the Games.

There was controversy over the number of tourists expected to visit Mexico during the Games. On the basis of one forecast of 200,000 tourists, the number of hotel rooms and other tourist facilities was expanded. Another forecast indicated that the number of visitors would not increase dramatically in view of the decrease in visitor numbers at the last three Olympic Games. This second forecast pointed out that Olympic tourists were different from 'ordinary' tourists. Also, Olympic tourists did not place a high value on accommodation, but had strong desires for admission tickets to the Games. The average tourist's stay during the Games was expected to be six days, which was the case at the Rome and Tokyo Games.

The Mexican Government forced regulations on the hotel industry to attract the foreign tourists who were the source of one-third of Mexico's foreign earnings. Under these regulations hotel prices were controlled by the Government Tourist Department. The Housing Control Office released rooms in blocks to travel agents. By September 1967, all rooms blocked in advance for the Games had been reserved. Mexico City was crowded, but not as crowded as expected, and some hotel rooms were available.

Munich Olympic Games, 1972

Three studies were completed to calculate the expected demand for lodgings at the 1972 Games. About 1.8m tourists (0.16m tourists per day) were expected to come to Munich during the Games. Consequently, 70,000 overnight lodgers per day were expected and 36,000 commercial beds needed to accommodate them.

The Tourist Trade Office of the City of Munich took over all the administrative tasks in the Central Accommodation Agency in the Olympic Information Centre and arranged accommodation for all German and foreign tourists. The Central Accommodation Agency arranged the reservation of about 60,000 beds. Roughly 6 per cent of these pre-paid beds remained unoccupied.

In contrast to other Olympics, there was a rush for prime space in Munich's best hotels, and their ballrooms and the more expensive night clubs were jammed as private parties flourished over the weekends during the Olympics.

Montreal Olympic Games, 1976

Olympic tourists were expected to number 1.5m. Demonstrations by Montreal taxi drivers and tightened entry regulations for Canada were two discouraging factors in attracting foreign tourists.

Tourists to the Montreal Olympic Games enjoyed their night life more than at any previous Olympics. As competition arenas closed, the streets were filled by tourists at night. Montreal became a city of pleasure seekers.

Ticket buyers found that seats for their favourite events were sold out by May 1975. However, thousands of tourists were able to buy final competition tickets less than two hours before the Games.

The allocation of tickets was controversial since 85 per cent of the tickets available were reserved for tourists from Canada and the USA, leaving only 15 per cent for the rest of the world. Only 41 per cent of the initial foreign allocations were sold abroad. The situation may have been exacerbated by world press scepticism of the feasibility of holding the Games in Montreal. The recorded attendance at the Montreal Olympic Games was 3.2m.

The Quebec Lodging Bureau controlled the reservations for hotel rooms. As with ticket sales, the hotel rooms were sold out several months before the Games. Cancellations produced openings on a night-to-night basis, and reservations were not necessary before tourists arrived at the 'Welcoming Centers'. Lodging requests were serviced at the 16 Welcoming Centers at major international crossing points, airports, railway stations and bus depots.

Moscow Olympic Games, 1980

The boycott of the 1980 Olympics by many nations was the main reason for the small number of tourists attending the Moscow Games.

The Organizing Committee for the 1980 Olympics estimated that visitors to Moscow during the Games would number between 30,000 and 300,000. Ticket sales totalled 5.3m.

Intourist was responsible for foreign tourism. It contracted with travel agencies in seventy-eight countries, which in turn sold over 1.3m admission tickets to visitors from seventy-one countries. Intourist published a free newsletter in the USA which served a dual purpose – imparting information on, e.g., package tours planned for Americans, and data gathering for a survey on length of stay, preferred Olympic events, and popular cities for Americans to visit in the USSR. According to the survey, 87 per cent of those who wanted to go had never been to the USSR and seeing Russia appeared more important than attending the Games.

Los Angeles Olympic Games, 1984

It was estimated that 625,000 tourists would attend the Games and that they would stay on average five days. However, only 400,000 tourists attended.

Neither the Olympic Organizing Committee nor the Greater Los Angeles Visitors Bureau made any housing arrangements for tourists during the Games, nor did they conduct promotional activities to attract tourists during the Olympics.

Heavy traffic congestion was expected in the Los Angeles area due to the influx of the estimated seven million spectators. However, despite warnings of traffic congestion, the traffic on the freeways flowed very smoothly during the Olympics.

A local editorial warned that price gouging might lose long-term local customers, and tourists might not return to Los Angeles. The majority of the popular Games tickets were distributed to people in the Southern California area who did not need to fly or stay overnight. The ticket distribution system of the Games prohibited ticket sales by blocks. The strength of the US dollar and the practice of assigning lesser quality tickets to non-US citizens disappointed foreign tourists and travel agencies. Consequently, the tour wholesalers and operators had to reduce the number of package plans, cancel planned tours to Los Angeles, and refrain from including tickets in the package tours as promised.

Despite the anticipated high demand for hotel and motel rooms, from 6,000 to 8,000 rooms remained unoccupied each night during the Games. Some hotels discounted their room charges.

Some restaurants reported sales of between 20 per cent and 40 per cent below their summer average during the first week of the Games and only average thereafter. Restaurateurs blamed the sales loss on regular customers shunning restaurants they assumed would be packed and on the spending habits of the Olympic tourists.

Most attractions in the Los Angeles area reported business down by 20 per cent to 35 per cent from the normal July and August traffic. It appeared that the visitors to Los Angeles during the Olympics were sports enthusiasts who came primarily to see the Games, but generated very little revenue in dining and sightseeing.

While the Games themselves generated an unprecedented profit, it was estimated that the loss of revenue for Los Angeles in general might be

Table 17.2 Factors influencing attendance at the Summer Olympic Games

Encouraging factors	Discouraging factors
Housing arrangements	Boycott of the Games
Simplified entry procedure	Tightened entry
Tax exemption	Unfavourable exchange rate
Block ticket sales	Suspect feasibility of the Games
	Confusing ticket distribution system
	Price gouging
	Overcrowding
	Traffic congestion, parking problems
	Incomprehensible road signs
	Smog

$331m, based upon a slow tourist summer nationally and in Southern California, as well as displacement caused by the Olympic Games.

Factors accounting for the relatively small number of tourists to the Los Angeles Olympic Games can be identified as:

● the general tourism sluggishness in 1984;
● the strong US dollar;
● the mass media coverage of anticipated traffic congestion and scarcity of hotel rooms;
● price gouging;
● ticket distribution policy;
● avoidance of the Olympic sites by out-of-town tourists and regional residents; and
● regional residents' spending on Olympic events rather than on other recreational activities in South California or outside the region.

Conclusion

The factors which have encouraged and discouraged travel to the host cities of the past six Olympic Games are listed in Table 17.2.

Beside these items, the Olympic tourists may be sensitive to language services, and may be discouraged by inefficiency and unavailability of relevant information. Food quality and sanitary conditions may also be important factors.

Two kinds of tourists visited Olympic Games host cities. One was the usual tourist, primarily interested in the host country and its culture, or in business not directly related to the Olympic events. The other was a sports enthusiast, with great interest in the Olympic events. The sports enthusiasts were less affluent than the usual tourists and not big spenders.

Many marketing implications can be drawn from the above findings about the special demands of Olympic tourists. First, regions with potential to generate a large number of tourists in general should be selected. Second, steps should be taken to find the people in each region interested in visiting the Olympic host city either as a usual tourist or a sports enthusiast. Third, in each target market, information designed to meet potential tourists' needs should be disseminated. Information geared to the different market characteristics should be designed to meet the needs of each given specific target market. Finally, special consideration should be given to tour operators since they are the intermediaries that facilitate mass tourism. Especially if tourists are not familiar with their destinations, they tend to purchase package tours. The tour operator can thus be utilized as an efficient promotional agent for the host city by furnishing incentives.

The short-term objective of the tourism sector during the Olympic Games is to attract a large number of tourists to offset part of the financial burdens of the host country's taxpayers. The long-term goal should be to upgrade the popularity of the host city as a desirable tourist destination through comprehensive public relations during the Olympic Games. Above all, the Olympic Games should be recognized as an investment for the future and an image-building event rather than a profit-generating opportunity.

Note

The reader is referred to the article published in the journal for an exhaustive list of the sources used in preparing it (vol. 9, no. 2, June 1988, pp. 137–44).

18 South Pacific tourism promotion

John Yacoumis

The recent advent of the Tourism Council of the South Pacific (TCSP) as a regional tourism organization, and its various activities under the EEC-financed Pacific Regional Tourism Development Programme have undoubtedly focused attention on the subject of regional tourism promotion. The concept of regional tourism promotion for the South Pacific is certainly not new. It is, however, doubtful whether there is general consensus as to its meaning and applicability. Attitudes range from seeing regional promotion as a panacea to dismissing it as altogether irrelevant and useless.

In Fiji there is some scepticism about regional tourism promotion, perhaps with reason. For one might conceivably wonder why Fiji, which is so far ahead of all other South Pacific island countries in tourism development, should be concerned with regional cooperative efforts. It is important to recognize prevailing perceptions and concerns and try to provide satisfactory answers to the following questions – Is regional tourism promotion necessary? Is it feasible? And is it sufficient by itself? It is also necessary to define what Fiji's role is in a regional promotion strategy, and how Fiji would benefit from it.

Before examining the role and rationale of regional tourism promotion in the South Pacific, it is useful to consider briefly the performance, trends and prospects of tourism in the region and suggest regional marketing objectives and strategy.

Performance, trends and prospects

In 1986, the least interrupted year, the South Pacific island region registered 454,000 international tourist arrivals, a mere 0.17 per cent of world tourist arrivals.[1] Of these nearly 60 per cent were recorded by Fiji. Following the two military coups in Fiji in 1987, tourist traffic to the country dropped dramatically, recording a calendar 1987 total of 190,000 arrivals.

This represented 48 per cent of the regional total, which also decreased to 393,000 arrivals. These figures alone are evidence that in global terms the South Pacific receives an almost negligible share of international tourism, and also, that Fiji dominates the region as the largest single tourist destination.

Six markets accounted for 84 per cent of all foreign tourist arrivals in 1986. These were, in descending order of importance, Australia, the USA, New Zealand, Europe, Canada and Japan. In 1987, their share dropped to 78 per cent.

A broad analysis of market developments up to 1987 points to two major trends. First, American and Canadian visitor arrivals were growing at a fairly high rate, resulting in a significant increase of their relative share of the total traffic to the South Pacific.

The second major trend was a dramatic development in the opposite direction. The Australian market was steadily declining; as far as Fiji's Australian market is concerned, there were indications of a downturn long before the 1987 political upheavals.

Other market developments during this time include the wide fluctuations of the New Zealand market which ultimately recorded no real growth, the steady decline of the Japanese market in sharp contrast to the spectacular growth rates of Japanese traffic achieved by Australia and New Zealand, and finally, during this period the European market showed a steady, if unspectacular, growth trend.

Australia and New Zealand have traditionally been the main tourist-generating markets for island countries in the South Pacific region and the mainstay of their tourist industries. The recent economic recovery and strengthening of their currencies promise renewed growth prospects. Although the growth potential of these two traditional short-haul markets is generally recognized, it has to be appreciated that future growth rates will not be dramatic. This is because some island countries have already achieved considerable penetration of the two markets and, as Australians and New Zealanders discover destinations further afield, growth, although feasible, will be slow and accomplished only through tough competitive action. In addition, it must always be remembered that the potential market in Australia and New Zealand is ultimately constrained by relatively small population bases.

It seems, therefore, that while South Pacific island countries will continue to depend for much of their visitor traffic on Australia and New Zealand, it is necessary to develop new source markets to ensure adequate and balanced traffic growth throughout the region. These new sources must be North America, Japan and Western Europe.

The North American traffic growth, which was recorded up to May 1987, was directly related to the recent substantial increase in trans-Pacific traffic flows to Australia and New Zealand, which created a large 'stopover' market for Fiji. This steady growth trend has been propelled by Australia and New Zealand's extensive and successful promotional efforts to establish themselves as major, permanent and high-volume destinations. Australia and New Zealand have not only focused an unprecedentedly high degree of attention on the South Pacific, but also created substantial traffic flows from long-haul markets into which the South Pacific islands can tap.

The future market strategy of South Pacific islands will have to recognize the dual role of Australia and New Zealand. First, as important bread-and-butter markets in their own right and, second, as channels and gateways for the long-haul markets through their increasing attractiveness as world tourist destinations.

The recent performance of the Japanese market in the South Pacific islands, essentially Fiji, has been a matter of grave concern, all the more so in view of its spectacular performance elsewhere. Even before the Japanese market virtually disappeared, as a result of the suspension and withdrawal of airline services after last year's events in Fiji, it was steadily declining. All this has been happening at a time when the Japanese outbound travel market has been booming, with South Pacific rim countries such as Australia and New Zealand experiencing an unprecedented influx of Japanese tourists.

Admittedly, the scope for attracting stopover traffic from Japan is quite limited, because of the largely single-destination, short-duration holiday travel patterns which characterize this market. However, the fact that neighbouring destinations in the Pacific receive a substantial and growing volume of Japanese visitors not only serves to demonstrate the existing potential, but also points to a market opportunity that the region seems to have been a little slow to grasp.

In the context of the Japanese government's current efforts to double the number of Japanese travelling overseas by 1991 as part of the so-called 10 Million Plan, the continuing strength of the Yen, the already established Japanese travel trends in the wider Pacific region, and Air Pacific's forthcoming air services between Tokyo and Nadi, it is perfectly justified to say that the Japanese market now offers the most exciting short-term growth prospects for Fiji and the rest of the South Pacific.

Need to widen product base

In order to ensure continued growth of the traditional markets of Australia and New Zealand and, especially, succeed in tapping new long-haul markets, the South Pacific region has to expand its tourist product base. Yet, throughout the region there is a dearth of developed tourist attractions and products that can readily meet identified potential demand.

Even in the traditional market of Australia, recent market research there, undertaken on behalf of Fiji, revealed that a differentiated demand pattern seems to be emerging away from conventional stay-put beach resort holidays to more varied travel experiences involving cultural, nature-related interests and hobbies. For example, scuba diving in the South Pacific fulfils, even exceeds, the criteria required by the dive travel market, namely clear and warm water, diverse marine life and living coral reefs. In addition the South Pacific has some of the most famous wreck dive spots in the world.

Recent market research in the USA estimated that in 1986 there was a total market of 1,200,000 to 1,400,000 active divers in that country, the largest diving population in the world.[2] The same research source estimated the number of active divers travelling overseas for dive holidays in 1986 at 550,000. Undoubtedly, the South Pacific, potentially the world's premier dive destination, has not yet tapped into this important market.

Regional marketing objectives and strategy

TCSP's specific marketing objectives are mainly:

- to attract an increased share of Australia and New Zealand bound trans-Pacific traffic for stopovers in the South Pacific;
- to increase long-haul 'destinational' traffic to the South Pacific, i.e. visitors whose primary, as opposed to stopover, destination is the South Pacific, thereby creating a larger pool of traffic for redistribution throughout the region; and
- to broaden the regional tourist-product base by cultivating special interest markets with already identified potential, such as the dive travel market, sport fishing market, and the adventure and nature tours markets.

In the short and medium term, TCSP will focus its resources on a tourist-product range which appeals to the largest potential segments of the markets. This range includes the following general and special interest tourist products available almost throughout the region:

- beach resort, single-destination, stay-put holidays, including family holidays;
- touring and sightseeing travel;
- pleasure cruising and sailing;

- honeymoon travel;
- visits to Second World War sites;
- scuba diving;
- sport fishing;
- adventure tours, i.e. hiking, trekking, bushwalks, four-wheel-drive expeditions or jeep safaris, white water rafting, caving and river expedition cruises; and
- nature tours, i.e. birdwatching, orchid viewing tours, butterfly viewing and collecting trips, wildlife and protected nature areas study tours.

The principal market segments targeted in the various source markets are as follows:

Australia and New Zealand

- beach resort holiday market;
- family holiday market;
- honeymoon travel market;
- dive travel market;
- sport fishing market;
- adventure tours market; and
- nature tours market.

North America (USA, Canada) and Japan

- general interest touring and sightseeing travel market;
- dive travel market;
- sport fishing market;
- adventure tours market;
- nature tours market;
- war veterans travel market;
- Australia and New Zealand bound stopover market; and
- additionally, in Japan the important honeymoon travel market.

Western Europe

- general interest touring and sightseeing travel market; and
- Australia and New Zealand bound stopover market.

Regional promotion

Travel behaviour patterns and perceptions of the South Pacific in source markets are important in formulating a promotional approach. First, we must distinguish between the traditional short-haul markets of Australia and New Zealand, which are essentially single destination travel markets with long average stays, and North America and Western Europe, which generate mostly multi-destination and stopover trips with relatively short average stay. By contrast, Japan is essentially a single-destination market, but is characterized by relatively short average stays.

Second, market perceptions of the South Pacific differ. In the traditional short-haul markets there is a greater degree of awareness and knowledge of the South Pacific than in long-haul markets. Thus, the Australian and New Zealand markets perceive the various South Pacific islands as separate destinations in their own right, each with a different image and identity.

The nature and strength of these images are a direct function of the nature and quantity of promotional activity by the island countries concerned. Obviously, some South Pacific island countries, notably Fiji, are more clearly perceived and better known in Australia and New Zealand than others. Direct flights from Australia or New Zealand to most of the South Pacific islands both reflect as well as reinforce single-destination travel patterns in these two markets.

On the other hand, the long-haul markets of North America and Western Europe perceive the South Pacific region, or subregions within it, as overall destination areas, in spite of the fact that such awareness is often limited to one or two major island destinations.

This distinction has significant strategic implications in terms of constructing regional tour patterns and general product packaging, as well as in terms of the emphasis and focus of regional promotion efforts. Recent market research by the Pacific Asia Travel Association (PATA) on the West Coast of the US[3] showed that the level of awareness of the South Pacific among both travel trade personnel and consumers ranges from low to vague. No doubt, these findings are still largely valid today, and presumably also reflect similar perceptions of the South Pacific in the other long-haul markets.

The major implications of the above survey findings in terms of a regional promotion strategy in the long-haul markets are as follows:

- There is a primary and urgent need to create and increase awareness and knowledge of the South Pacific islands, other than Fiji, among both the travel trade and potential consumers.
- Fiji enjoys a higher level of awareness in, and has achieved a greater

penetration of, the long-haul markets, particularly North America. It seems, therefore, advisable for other South Pacific island countries to take advantage of Fiji's market leadership to gain entry into the long-haul markets through appropriate tour packaging and promotion.

Promotion objectives

1   The overriding aim of all regional promotional activities at all times is the creation of awareness of the South Pacific region in the target markets of Australia, New Zealand, North America, Japan, and Western Europe.
2   All promotional activities undertaken by the TCSP will always be part of a process of 'softening up' potential markets for member countries and their tourist industries. Within the positive market climate created by the TCSP in target markets individual country and supplier promotion will be more purposeful and cost effective.
3   While general destination promotion of individual island countries in the short-haul markets of Australia and New Zealand will remain the responsibility of the respective national tourism organizations, the TCSP will focus its regional promotional efforts on the development of potential special interest target markets.
4   The underlying principle of the South Pacific regional promotion strategy is close cooperation between all parties concerned – TCSP member national tourism organizations, the private sector within the region, airlines serving the region, and the travel trade in target markets.

Role of airlines

Airlines play an important role in the success or otherwise of regional tourism promotion in the South Pacific. There are a number of concerns which TCSP share with numerous organizations and individuals in the region. First, that large metropolitan air carriers are themselves also subject to domestic political or business pressures in their respective countries and seem by and large to have no binding ties and loyalties to the islands, other than pure commercial interests. So they can influence the entire tourism sector of the region, and their fickleness can wreak havoc on the tourist industries of the islands.

Second, inter-island air travel remains a serious constraint to regional tourism movements, in spite of Air Pacific's commendable initiatives with the introduction of the ATR 42s and the special Air Pass fares. Inter-island travel is still disproportionately expensive. There is an urgent need for greater cooperation between airlines with a view to introducing a greater degree of interlining and generally rationalizing fare structures and coordinating flight schedules.

Third, TCSP is deeply concerned with the fragmentation of regional airline operations into small and commercially unviable airlines. Small island countries with limited populations and embryonic visitor industries cannot possibly sustain viable independent national air carriers operating large jet aircraft. Greater cooperation and integration of air transport operations in the islands is a precondition of long-term success in tourism development.

Role of Fiji

Fiji is the major regional gateway for trans-Pacific flights. Disregarding the temporary setback brought about by the recent political events, Fiji is the only destination in the South Pacific which has recorded a substantial traffic increase from long-haul markets, particularly North America. In addition, Air Pacific's increased intraregional frequencies with the introduction of the ATR 42s, together with the special Air Pass fares, probably offer the most valuable marketing opportunity to date for other island countries to tap the North American and Western European visitor traffic to Fiji.

Thus, in a short-term regional promotional context, Fiji is seen not only as a gateway for the redistribution of tourist traffic flows to other island countries, but also as the market leader on which they can 'piggy-back' in order to achieve entry into the target markets. The practical implication of Fiji's strategically important role is the promotion of regional or sub-regional tour packages using Fiji as a hub.

Regional tourism promotion initiatives

During the three-year period 1989–91 the TCSP intends to seek assistance from aid donors to establish a field marketing organization. This will comprise regional tourism marketing representations in North America, Japan and Western Europe. Similar representations in Australia and New Zealand are not considered necessary.

These South Pacific tourism marketing representations will be responsible not only for implementing a number of collective promotional activities sponsored by the TCSP, but also for coordinating all other resources available for regional promotion, such as airlines, individual country representations, where such exist, travel wholesalers and retailers, and the media. It is this coordinating role, which aims to maximize the marketing opportunities available to the region, that ultimately justifies this organizational initiative of the TCSP.

In the meantime, TCSP has taken over coordination of participation in major international travel and tourism fairs. These are the International Tourism Exchange (ITB) Berlin, the World Travel Market (WTM) London, the International Travel Industry Exposition (ITIX) Chicago, and the Sydney Holiday and Travel Show. As regional coordinator TCSP is responsible for the implementation of the combined regional exhibition stand called 'South Pacific Village'. The design concept of the village is flexible, taking into account the nature of each fair and the promotional objectives of the region in each case. However, it always aims to project a regional identity, while at the same time allowing each individual country to pursue its own promotional objectives. It is an excellent example of regional cooperation in tourism promotion, whereby pooling of resources results in economies of scale and generally increased promotional benefits to all concerned.

To increase awareness and knowledge about the South Pacific as a tourist destination, the TCSP has undertaken the production of a series of twelve films – eleven documentary films and one purely tourist promotional film. These eleven films are by definition documentaries rather than the conventional type of tourist publicity film, and are being produced to television screening specifications and standards, with a view to achieving wide network transmission in all overseas target markets.

At the same time, all films will be transferred on to video tape and large numbers of copies will be produced for extensive distribution through overseas marketing representations, national tourism organizations, airlines, tour wholesalers and travel agents. In addition, wide distribution will be sought through film libraries.

In addition to the film series, TCSP has completed production of a range of eight regional promotion publications. They aim to create and enhance awareness and knowledge about the South Pacific as a desirable tourist destination not only in the general travel market, but also in a number of special interest travel markets. In addition, they aim to help travel agents and tour wholesalers in tour planning and travel counselling. In positioning the South Pacific and projecting a distinctive image of it as a tourist destination, these publications emphasize the following major unique selling points:

- the variety of visitor experience based on the diversity of countries, environments, cultures and life-styles found in the South Pacific;
- the romance, mystique and exoticism of the South Pacific;

● the superlative recreation marine environment, a premier world playground; and
● a friendly, unspoilt and increasingly accessible part of the world, which is yet to be discovered.

A slogan or theme has been developed which epitomizes the South Pacific. It goes beyond the sun, islands and palm trees, lagoons, white-sand beaches and living coral reefs, which other parts of the world may also boast of. It is rooted in and evokes the way of life – 'The South Pacific Way'. On its own it has many connotations – geographical, emotional and descriptive. But when combined with another element, i.e. words which are also descriptive and demonstrative of what that 'way' actually is, the theme becomes not only uniquely adaptable, but also virtually inexhaustible in its applications.

Half a million copies have been printed initially. Apart from English, some of the brochures have also been produced in German and French. There is provision to produce Japanese versions in the near future. The eight regional tourist promotion publications are the following:

1 *Travel manual* This key promotional and sales tool is intended to be an annual publication. It will aim to provide factual, reliable and up-to-date information on the region to tour wholesalers and travel agents and thus increase product knowledge, improve client counselling and facilitate organizing and selling travel to the South Pacific. In the first year 40,000 copies have been printed.
2 *Tourist map folder* This 24-panel standard rack size folder aims to introduce potential visitors to South Pacific island countries and create awareness of the region as a tourism destination area. It is intended for large-scale distribution and will be particularly useful at travel fairs and trade shows. There have been 125,000 copies printed.
3 *Posters* A series of four large format posters – with 30,000 copies of each – has been printed initially. The posters are intended as basic display material projecting and reinforcing the desired image, while at the same time creating and enhancing awareness of the region.
4 *Diving brochure* This 16-page, A4-size, full-colour brochure is intended as a specialized promotional tool for the divetravel market. It aims to increase awareness of the South Pacific as a superb diving destination. There have been 75,000 copies printed.
5 *Sport-fishing brochure* This 12-page, A4-size, full-colour brochure is intended as a specialized promotional tool for the sport-fishing market, with 50,000 copies printed.
6 *Adventure tours brochure* This 12-page, A4-size, full colour brochure for the adventure tours market features trekking and hiking expeditions, bushwalking, four-wheel drive or jeep safaris, white-water raft-

ing, caving and river expedition cruises. It aims to create awareness of all these special interest travel possibilities in the South Pacific. There have been 100,000 copies printed.

7 *Nature tours brochure* This 12-page, A4-size, full-colour brochure focuses on the fauna and flora and the protected nature areas of the South Pacific region. It highlights such nature-related attractions as national parks and reserves, specific forests and botanic localities, bird watching, butterflies, wildlife, etc. There have been 100,000 copies printed.

8 *Press kit* 2,000 press kits have been produced.

Other promotional activities

In time TCSP will become more actively involved in a number of 'sharp end' promotional activities in target markets, such as travel agents' workshops and seminars, travel marts, familiarization tours, media trips, etc. This involvement will take place only if the activities are clearly of a regional nature, and a regional approach makes both marketing and financial sense to all parties concerned, so there will be a need for coordination.

Effective marketing and promotion of the region as a whole, and of individual countries, need detailed and reliable market data and information. TCSP intends to organize and carry out market studies as part of its continuing research programme, in order to generate the marketing intelligence needed to refine marketing and promotion planning and monitor the effectiveness of promotional activities. This is clearly an area where a coordinated regional approach will result in considerable economies of scale to individual countries.

Role and rationale of regional promotion

Having outlined the regional marketing strategy and the main promotional initiatives of the TCSP, it is necessary to define the role and rationale of regional tourism promotion, and provide answers to the questions posed at the outset.

Is regional tourism promotion necessary?

Two main factors imply the necessity of regional tourism promotion. First, there are practical considerations of a financial nature and of human and material resource allocation, which dictate a regional cooperative approach to tourism promotion. Most island countries could never afford to undertake a comprehensive promotion campaign entirely on their own.

Second, there are intrinsic marketing reasons why regional promotion is necessary. In North America, and Western Europe by and large, the whole region is perceived as the destination area. As such, the region as a whole has to be promoted. Even in predominantly single-destination markets such as Australia, New Zealand and Japan, regional promotional initiatives to cultivate potential special-interest markets seem to be the most sensible course of action.

Is regional promotion feasible?

Regional cooperation in international travel fairs coordinated by TCSP has already demonstrated the feasibility of effective regional cooperative promotion. So have the continuing projects for the production of films and marketing publications.

Is regional tourism promotion sufficient by itself?

Regional tourism promotion is intended to supplement and complement individual destination and supplier promotion, not replace it. Regional promotion of the South Pacific essentially aims to create a positive climate in target markets in which individual countries and the private sector can promote themselves more cost effectively. It would be naive if TCSP believed that it could do more than coordinate efforts and resources, soften up markets, generate economies of scale for individuals and their tourist industries and maximize the synergy of collective efforts. TCSP appreciates fully the scope and limitations of regional promotion. But it would be just as naive, indeed dangerous, if any island country relied on TCSP to carry out its own destination promotion.

Benefits for Fiji

It is now only reasonable to ask why, given Fiji's privileged situation on trans-Pacific air routes and its position of market leadership, it should help other island countries to gain entry into markets. First of all, no market leader has ever suffered from the effects of generic product promotion. Indeed, given its central position and market leadership, Fiji stands to gain a great deal from increased awareness of the South Pacific as a tourist destination area. The more TCSP helps to focus attention on, and create interest in, the South Pacific, the more Fiji stands to benefit.

Second, there are undeniable financial and other practical benefits for Fiji from participating in several regional cooperative promotional activities, which would be unnecessarily costly to undertake independently. These include international trade shows, travel marts, agents' seminars, promotional publications such as the travel agent's manual, etc., and of course market research activities.

Third, and perhaps more important from Fiji's point of view, a regional promotional approach is necessary if continued and long-term growth is to be maintained in the North American and Western European markets. This is because of the regional product perceptions and multi-destination travel patterns which characterize these two markets. In fact, if necessary, Fiji itself should promote neighbouring island destinations, because ultimately it needs them as vital elements of product diversification and innovation. This idea is well understood and appreciated by Air Pacific and is best exemplified by the special Air Pass fares.

Finally, and in a wider context, in the same way that Air Pacific perceives Nadi as a regional hub and itself as a regional airline for the South Pacific, so must Fiji see itself as an integral part of a wider tourist destination area. As a regional centre and leader, Fiji has the opportunity to become the locomotive of tourism development in the region. The corollary of this role is not only the need to adopt a regional tourism marketing perspective, but also to appreciate and seize the expansion opportunities offered by neighbouring countries through investment and participation in their tourism plant and export of tourism skills and expertise.

Notes and references

1   The South Pacific island region includes Fiji, Papua New Guinea, Solomon Islands, Vanuatu, Tonga, Western Samoa, American Samoa, Cook Islands, Niue, Kiribati and Tuvalu.
2   'Market research report in worldwide trends on dive travel', *Skin Diver Magazine*, Los Angeles, USA, 1986.
3   Pacific Asia Travel Association, *Perceptions of the South Pacific in the USA – a survey of tour operators and travel agents on the West Coast*, PATA, 1984.

Acknowledgement

This chapter is a revised version of an address delivered at the 1988 Fiji Tourism Convention.

Further reading

Further reading on marketing in *Tourism Management* 1980–9

Bonnett, J., 'Implications of marketing and promotion for the development of tourism', vol. 3, no. 4, December 1982, pp. 242–7.

Clements, M. A., 'Selecting tourist traffic by demarketing', vol. 10, no. 2, June 1989, pp. 89–94.

Gilbert, D., 'Rural tourism and marketing: synthesis and new ways of working', vol. 10, no. 1, March 1989, pp. 39–50.

Johnson, W. H., 'Tomorrow's traveller – a marketing analysis', vol. 4, no. 2, June 1983, pp. 129–31.

Kaynak, E., 'Developing marketing strategy for a resource-based industry', vol. 6, no. 3, September 1985, pp. 184–93.

Krippendorf, J., 'Ecological approach to tourism marketing', vol. 8, no. 2, June 1987, pp. 174–8.

Middleton, V. T. C., 'Marketing implications for attractions', vol. 10, no. 3, September 1989, pp. 229–32.

Morse, J., 'Tourism: Australia's fastest growing industry', vol. 10, no. 3, September 1989, pp. 225–8.

Taylor, G. D., 'How to match plant with demand: a matrix for marketing', vol. 1, no. 1, March 1980, pp. 56–60.

Taylor, G. D., 'Multi-dimensional segmentation of the Canadian pleasure travel market', vol. 7, no. 3, September 1986, pp. 146–67.

Part Seven

Managing the Tourists

Whilst tourist attractions and facilities are increasingly more competitive, many are also experiencing increasing visitor pressures. A growing response to both on the part of their operators is to pay more attention to the quality of the tourist experience and to seek approaches and techniques to enhance formerly neglected aspects of the tourist product. In this part of the book three selected articles consider in turn queue management, interpretation and animation.

In 'Towards the better management of tourist queues' Philip Pearce of the James Cook University in Australia brings psychology to bear on one of the less enjoyable features of visiting tourist attractions and sites, and puts forward practical suggestions for various travel and tourism situations.

In 'The technique of interpretation' Chris Cooper of the University of Surrey in the UK describes the uses and significance of interpretation in providing an interface between the tourist destination and the visitor, and enhancing the visitor experience by making its attributes more comprehensible.

'The concept of animation', which is examined here by Wilhelm Pompl of the Fachhochschule Heilbronn in the Federal Republic of Germany, is not new but has so far received little attention in English tourism literature, and the author explains its aims, characteristics and requirements.

Further articles with a bearing on the theme of this part of the book published in *Tourism Management* from 1980–9 are listed on page 239. See also Chapter 11, 'Heritage management for heritage tourism' and Chapter 14, 'Hub operations and airline competition'.

19 Towards the better management of tourist queues

Philip L. Pearce

For many tourists one of the less enjoyable features of visiting tourist attractions and sites is the process of waiting in line. Yet the inevitability of waiting seems likely to increase as larger numbers of people visit locations where the size of the resource or attraction cannot be altered. Additionally, the use of queues is a standard procedure in immigration and passport control as well as for tourist transport and food services. As a general form of social behaviour, waiting in line exists in many everyday-life situations with long waiting times being common in gaining access to films, concerts, sports events, shopping and even waiting for the publication of academic articles.

One perspective on queues at tourist attractions has already been given attention in this journal.[1] Wanhill examined the topic of congestion at tourist attractions and used an economic modelling approach to explore the social costs of waiting to view an attraction. This approach, a derivative of social cost-benefit analysis, works towards eliminating queues through the pricing mechanism. Even if such pricing control approaches were widely adopted, queues are still likely to form in a host of tourist settings, e.g. within theme parks, museums and art galleries, at international fairs and expositions, and in many transport and service venues.

This article seeks to promote better management of tourist queues by describing some of the psychological processes operating within and among individuals as they wait in line. It is argued here that the social, cognitive and behavioural needs of people all warrant attention in understanding the frustrations of waiting in line and that management actions directed at satisfying these needs should promote more satisfied tourist clients.

Psychological background

In order to understand the psychological needs and processes operating within a population of waiting visitors it is valuable to review some earlier work by psychologists in this area. The work of Mann and Taylor (1969), Mann (1970) and Mann (1977) represents one coherent line of inquiry tackling social and cognitive features implicated in people's in-line behaviour.[2] The combined results of these studies suggested that subjects before the critical point (where the commodity is likely to become unavailable) tend to overestimate the numbers waiting ahead whereas subjects after the critical point tend to underestimate their position in line.

In a further paper on queues Mann (1977) observed that six people were required to elicit queue joining.[3] This finding, the result of a carefully planned field study of bus queues, is of course linked to specific cultural and situational contexts (specifically bus queues in Israel) but Hall has observed, where the cultural values of egalitarianism and orderliness prevail, line forming is likely to occur even when less than six people are present.[4] These research observations on estimating queue sizes may be supplemented by other more general psychological inputs.

Time perception

For example, one of the critical concepts germane to queuing is the individual's perception of time. Fraisse (1963) has proposed that every time we turn our attention to the course of time it seems to grow longer.[5] He argued that two forces were at work here – first overestimating the obstacle (in this case the speed at which the queue is moving) and paying heightened attention to the changes which separate the person from the end goal. Fraisse observes that the common experience of waiting five minutes for someone to come can seem much longer, whereas watching an enjoyable five minute television programme can seem to have taken much less time. Fraisse argues that the cliché 'time flies when we are happy' is best understood by conceptualizing it as time is unnoticed when we are happy, and it is the process of not paying attention to time which makes it pass quickly.

Several studies, some conducted over half a century ago, confirm Fraisse's arguments. Other studies have confirmed that people who are highly motivated provide truncated time estimates. Similarly, active as opposed to passive subjects report that time passes more quickly, as evidenced in the comparison between lecturers and their students where typically, the passive listeners find the lecture longer than their mentor, who is active and whose task involves a greater unity of purpose and a higher motivation to stay awake.

Needs of the waiting public

There are already several implications here for queue management (such as the need to make queue members active rather than passive) but they can be expressed more powerfully by considering the ramifications of other psychological research on human information processing. Many perspectives in psychology emphasize the need for people to operate in an optimum level of information processing – having to deal with too much information is stress inducing, having to deal with too little information also produces stress through the process of lack of control and its consequences of boredom and fatigue.[6] Typically, queue members suffer from a lack of information in their environment. They are unsure of how long they will be waiting, they are uncertain as to how crowded the attraction/feature will be when they arrive at the end of the queue and, as discussed before, they are often unable to estimate accurately the number of people in the queue or the time they have been there. Frustration, boredom and a range of negative, emotional effects follow from this lack of information to the waiting public.

A final, but not trivial, consideration in planning for better queue management relates to the physical needs of people who are standing in line. There is a need to provide resting opportunities, drinking fountains, and possibly the scope for a passout card or access to toilet facilities in the longest queues. Additionally, it is desirable that family members can stand side by side in the queue since this facilitates conversation compared to a strict linear queue arrangement. Queue 'width' is also important for children who benefit from a wider queue by having more room to stretch, interact and relate to their care-givers than is possible in confined, one-person wide corridors.

These psychological and physical needs of people in queues can be met with a range of innovative queue management techniques. These include detailed attention to the shape of the queue (see Figure 19.1). Outside queues which follow form (5) can be easily provided with shade/shelter protection by adding to the exterior of the relevant building. Effectively then, the attraction starts the moment one joins the queue, rather than simply being a dull preliminary to the main event.

This approach of incorporating the queue into the design of the building exhibition or tourist display can serve additional functions in psychological terms. For example, it is possible to have small displays which preview the main interests of the exhibition alongside the rails which structure the queue formation. These information panels, which need to be durable, can mentally stimulate visitors and structure their thinking towards the attraction or facility itself. Display panels or sheets which ask the waiting public questions, or which set them tasks to solve, assist both

(1) Traditional single line queue – one service person

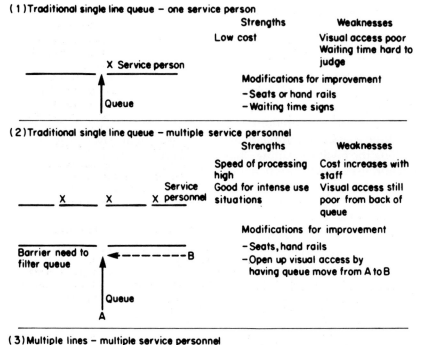

Strengths	Weaknesses
Low cost	Visual access poor
	Waiting time hard to judge

Modifications for improvement
- Seats or hand rails
- Waiting time signs

(2) Traditional single line queue – multiple service personnel

Strengths	Weaknesses
Speed of processing high	Cost increases with staff
Good for intense use situations	Visual access still poor from back of queue

Modifications for improvement
- Seats, hand rails
- Open up visual access by having queue move from A to B

(3) Multiple lines – multiple service personnel

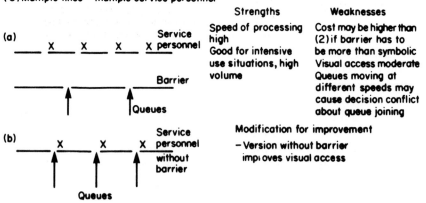

Strengths	Weaknesses
Speed of processing high	Cost may be higher than (2) if barrier has to be more than symbolic
Good for intensive use situations, high volume	Visual access moderate
	Queues moving at different speeds may cause decision conflict about queue joining

Modification for improvement
- Version without barrier improves visual access

Figure 19.1 Queue forms and their features

(4)Multiple lines – single service person

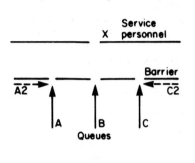

Strengths	**Weaknesses**
Visual access	Orderly turn taking
moderate	among queue leaders
Cost of personnel low	is important
	Cost increases if
	barrier has to be more
	than symbolic
	Decision conflicts in
	queue joiners

Modification for improvement

– Visual access can be improved
having queue A move to A2
and queue C to C2

(5)Themed or integrated queue

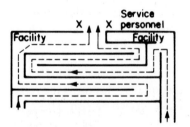

Strengths	**Weaknesses**
Visual access (and	Increased costs
time judgments)	applicable to theme
improved	park, zoo, heritage
Information can be	entrances, rides,
displayed	attractions
Physical comfort can	
be built into queue form	

Modifications for improvement

– Single queue form also possible
Themed queue along the side of
a building a further alternative

the information needs of the public and their perception of time since, as outlined in the research on time, 'filled time' is not likely to seem as long. Queues which provide visual access to the entrance/point of departure or end of the queue are also to be recommended in design terms, since the waiting public can attend to the speed of progress at the end of the line and possibly preview some of the attraction itself. A simple but effective management aid which serves this same goal of informing the waiting public is the provision of 'wait time' signs which indicate that it is, say ten minutes or fifteen minutes to the end of the queue from a specific point.

The physical features which can make waiting more comfortable include the provision of water fountains, and the supply of occasional benches or seats moulded into the corners of queues. In other areas of tourist study, such as behavioural observations in museums and visitor centres, it has been demonstrated that people relieve fatigue by leaning, stooping and propping themselves against bars, rails and barriers.[7]

In Table 19.1 some recommendations are made for queue organization in relation to specific tourist settings. The matrix proposed here makes suggestions for eight tourist queue settings. These recommendations are based on the principles discussed previously in this article, notably the mental and physical needs of those waiting in line. The recommendations cannot be definitive since the size of the queues, the space of the particular facility and cost factors in personnel may prevent some choices being made. Nevertheless, the matrix is provided to challenge and stimulate thinking about future queue management in tourist settings.

For transport service (taxis, bus stops) and small restaurants the recommended queue type is the single line with one service person. This queue type is serviceable when the waiting lines are fast moving and space for other queue forms is limited. In many situations, providing direct information on the service to be used (e.g. cab hire fees, restaurant menus), as well as more general contextual information such as regional attractions would add to the visitor experience. Queue width (at least 2 metres) and leaning rails are helpful in transport services where passengers have luggage and are likely to be in small groups.

The single line with multiple service personnel queue type is recommended for longer queues where space is constricted into tunnels, hallways and corridors. Much can and should be done in these settings to relieve consumer frustration and boredom by employing information (wait times, entertainment, e.g. videos, and precise instructions) and physical comfort options (seats, moving platforms, toilets).

A better queue type for most large open spaces found in airport as well as in food and customs/immigration facilities is the multiple lines, multiple service personnel system. Here visitors regain some sense of psychological control by being able to see the end of the queue, the speed of

Table 19.1 Generalized matrix of recommended queue forms for different tourist attractions/facilities

Queue type	Customs immigration	Airport check-in	Transport (taxi, bus stop)	Restaurant waiting	Food service counter	Theme park entrance/ attraction	Theme park ride	Theatre–film cultural attractions
					Attraction/facility			
(1) single line – one service person			R	R				
Extras: Physical			√	√				
Information			√	√				
(2) Single line – multiple service personnel	R							
Extras: Physical	√							
Information	√							
(3) Multiple line – multiple service personnel	R				R (for intense use)			R (for intense use)
Extras: Physical		√			√			√
Information		√			√			
(4) Multiple lines – single service personnel					R			
Extras: Physical					√			
Information					√			
(5) Themed queue				R		R	R	R
Extras: Physical				√		Im	Im	√Im
Information				√		Im	Im	√Im

Note: R = recommended; Im = implicit.

processing of the queue and, if information is well organized, their choices and options at the service point. Where such queues are likely to be slow moving, seating and physical facilities options, e.g. leaning rails and water fountains, in the queue can add interest and facilitate visitor comfort. Designers working on the layout of these queue facilities should be guided by Fraisse's maxim that it is 'not paying attention to time which makes it pass quickly'. Consequently the queue shape and associated facilities should aim to mentally stimulate and physically relax its participants.

Multiple lines with single service personnel can be recommended for less intense use periods in such situations as theatre or film ticket purchase and food service counters. While the multiple service personnel option is still preferable in these settings, management costs may prevent using multiple staff. Nevertheless, the multiple lines queue will usually be better for the customer than the single line queue since more individuals in the queue can visually monitor the service point, they can see more of a service/attraction and they can better share any information/entertainment services provided than would be possible in a single queue. The potential sociability of such queues is much greater than for the single line queue type.

One of the strongest recommendations on waiting in line situations which emerges from this discussion is the considerable advantage of using themed queues. Indeed in most situations where space is adequate it is recommended that queues be built into the structure of facilities such as large restaurants, theme park entrances, rides and cultural attractions (such as heritage buildings and art galleries). By specifically designing the queue as part of the fabric of the attraction the visitor experience begins on arrival at the destination. Much can be achieved with awnings, verandahs, rails, seats, interpretive signs and games in the theming process. In larger settings, the 'take a ticket' numbering system can free people from the queuing process which further permits an entrance space to become a room or exhibit area with full physical facilities.

In summary, queues do not have to be a bleak introduction to a tourist attraction. Instead they can be integrated into the design of a facility, they can provide an opportunity to orientate people towards that facility with questions and display panels, and they can be less onerous physically with the provision of resting opportunities, occasional seats, water fountains, and indicators of time. In some settings it is possible to provide videos as information sources to the waiting public while in others live entertainment can engage the minds of the audience. The critical issue to be addressed at tourist attractions is the need to attend to the visitor at all times and people in queues should not be exempt from this attentive service.

References

1 Wanhill, S. R. C., 'Charging for congestion at tourist attractions', *International Journal of Tourism Management*, vol. 1, 1980, pp. 168–74.
2 Mann, L. and Taylor, K. F., 'Queue counting: the effect of motives upon estimates of numbers in waiting lines', *Journal of Personality and Social Psychology*, vol. 12, 1969, pp. 95–103; Mann, L., 'Social psychology of waiting lines', *American Scientist*, vol. 58, 1970, pp. 390–8; and Mann, L., 'The effect of stimulus queues on queue joining behaviour', *Journal of Personality and Social Psychology*, vol. 35, 1977, pp. 437–42.
3 *ibid.*
4 Hall, E. T., *The Silent Language*, New York: Doubleday, 1959; and Hall, E. T., *The Hidden Dimension*, New York: Doubleday, 1964.
5 Fraisse, P., *The Psychology of Time*, London: Eyre and Spottiswoode, 1963.
6 Eysenck, M. A., *Handbook of Cognitive Psychology*, Hillsdale, NJ: Laurence Erlbaum, 1984, pp. 331–42.
7 Melton, A. W., 'Visitor behaviour in museums: some early research in environmental design', *Human Factors*, vol. 14, 1972, pp. 393–403; and Melton, A. W., 'Studies of installation at the Pennsylvania Museum of Art', *Museum News*, vol. 12, 1933, pp. 5–8.

20 The technique of interpretation

Chris Cooper

The destination is the raison d'être of tourism. It is the location which attracts the visit and so energizes the tourism system. It is where the most significant and dramatic aspects of tourism occur and is the location of many parts of the tourism industry – attractions, accommodation, entertainment, and support facilities. Yet destinations around the world are coming under increasing pressure as tourism demand grows and it is essential that we plan and manage to maintain the integrity of destinations. This means maintaining the individual qualities which attract the tourist in the first place while ensuring that the tourist is given an enjoyable, rewarding and high-quality experience.

Tourist destinations

Tourist destinations have distinctive characteristics, which demand effective planning and management. First, they are perishable in that, as demand to visit grows, some destinations are subject to excessive visitor numbers and may deteriorate. Only effective planning and management can save such destinations – after all, tourism is attracted to the fragile and unique places in the world and these sites must be protected. Heritage tourism is already big business in Western Europe, and clear conflicts are emerging – e.g. between those who view heritage as an irreplaceable national asset, and those who view it as a commodity to be consumed, or between those who demand access to heritage attractions and those who strive to ration access and impact on the heritage.

Yet until tourism begins to measure success in terms of quality experiences rather than numbers through the door, these dilemmas will be exacerbated. This is particularly acute in market economies, where volume represents income, but also wear and tear on the resource itself. 'A low volume, high quality, high value added' tourism is the future philosophy for destinations. But this presupposes rationing, which can be divisive, denying access to some and often prejudicing educational use.

Second, destinations are commonly shared with other users. The coast for example, with shipping, and forests with timber production, and again this demands effective management of multiple uses and resolution of conflicts.

Finally, destinations are cultural appraisals. They are not deemed worthy of visiting unless society has placed a value on them. Of course, these values are always changing. In Britain, for example, there is a 'new' industrial heritage of factories, railways and canals, which is now a major tourist attraction. Yet fifty years ago this would have been inconceivable. As we move towards the year 2000, these values are continuing to change and the tourist of the 1990s will be seeking certain utilities from his visit to the destination. Destinations must recognize that tourists are individuals with their own preferences, past experiences, education and expectations of a destination. At the same time, they generally come to a site in groups, so personal interactions should be encouraged. The tourist of the 1990s will have new skills and expectations which must be built into tourism planning at the destination.

Clearly, these trends introduce a number of potential problems to tourist destinations and the solutions must lie in effective planning, management and interpretive/presentation techniques. In the 1990s good heritage management will ensure that the potentially conflicting aims of tourism and conservation are reconciled by maintaining a balance between the needs of the resource and of the visitor.

Interpreting destinations

Tourist destinations must make the visitor aware of their importance, significance, and major features by effective presentation. Interpretation provides this service by the imaginative display of information in the form of trails, signboards, visitor centres, and audio-visual media to enhance and shape visitors' experiences and bring the destination to life. Interpretation also assists in site management as it represents a communication link between the resource and visitor. Yet many tourism practitioners are ignorant of interpretation and its role while others fail to see its relevance to the tourism industry.[1] But, as the industry matures and consumers become more sophisticated in their demands at the destination, interpretation provides a potent technique with which to offer an enhanced experience while at the same time providing a positive management tool to help ameliorate the potential impacts of increased tourist contact with the resource or host society.

Interpretation as it is now understood began in North American national parks around the turn of the century and was well developed by the Second World War. It spread to the UK after the War when it was stimulated first by the conservation movements' initiatives to make the public aware of the value of the countryside, townscape and industrial heritage, and second by its roots in the environmental education movement both in North America and the UK.

A third influence has been the planners' recognition of the need to plan and manage tourist resources in the face of burgeoning demand set against static supply. As planning for tourism and recreation moves away from defensive management for resource protection and becomes orientated towards the visitor and his needs, interpretation is seen as a sophisticated management tool to achieve these goals. Interpretation is now firmly established as a technique on both sides of the Atlantic with its own professional bodies, journals, and small community (around 2500 practitioners in North America and 200 in England and Wales).[2]

Interpretation offers a number of benefits. First, it assists the visitor in developing a keener awareness and understanding of the destination, enhancing his experience and enjoyment.[3] Second, it is an effective management tool – by controlling the information content and positioning of interpretation, visitors can be hurried through pressure points, distributed along a trail, or steered away from sensitive areas. It is also felt to change visitor attitudes toward the resource by fostering a desire to protect and thereby influence behaviour.[4] Third, interpretation is increasingly seen as a means to revitalize run-down urban or rural areas not only by attracting tourist spending but also by rekindling residents' sense of community.[5]

Interpretive planning process

The interpretive plan is central to any interpretive project and is normally integral to the management plan.[6] The interpretive plan follows a flexible and interactive sequence:

● objectives;
● inventory;
● themes;
● media selection;
● interpretive emphasis; and
● evaluation

The interpretive planning process begins by setting objectives – either

Figure 20.1 Possible interpretive media

general ones, e.g. visitors will leave the destination having enjoyed their time there, or specific, e.g. the visitor will have understood the way of life of the Vikings.[7]

Objectives are important, laying down the priorities for the plan and acting as a guide for teamwork, and allowing interpretation to be monitored and evaluated against a measurable standard.

Once objectives are established the second stage is inventory or stocktaking where the available resources are closely scrutinized and decisions taken as to which should be interpreted. Other sites in the catchment area will also be examined at this stage to prevent duplication.

Themes and stories are then sifted out. Themes drive the interpretive process as, once determined, any exhibits or information discordant to the theme must be rejected – it is one of the most common failings of interpretation to include as many themes as possible thus confusing the message and the visitor. It is at this stage that creativity becomes important in the process rather than any guidelines or set formulae. Similarly the final stages of the interpretive plan – media selection and interpretive emphasis (or positioning) – also demand considerable flair and insight as they allow the theme or story to be told.

Media selection involves choosing the facilities and services most appropriate to the theme, the resource, and the visitor. There is a plethora of media available including not only the familiar signboards, trails, and visitor centres but also interactive video, computer-driven interpretation

Inventory	Theme	Media choices	
		Personal	Non-personal

Figure 20.2 A media matrix

and a wide range of audio visual techniques (Figure 20.1).[8] Interpretive media may either be in the form of personal or attended services:

- information duty;
- conducted activity;
- talks to groups; and
- living interpretation.

Or in the form of non-personal or unattended services:

- audio-visual devices;
- written material;
- self-guided activity;
- indoor exhibits;
- visitor centres; and
- off-site/off-season media.

Three considerations are taken into account in media selection. First, the nature of the media themselves as each is appropriate in its own particular setting and each has its strengths and weaknesses, e.g. guided trails allow two-way communication but often preach to the converted – self-guided trails are inexpensive and accessible but lack the immediacy of personal contact.

Of course media complement each other – the visitor centre orientates, trails allow exploration, and leaflets act as a reminder of the visit. But media can also compete for attention creating a site that is too 'busy', and diffusing interest. Considerations of cost and durability are also important. Second, the visitor must be considered and the media and content should be appropriate to the target audience – which may be the blind, children, etc. At the same time choice of media should encourage shared experiences, consider and influence the pace of movement around the destination, ensure a variety of content to attract repeat visits, and protect the visitor from any hazards of the resource. The resource itself is a final influence on choice, in particular the consideration of visual or oral intrusion from the media and the need to protect sensitive areas from overuse while influencing movement to hardened areas. A media matrix can be constructed to assist the planner in these decisions (Figure 20.2).

The final stage is monitoring to ensure that interpretation is meeting its objectives. This can be done either informally (staff observing behaviour) or more formally (e.g. by questionnaire). Throughout the planning process evaluation can be applied in order to test the effectiveness and success of the interpretation. Prince has identified three stages of evaluation:

- front-end analysis which is research done before the plan is implemented;
- formative evaluation, done while the project is underway; and
- summative evaluation which involves testing once the project is complete.[9]

Wider applications

Interpretive planning is being considered at geographical scales other than simply a single destination.[10] Regional and even national interpretive plans are possible and have a number of advantages. For example, a higher level approach acts as a framework for interpreting a group of sites and allows the development of themes and sub-themes regionally which can be linked to the marketing of the destination. At the same time this approach avoids duplication of interpretive effort and acts as a catalyst for public and private sector cooperation. A number of regional plans now exist and more ambitiously MacFarlane suggests national plans geared to a world interpretation and presentation strategy.[11] However, this scale of operation demands a comprehensive database and often the typical ordinary site demonstrates a region's personality rather than the rare, special, but popular attractions.

Discussion

However, interpretation has it critics, many of whom argue that manipulation of information is inherently suspect and that the 'gatekeeping' role of interpreters can be abused. For example, while interpretation supposedly enhances the experience of the visitor there is a danger that it removes inspiration and dampens the need to discover – after all does not the interpreter tell the visitor all he needs to know?[12] Yet, Nyberg argues, this is the interpreter's professional reality, suggesting the visitor's preconceptions are delusion.[13] At the same time the communication process can be patronizing, particularly if the message is unrelated to the audience. And it does not just patronize the audience, it is common for interpretive content to be devoid of social comment, ignoring for example the plight of the rural poor or exploited industrial workforce in the breathless and uncritical exposition of, say, Victorian farming or industrial heritage sites.[14]

The obvious gatekeeping role also causes concern when agencies use interpretation overtly to sell their aims, objectives and point of view. There is also increasing evidence that interpretation preaches to the converted, this contradicting those who defend interpretation on the grounds of increasing understanding and thus protection of sensitive issues or fragile resources.

Despite these caveats, interpretation deserves a wider audience and understanding among tourism practitioners. Its particular strength lies in its ability to provide an enhanced experience at the destination while at the same time reducing the impact on host societies and landscapes – surely a virtue when tourist resources are coming under increased pressure and the tourist is searching for a 'quality' experience at the destination.

References

1   Machin, A., 'Changing the viewpoint', *Heritage Interpretation'*, Winter 1986, pp. 4–5.
2   Stevens, T., *Interpretation. Who does it, how, and why*, Centre for Environmental Interpretation Occasional Paper 2, Manchester, 1983.
3   Sharpe, G. W. (ed), *Interpreting the environment*, New York: Wiley, 1982.
4   Tilden, F., *Interpreting our heritage*, Chapel Hill, USA: University of North Carolina Press, 1957.
5   Civic Trust/Centre for Environmental Interpretation, *Up Greenhill and Down the Dale. An interpretive plan for Wirksworth, Derbyshire*, London: Civic Trust, 1983.
6   Countryside Commission, *Guide to countryside interpretation Part 1. Principles of interpretive planning*, Cheltenham: Countryside Commission, 1975.
7   Putney, A. D. and Wagar, J. A., 'Objectives and evaluation in interpretive planning', *Journal of Environmental Education*, 1973, vol. 5, no. 1, pp. 43–4.
8   Countryside Commission, *Guide to countryside interpretation Part 2. Interpretive media and facilities*, Cheltenham: Countryside Commission, 1975.
9   Prince, D., *Evaluating interpretation. A discussion paper*, Centre for Environmental Interpretation Occasional Paper 1, Manchester, 1982.
10 Goodey, B., 'The interpretive boom', *Area*, 1979, vol. 11, no. 4, pp. 285–8.
11 Macfarlane, J. M., 'Cordillera Communications', *Heritage Interpretation*, Winter 1986, p. 5.
12 Nyberg, K. L., 'Some radical comments on interpretation', in Machlis, G. E., and Field, D. R. (eds), *On interpretation. Sociology for interpreters of natural and cultural history*, Corvallis, USA: Oregon State University Press, 1984, pp. 151–5.
13 *Ibid.*
14 Goodey, *op. cit.*, reference 10.

21 The concept of animation

Wilhelm Pompl

Where would it all end, if the masses set out on holiday on their own and came back as individuals?

Friderich Sieburg

One of the structural changes in the tourism industry has been the development of the former seller's market into a buyer's market. And if price competition in this market with a decreasing rate of growth was not to be ruinous, product design had to be viewed increasingly within set parameters of competition. The more similar the various package tours to specific holiday destinations were, then the easier it would be for travel agents and firms to be interchanged (and with them the hotels) – the customer books the cheapest holiday if he is not offered other *qualitative advantages*. These could only lie within the range of services. The services offered by a travel company as part of the holiday package were the only remaining aspects of the holiday package available whereby a company could present itself as a distinctive 'brand' to the customer, as other parts of the package tour (flight, hotel, transfers, excursions) were often sold to the competing agencies by the same source.

The availability of purposeful holidays is becoming important to an increasing number of tourists who want more from their holiday than to lie passively in the sun yet who, at the same time, lack the ability or initiative to organize their holidays for themselves. The desire 'to change the wallpaper' and to escape from routine or work is the basic motivation of those who search during their holidays for a contrast to their usual daily experiences. These are people who want to experience a happy fulfilled 'new' world, for a limited time, but who cannot actually achieve such a change through a fulfilling holiday because of limited travel experience, inadequate language abilities, insecurity and fears in a foreign environment, the lack of individual initiative and a general inability to make contact. Offering help in overcoming the 'truth barriers' in relation to holiday experiences provides the contents of the service known as animation. It can be defined as a stimulus for the body, for the mind and for the pursuit of social activities. These stimuli can come from people (human animation), media (media animation) or material (material animation).

Economic aspects

Animation will incur costs for the company offering such services, yet it can be deployed successfully and profitably in different areas by framing company policies relating to animation services so as to achieve specific goals:

- Innovative competitive behaviour can be converted into product policies by creating a new type of product (such as a club holiday or a sports hotel) that exploits gaps in the market, because holidays with activities 'à la carte' differ substantially from the existing package holiday.
- Better use can be made of the capacity available in the poorly booked 'out of season' months, through offering an animation programme which makes a hotel stay and the associated activities independent of the activities and entertainment available in the holiday resort, and such alternative programmes can partly compensate for bad weather.
- Success in animation helps to increase customer satisfaction. Two factors are mainly responsible for higher rates of bookings and lower advertisement costs – first, word-of-mouth recommendations (an important factor in tourism) and second, an increase in the number of tourists who re-book a particular holiday.
- Guests who participate in an animation programme remain in the hotel and thus increase turnover in the food and beverage section, through higher spending. They also take advantage of supplementary offers.
- In addition to such financial return, animation can support marketing goals through achieving a better image and position in the market.

From the financial viewpoint a realistic assumption is that the costs of offering an animation programme are roughly 10–15 per cent of the price for full-board. In many clubs, expensive sports have to be paid for as extras. In general, it can be said that the degree of success of investment in animation programmes can only be appraised over the long term.

Human animation has the advantage that, by comparison with material animation, only a small amount of material outlay is necessary. Thus less investment is needed at the outset, there is less 'tying-up' of long-term money, and there are no high upkeep costs. It would, however, certainly be wrong to equip a programme with an untrained and badly-paid 'casual animator', who would perhaps achieve rather more negative than positive results, just as ill-serviced or half-functional facilities or services have a negative effect.

Target groups and organizers

A review of animation programmes that have been pursued in both West Germany and abroad shows that such programmes have appealed to nearly all age groups – children, adolescents, young families with children, older people or uncategorized 'adults'. Under the category 'booked accommodation', one finds hotels, holiday clubs, camp sites, accommodation in private homes, holiday flats, convalescent holidays in sanatoriums and other forms of accommodation. If one segments the animation programmes offered according to holiday activities, then animation exists in really all areas – sport, getting to know country and people, hiking, social gatherings, hobbies or relaxation. Although the specific kind of programme depends on climatic conditions and seasonal requirements, it is clear that, in principle, animation programmes can be arranged at any time of the year, from winter sledge rides, to nature sightseeing tours in spring, to beach gymnastics.

But the main providers of animation programmes at present are travel agencies and holiday hotels. Among the holiday providers with the greatest range of programmes and the widest experience in this area is the French Club Mediterranée, which has nearly 100 club villages worldwide and has a share in the Italian company, Valtur Servizzi (twelve holiday compounds). Among the major German companies that provide and develop 'animation on holiday' are Touristik Union International Hanover and NUR Frankfurt. In its programme, Touristik Union International, the biggest European package tour organization, offers the thirteen 'Robinson Clubs', from Austria to Kenya; 'Twen Tours' for young people; Club Mallorquin – a long-term programme for older people; and a special animation programme for children in big hotels. In addition, they have developed their own concept of 'studying other nations' which includes excursions and hikes in the holiday resorts.

Non-profit making trustee holiday organizations (churches, trade unions, sports clubs and communes) mainly orientate their programmes to the specific needs of older people and adolescents, as well as intercultural studies. Some towns connected with tourism in Germany have realized the necessity and advantage of looking after their guests actively; animation through local support personnel can be found, for example in Groemitz, Ruhpolding, Bad Achern or Freudenstadt.

Aims of animation

In general, animation should help towards realizing holiday wishes and desires. In this respect it goes beyond being simply a way of occupying or spending time, and demands at the very least a prior understanding of what tourists actually want and can achieve: this means knowledge of the motives and needs of tourists on the one hand, and their abilities and inabilities, on the other. In places where animation is more than just the supply of rooms and organization, it is necessary for it to overcome for some tourists the discrepancies between wishes and abilities. This can be achieved through well thought out planning (what can one do in this hotel, or in this place), through stimulating suggestions for a varied programme, through providing helpful examples, and through active participation.

In their book, *Animation im Urlaub* (Starnberg, 1975), K. Finger and co-authors summarize the possible effects of animation as follows:

- augmentation of contacts;
- increase in communication;
- greater variety of holiday activities;
- more intensive holiday experiences;
- increase in fun, happiness and pleasure;
- development of own initiative;
- realization of needs;
- chance to develop further the experiences undergone.

This formulation points to the need for a more thoroughgoing understanding of the concept of animation, one that does not just see it as an entertaining service, but also as an educational start in personality development. The programmes practised, so far, must be qualitatively measured against these goals, even though the intentions behind them have tended to be on a much lower level.

Areas of animation

Although individual animation activities ideally concern several dimensions of behaviour and experience and thus occur simultaneously, we can, however, try to divide analytically the 'animation areas'.

- *Sport* as an area of animation is far less an educational experience or training in a specific sport, but rather 'games', in which enjoyment in movement and the fun derived from playing represents far more the art of communication than competition. Examples: beach gymnastics, volleyball for all, watergames, darts.
- *Hobbies* that the guests pursue, or would like to pursue at home. Here, however, instead of an activity being undertaken pedantically by

following precise 'do it yourself' instructions, fun 'without pressure' should dominate in an attempt to develop creativity. Examples: mosaics, batiks, wood carvings, pottery.

● *Entertainment programmes* serve as a *divertissement*, as a social gathering, or as amusement, because they stimulate the guests to take part and become involved. Examples: fancy dress parties, shuffleboard tournaments, bingo, folklore.

● *'Experiences'* for the ordinary tourist are not the 'danger of adventure' whereby the tourist pushes his or her body to its limit, but rather the 'small happenings' that remain in the mind as highlights of the holiday – not, for example, shooting rapids or crossing deserts but instead a night in the open, a self-organized bonfire, a hike over the hills, trying the local cuisine (outside the hotel), or attending a local church service.

● *Excursions*, as organized trips, hikes or guided tours, the main idea not being that of 'seeing the sights' and passive consumption of 'musts' (e.g. visiting cathedrals, art galleries, museums etc.), but rather centring excursions around the current events in the holiday resort and its tourists and the local population. Examples: guided botanical tours around the hotel park, information rallies, walks at night, visits to a productive farm (instead of a farm museum).

● Animation as *a guide to employing time* seems to be a contradiction in terms. Yet the intentional provision of quiet rooms or places, quiet periods, reflective activities, the use of otherwise 'dead' periods (for example the time between being on the beach and dinner) can be stimulating instead of boring. Examples: stories by the fireside, classical music by candlelight, yoga, the discotheque as a meditation room in the late afternoon.

● *Improvement of communication* is actually a goal, which runs through all the areas mentioned so far. On the other hand, it can be a programme point on its own, if it is necessary to integrate groups of newcomers, to create an easy atmosphere, or to hasten introductions between guests.

Didactical principles and requirements

The principles behind a well thought out and correctly employed animation programme, as defined here, are based, on the one hand, on the fundamental condition of voluntary participation, and on the other, on the methods of psychological group dynamics.

Voluntary participation is regarded as the foremost principle: animation programmes are not obligatory, the guest should not feel a requirement to participate, he or she should not be talked into something, nor be caught unawares. This voluntary participation obviously calls for the provision of a wide range of programmes to choose from or to refuse.

Participation through demonstration makes use of the interest to imitate in place of the direct request. The guest should have interest stimulated and be encouraged to be sufficiently curious about an activity to want to try 'it' for himself: through encouragement and incentive, involvement will naturally come about.

Starting with the needs of the individual and the group, neither the prepared programme nor the qualities and knowledge of the animator determine the content or intensity of a guest's actions or level of involvement, but rather the abilities and interests of the participants. These should be allowed to develop and flourish, and even produce unsanctioned 'mishappenings', if creative development is the aim of animation rather than standardized responses.

Situation-oriented programme organization applies primarily to what the guest sees, hears, smells and feels, and also takes into account the connection between the size of the group and the activities: no romantic boat trips with lanterns and guitar music for hundreds, and no information rallies for only three participants.

Fun instead of achievement should be the norm. By this is meant having fun instead of attaining perfection in pottery, playing instead of fighting in sports, creativity in batik being far more important than the result, personal experiences on an excursion being more important than checking off a complete list of sights.

No discrimination of individuals. Many games or so-called amusing interludes derive from the fact that the audience amuses itself at the expense of other guests, for example, feeding each other with spaghetti while blindfolded, or going on stage during a pantomime and unwillingly making fools of themselves.

Well-organized preparation is not always a ready recipe for success. Preparation also requires an ever-ready 'reserve programme', when for example the weather is not suitable, or when the guests do not respond to the activities offered.

Lastly, *no therapy methods.* Animation on holiday cannot alter personalities, nor can it get rid of behavioural deficiencies. It can offer support, minimize fears and inhibitions, and develop self-confidence.

Personality of the animator

In distinction to a tour leader or escort, an animator is not concerned with the operational aspects of the holiday trip (such as arranging transfers, selling excursions, or sorting out complaints). Rather, the animator's main duties are concerned with organizing the animation programme that is offered in the holiday resort or club hotel. The animator usually receives a fixed salary, and does not depend on commission. The employers of the animator may be tour operators, hotels, or local tourist offices.

Talent and inclination are the main personal qualifications needed for the job of an animator. For while a sport, the rules of a game, or the techniques of a hobby can be learnt, sympathy, the ability to make contact with people, sociability, social competence or creative skills are only acquired – if acquired they can be – through a long learning process. Most of the present animators come from related professions, e.g. teachers, social workers or artists.

Personal animation is closely related to the personalities of the animators. A disinterested animator, who is bored and feels nothing but indifference towards the participants, does more damage than good to both business and guests. It is, therefore, essential to choose people carefully, according to specific criteria, just as it is essential to give psychological advice and supporting supervision.

Animation through manipulation?

Criticism of the present practice of animation in tourism can be summarized thus:

● The quality of animators is below standard. They are often badly trained or not trained at all, often arrogant and not motivated enough themselves to motivate others.

● Permanent programme offers, and the all-inclusive, pre-paid package tour price create a new kind of holiday stress. Despite voluntary participation in animation programmes being desirable in order to get the most out of the holiday programme, some guests – because they have paid an 'all-in' price, force themselves to take part in almost every activity. Thus, the internalized norm of performance comes into play during the holiday.

● Commercialized animation programmes come under pressure from the requirement for short-term success. This is pursued through 'ready for consumption' activities, the search for constant amusement and entertainment, which requires little commitment from the participant. An unreal holiday world (no cash, no professional ties, Christian name terms) is thus created – a pre-fabricated kind of holiday happiness (directed towards increasing the tourism providers' profits) which neglects the reality of everyday life and reduces the value of human existence. If the experience and newly-acquired skills gained during the holidays are intended to affect everyday life, then the actual needs of people have been neglected by the holiday clubs in these 'concrete utopias'. Pre-arranged holiday happiness often proves to be cleverly sold manipulation.

Prospects

Holiday trips, on the whole, are becoming more and more popular, and weekend trips too are affected by this growing trend. A weekend trip to a hotel that is good value for money and easy to reach, can represent a very interesting tourist product when additional activities are available in addition to an already attractive basic product (for example, an overnight stay in a castle hotel). Such 'extras' might include concerts in castle grounds, a high standard of cuisine with a regional instead of international menu, horse-riding or art workshops. Not to be forgotten are the animation programmes for children – these unburden the parents, and the very young guests are thus not treated as inconvenient nuisances.

Even if one does not share the view that a holiday should stimulate social communication and that the holiday experience should trigger off changes in outlook and attitudes to everyday life, animation programmes will still have to come to terms with criticisms made of aspects of current programmes.

Further reading

Further reading on managing the tourists and related topics in *Tourism Management* 1980–9

Canter, D., 'Psychology and tourism management', vol. 3, no. 3, September 1982, pp. 193–5.

Gantzer, H. and C., 'Managing tourists and politicians in India', vol. 4, no. 2, June 1983, pp. 118–25.

Graham, R., Nilsen, P. and Payne, R. J., 'Visitor management in Canadian national parks', vol. 9, no. 1, March 1988, pp. 44–62.

Hughes, H. L., 'A tourism tax – the cases for and against', vol. 2, no. 3, September 1981, pp. 196–206.

Pearce, P. L. and Moscardo, G., 'Making sense of tourists' complaints', vol. 5, no. 1, March 1984, pp. 20–3.

Shackleford, P., 'Keeping tabs on tourism: a manager's guide to statistics', vol. 1, no. 3, September 1980, pp. 148–57.

Travis, A. S. 'Managing the environmental and cultural impacts of tourism and leisure', vol. 3, no. 4, December 1982, pp. 256–62.

Vine, P. A. L., 'Hotel classification – art or science?', vol. 2, no. 1, March 1981, pp. 18–29.

Wanhill, S. R. C., 'Charging for congestion at tourist attractions', vol. 1, no. 3, September 1980, pp. 168–74.

Wei, L., Crompton, J. L. and Reid, L. M., 'Cultural conflicts – experiences of US visitors to China', vol. 10, no. 4, December 1989, pp. 322–32.

Part Eight

New Technologies

Since the advent of computer technology some of its most fruitful applications have been in the travel and tourism industries, where the first ten years of *Tourism Management* coincided with rapid technological change. In this part of the book are included three articles on computer applications and their impacts published in the journal in the late 1980s.

In 'New technology and the future of tourism' Margaret Bruce of the University of Manchester Institute of Science and Technology (UMIST), UK, reviews some of the main technological developments and considers various trends in terms of their opportunities and threats. Projections are made of possible developments in the 1990s, which open up opportunities for the future.

In 'Expansion and development of central reservation systems' David Collier, at the time of writing with the SEMA Group, a multi-national systems company, and latterly with SABRE American Airlines, highlights the opportunities continuing development offers tourism vendors and national tourist boards, as CRS are expanding their services to become travel and tourism distribution systems.

In 'Developing effective computer systems for tourism' Paul Gamble of the University of Surrey, UK, finds that some computer-based travel trade systems are not working as well as expected and fail to exploit their potential. Explanations are put forward and implications are considered for improving management performance.

Further articles on computer applications and their impacts in travel and tourism published in *Tourism Management* from 1980–9 are listed on page 266.

22 New technology and the future of tourism

Margaret Bruce

Pleasure, sea, blue skies, fun, adventure, change ... are some of the words conjured up by the offerings of the travel industry. Yet behind these happy vistas, the structure of the UK travel industry is competitive, conflict-ridden, and undergoing immense technological change. The main forms of competitive strategies adopted by the protagonists, i.e. the principals of the wholesale side of the industry, are price-cutting, providing a differentiated range of travel products and a focus on particular market segments, e.g. the provision of longer-stay holidays for the elderly, or a mixture of these. Rivalries between the main suppliers of travel products are notorious as well as potential conflicts between those in the wholesale and those in the retail end of the business. Technology is affecting the travel industry through changing the way the industry is organized and how tasks are done, e.g. public access ticket machines for airflight bookings. It is also changing the competitive 'rules of the game' of the industry because those companies that effectively exploit new technologies can enhance their own competitive performance in the industry. In order to move into the 1990s effectively, travel companies will have to assess available technological and marketing options and relate these to their own corporate strategies.

1980s in retrospect

The most recent and widespread technological change in the UK travel industry has been the adoption of interactive videotex. Within five years of its introduction to the industry late in 1979 about 90 per cent of all UK travel agencies used videotex systems for at least checking latest availability, up-to-date prices and general travel information, such as currency exchange rates. Over 85 per cent of all package bookings are now made through videotex. As well as the travel services available through British Telecom's Prestel service, there are private videotex systems designed and operated by principals and carriers. The most famous of these are perhaps Thomson Holidays' 'TOPS' system and the videotex networks provided by Istel and Fastrak. Videotex technology has become an integral part of the communications infrastructure of the travel industry, so it is not possible for any particular group of the industry to work effectively without interactive videotex.

Videotex has been used mainly to improve communications between the tour operations and travel agencies. Why was interactive videotex taken up so rapidly by all sectors of the industry? Up to the 1980s, the main communications channels between the carriers, travel principals, and the geographically dispersed agents about travel offerings had been via telephone, paper and telex. Booking and confirmation procedures were time consuming, with loss of potential custom and travel companies were unable to realize the full value of their products. Interactive videotex offered significant advantages for improving the distribution of travel products, in particular information about availability of airline seats and hotel accommodation, and the opportunity of making electronic confirmation of reservations.

The travel principals and agencies initially adopting videotex were able to gain a competitive advantage by cheapening the cost of communications between principals and agents, for example with the reduction in the production and postage of written information and by improving communications especially in the dissemination of up-to-date information about their travel products, such as prices and availability. The service to the customer has improved too, resulting in increased custom for those companies with electronic information systems.

Videotex applications

The companies taking up interactive videotex exploited its potential in different ways. One effective technological/competitive strategy with regard to videotex was that of Thomson Holidays. At the beginning, the company designed and developed its own private videotex system, 'TOPS'. This system restricted access to Thomson Holidays' travel information to those agents trained to use TOPS, which ensured that its travel information was easily selected by the agent selling its travel products. Also, the system meant that the principal's information was secure; its competitors could not find commercially-sensitive information about, for example, the company's load factors. TOPS also led to cost savings in the communications between Thomson Holidays and the agencies which distribute its products. Then in December 1986, Thomson Holidays made all its holiday bookings available via interactive videotex only. Indeed, during 1986, the company doubled its business, increased its market share from 20 per cent to 30 per cent and kept its average holiday prices at the 1984 level. Colin Palmer, Deputy Director, claims that the TOPS videotex system is responsible for this success:

> This has allowed us to shake up the market with dramatic pricing moves in the sure knowledge that we had the systems in place to soak up the extra demand! The ability to handle bookings on a massive scale and to cope with the huge surges in demand that are a feature of the package holiday business has been an important factor in keeping Thomson in front of every other UK tour operator year after year.[1]

The success of Thomson Holidays in exploiting the competitive advantages offered by interactive videotex has not been shared by all principals. Thomson Holidays with its offensive strategy in the travel trade is perhaps the 'shaper' of technological change in the industry with the other principals responding to it. What constitutes an opportunity to some poses a threat to others!

As regards the retailers or travel agencies, the adoption of videotex has been advantageous in:

- being cost-effective, mainly because a greater volume of business could be handled by the agencies without incurring substantially greater costs; and
- making the process of booking, confirmation and finding out the latest availability of prices of travel offerings so much easier.

Improved customer service has meant that the agencies with videotex gained a larger market share in the areas in which they were operating.

Trends

It is possible to discern certain trends coinciding with the use of interactive videotex in the UK travel industry. The technological changes occurring with videotex were accompanied by a process of greater rationalization and centralization of the travel industry.[2] Principals have taken some control over the communications network and distribution of travel products through, for example, locking agencies into videotex systems designed and operated by principals and by expanding chains of agencies owned by principals. The latter process is intensifying. The smaller and independent agency is particularly under survival threat because of being unable to sustain the loss of revenue as their high-street competitors invest in electronic technology and take a significant proportion of their business.

Jobs have been lost in the reservation and information offices of tour operators and carriers but new jobs are being created and new skills are required, e.g. keyboard and information retrieval skills, learning how to sell travel products while using a visual display unit to carry out the transaction, and how to make bookings. The task of providing training and education for these new skills is being addressed by private companies and managers of travel agencies, and some colleges have courses with an information technology component.

The interactive videotex wave of technological change in the travel industry is nearly over. Videotex has become one of the industry's main standards and has led to the automation of the travel industry. Now companies are looking for new technological changes to exploit and to gain a competitive advantage.

Forward into the 1990s

There has been a phenomenal growth in the amount of information technology available which is expected to continue so that by the year 2000, satellite, speech facsimile, telemetry and so on will be commonplace. The choice is overwhelming. But which technologies are of relevance to the travel industry, and if adopted, what will the consequences be?

Many of the forecasts of future society assume that there will be a greater quantity of information technologies around at home, in the community and in workplaces.[3] These societal changes will facilitate new forms of distribution of travel products, especially for the next generation who will be so much more familiar with computers. Not only will the consumer's role change with the provision of more self-service ticketing facilities but so too will the principal's and the agent's roles change.

Short-term technological advances

In the shorter term, there are problems with information technology as it is currently used in the agencies. These can be rectified and, in so doing, may lead to an improved customer service. Some of these problems are listed here. It can take the agency staff a day to enter or 'log-on' to the databases of some of the principals and carriers in order to check availability and make bookings. This can lead to bottlenecks, loss of custom and empty seats; and the procedure is time-consuming and frustrating for both staff and customers. Automatic dial-up facilities to search the different computerized reservation systems of the principals and carriers is required for agents. Installing ticket facilities in the retailers would be helpful especially for late bookings – more common than not for business travellers – and deposit bookings. Providing 'print-outs' for customers to take away with them can prevent misunderstandings and provide reassurance for the customer. Separating the administration tasks from making bookings would release agency staff's time so they could focus on the selling of travel products. Introducing microcomputers and word processors can assist the agencies' administrative tasks. Also, word processors can lead to new tasks, e.g. mailshots to businesses to advertise the agent's services. It would be helpful to have two terminals on the desks of travel-agency clerks so that the customer can see the screen at the same time as the clerk and so follow through the booking process. Paying attention to the customer's needs is to do with people as well as technology. One prime example of this is the failure of the requirements of the female business traveller to be taken into account. Many times, a female business traveller is assumed to be a 'person' defined as 'male' which can lead to embarrassing situations.[4] All of these suggested improvements can be implemented now and with little investment in technological change.

Why have such issues not been dealt with before? Partly because there has been a focus on installing or implementing technology without fully considering the effect on the customer. Indeed, a survey of north-west UK agencies to investigate the effects of new technology on the motivation of staff in travel agencies supports this.[5] The research shows that automation beyond a certain threshold depresses staff motivation and affects their interaction with potential customers. Dealing with some of these problems may help to bring about a balance between a technological focus and a customer orientation. Getting this balance right is crucial.

Looking further ahead into the future, it is likely that current experiments with public-access ticketing machines located at railway stations and airports for the customer to purchase rail tickets and tickets for internal flights directly will become increasingly widespread; and will be used for other standardized travel products. As with retailers in other service sectors this trend to 'self-service' will grow.[6] Although the travel consumer has to be confident when booking electronically that the information to go through the transaction is comprehensive, accurate and reliable, and that liability is guaranteed if something goes wrong. Indeed this form of distribution of travel products may require changes to the laws of product liability. Another trend is the introduction of videotex/videodisc equipment in agencies. The customer will be able to watch videos of holiday destinations and simultaneously acquire information about availability and price.[7]

Approaching the 1990s

Travel agencies are concerned about their survival, in the longer term, precisely because new information technologies offer opportunities for travel principals and carriers to sell their products direct to the consumer. However, travel agencies themselves can gain some control over the design and implementation of information technologies and act creatively on the opportunities new technology can give them. One innovation is that of 'Travel Desk', an information service available through Prestel. It is Prestel's first electronic travel agency and it enables the travel agency providing Travel Desk to take its 'shop' directly into clients' living rooms and offices. This service offers quotes and booking facilities on Prestel for airline tickets, car hire, travel insurance, etc. This is one example of the 'paperless travel agency'. Alternative high-technology armchair agencies may be those acting as consultancies rather than high-street booking shops. The travel consultants could focus on particular market segments, e.g. holidays in the UK for the over thirties, or offering exotic travel packages in the Far East. This assumes that the agencies would segment the market for the area in which they are based and make offerings for their market segments. These agencies could use information technologies to 'mix and match' travel products to suit individual requirements and tastes. This development would, perhaps, counter the conformity of standardized travel packages offered via electronic 'self-service' outlets.

During the course of the 1990s, cable and satellite communications will be more and more prevalent. Again, these may not be entirely in the hands of principals. It may well be the case that travel agencies can exploit these technologies and arrange hotel accommodation themselves with hoteliers in Spain, Greece or wherever and so bypass the principals.

Another significant development is that of the 'fifth generation' software, e.g. 'expert systems'.[8] This type of software would enable the consumer booking at home or through an agency to give certain parameters defining travel arrangements, e.g. date of travel, length of stay, price, etc., to the reservation system. This would then automatically generate a list of travel products and present these to the consumer to help the customer choose. Another application of expert systems is in helping to plan travel routes, e.g. a train journey in southern France. However, with developments in communications technologies, it may be that the amount of movement of people will start to decrease. Instead business people may well hold teleconferences, and other potential travellers will take instant trips with audio-visual images. Perhaps these are new market opportunities for travel companies. If travel companies do not move into such areas, other companies outside the industry will.

These are some of the discernible technological trends which are likely to take the travel industry into the 1990s and affect the industry in the next decade. But technology is not the only issue for tourism in the 1990s. Marketing is also important.

Marketing strategies

Harnessing technological changes can be used by travel companies to develop an effective competitive strategy by lowering the cost of distribution and improving the service provided to the consumer. But what has tended to happen is a 'technocist focus' and a neglect of other factors influencing the consumer's purchase behaviour. One marketing strategy which is likely to be effective and initiated by other retailers is that of a travel agency business in the north-west UK. Speakman's Travel has revamped its retail outlets and renamed these Abroad.[9] This travel agency has invested resources in the development of computer software to improve and speed up the access and the search of principals' and carriers' databases of travel products and so to enhance the customer service. At the same time, the company provides a pleasurable shopping experience for the customer. The ambience of the retail outlets is relaxed and the staff are professionally trained to sell the travel products, the consumer can peruse the printed information in comfort and also sit and watch videos of the travel products available. Abroad intends to cater for the entire needs of the travellers by selling Abroad sunglasses, Abroad suntan lotion and so on.

Other marketing strategies can be employed – these include segmenting the market and generating travel offerings for particular segments, e.g. holidays in the UK for the over thirties. Agencies could combine with local retailers to have joint marketing ventures, e.g. for winter ski holidays the agency could collaborate with a sport retailer to provide special offers of ski clothes. New technologies could be employed to assist marketing ventures. Microcomputers and word processors can help in the administration of surveys, to find out what the demands are in the local marketplace, and of mailshots to, e.g. local businesses to advertise its particular travel products.

Technology in the 1990s

It is clear that the quantity of information technology utilized by the travel industry will increase. The main applications will be in improving the distribution of travel products by the principals and carriers both to agencies and to the potential consumers directly, e.g. experiments with videotex/videodiscs and with public-access ticket machines. So, the outcome of technological change will be a continuation of efforts to cheapen the communications costs for the distribution of travel products and to improve the purchase process.

Focusing on technological change can mean a neglect of a 'customer orientation'. A balance has to be made between the improvements technology can bring and other changes, such as a greater investment in marketing. Effort at the retail end of the industry to make the selling experience more professional and pleasurable, the introduction of marketing ideas, e.g. market segmentation and catering for the entire needs of the travel consumer, would be at least as effective as introducing more technology. Already trends are discernible in this direction with, e.g. the revamping of agencies in accordance with new concepts like that of Abroad and other agencies paying attention to such aspects of their business. Maybe there will be a move towards a greater specialization within the industry with some companies focusing on particular market segments and providing products for these. A new type of agency may emerge which moves away from the high-street booking shop to more of a travel consultancy providing individualized travel packages made up of a 'mix and match' of available travel offerings. Sophisticated information systems could be used to achieve the optimum travel package.

The rate of adoption of technological change in the travel trade is related to the competitive strategies of the travel companies. Companies that have effectively taken up and used technology in the past will be more likely to continue to do so and to make the introduction of new technology an integral part of their corporate strategy. Such 'shapers' of technological change set up procedures – e.g. think-tanks with people from different departments in their own company and with representatives from equipment suppliers and so on – to search for developments in technology, assess these and relate them to their own position in the travel industry. The harnessing of technology can affect the competitive 'rules of the game' as interactive videotex has done, for the travel industry with some companies gaining a sustainable competitive advantage over time through their ability to exploit the technology.

There are various 'technofears' in the industry about the impact of automation on job design and on the displacement of jobs. Will the small agencies survive? Will cable and satellite lead to agencies bypassing principals and so taking business away from the principals? Will the offerings available to the consumer be limited as agencies look into the electronic information systems of a handful of principals? Or will the range open up as agencies survey a range of databases? These are all pertinent questions which need to be raised and continually assessed by members of the travel industry. Technology is not 'out of control', and it rarely has sudden impact. Consequently a greater awareness within the industry of technological developments, anticipating 'what would happen if technology x were introduced . . .', a closer interaction between travel companies and equipment suppliers to introduce joint development of information systems appropriate for the needs of the travel industry, and the instigation of think-tanks or planning procedures within travel companies to enable them to cope with change, may lead to the effective introduction of new technologies within the industry. Opportunities for some particular groups may represent threats for others. The issues of 'who controls' (the principals and carriers or agencies) the rate and direction of technological change is relevant to such assessments.

Addressing technological futures, and working out plans of action in accordance with an understanding of corporate strategy and an awareness of a marketing orientation, is an effective approach for the tourist industry entering the 1990s.

References

1 *Videotex Viewpoint*, 17 December 1986.
2 Bruce, M., 'Information technology: changes in the travel trade', *Tourism Management*, vol. 4, no. 4, 1983, pp. 290–5.
3 Long Term Perspectives Group, *IT Futures Surveyed*, NEDO, London 1986.
4 'Hi-Tech Hitches are Human Nature', *Travel News*, 8 August 1986.
5 Khan, H., *Information Technology and Job Satisfaction*, Work in progress, Management Sciences, Manchester: UMIST, 1987.
6 Gershuny, J., *After Industrial Society? The Emerging Self-service Economy*, London: Macmillan, 1978.
7 Kwok, L., Jackson C. and Teskey, F., 'A combined videotex/videodisc system for tourist information', *Journal of Information Technology*, September 1986.
8 Feigenbaum, E. and McCorduck, P., *The Fifth Generation: Artificial Intelligence and Japan's Challenge to the World*, London: Michael Joseph, 1984.
9 Bruce, M., Speakman's Travel, Swinton, UK, personal interview, 1986.

Acknowledgement

This chapter is based on a contribution to an international conference on tourism in the 1990s organized by *Tourism Management* and the Department of Hotel, Catering and Tourism Management, University of Surrey, in London in November 1986.

23 Expansion and development of central reservation systems

David Collier

Looking back at the growth of central reservation systems (CRS), we can see that deregulation of the airline industry in the USA created a fundamental change in the role of CRS. They had been developed as airline information and booking systems in the 1960s. They handled airline schedules and coped with the limited number of fare changes that were made during the year.

In regulated markets multi-access systems were adequate for the demands of retailers. These systems acted essentially as a switching system to gain access to the individual databases of airlines. They did not access a central database, which consolidated fare offerings from a number of different carriers and, therefore, there was a tendency to 'camp' in one of the databases offered to the retailer through the system.

Deregulated markets, however, offered new opportunities to the traveller and, therefore, placed new demands on both retailers and vendors. CRS had to expand their role. No longer could they be merely information and booking systems; they had to grow into marketing and distribution systems.

Why was this the case? Deregulation brings a broad choice of fares. The CRS had to be able to cope with one million changes to air fares per day and to present these fares to agents who were being asked to find the most competitive offers. As a result single-access systems were required. The technology had to access information from a broad range of airlines and to present this information to the agent on a screen in cost or time ranking.

Both for the airlines and for travel agents in the free market economy these systems soon became essential to the provision of customer information and service, which resulted in the development of the largest private computer systems in the world.

Recent developments

Recently we have witnessed a massive growth in the international expansion of CRS. This is because travel must service the customer àt both the point of departure/sale and at the destination. In recent years there has been rapid growth in international travel both for business and leisure. There have also been moves towards liberalization of air tariffs in Europe and in the Far East. This produces a reduction in the price differential between charter and scheduled services. As a result the consumer can create his own itinerary, which is not significantly more expensive than a tour offering.

If agents are to provide the facility to create bespoke itineraries, they do require a wealth of information on value-added services, in particular accommodation and land transport. CRS will match the needs of the agents by providing access to vendor products at destinations worldwide.

The CRS have made a huge investment in the development of these systems. Their return arises from generating transactions. To generate transactions, one requires a customer, usually serviced by an agent, and a vendor. For the CRS to create additional transactions, they needed to expand the number of sales outlets and this was best achieved by international expansion.

We now move on to the new breed of CRS which will include Galileo, Amadeus, Sabre, Abacus, Pars, Gemini and Fantasia. In order to attract retail outlets to use their systems, CRS have to offer value-added services. This will include not only back-office systems for travel agents, but also a broader range of travel products for sale.

Growing importance

The importance of CRS, therefore, grows. They are no longer a pure marketing system for an airline, but they are an industry in their own right, and they will significantly alter the pattern of world tourism over the next decade.

At first glance this statement might appear far-fetched but there are sound reasons for coming to this conclusion. If we consider just one of these distribution systems, Sabre, we find that in 1986 it handled over 100,000 terminals (60,000 in travel agencies and 40,000 operated by airlines). These terminals were supported by 700,000 miles of network data circuits. In the USA the proportion of airline tickets sold through agents rose from 50 per cent in 1976 to 70 per cent in 1989, with over 95 per cent of tickets sold by agents handled through CRS. This is not an airline booking system, or a marketing system, but a huge travel distribution network.

The way in which travel and tourism is sold will follow the experiences of the airlines. The airlines through their investment have produced new channels for travel distribution. For the consumers this should result in greater choice and the ability to book the trip they demand. For both the tourism vendor and for the CRS there is a need for complementary activity. The CRS will provide the distribution channels the vendors need to supply access to their product.

CRS are providing the route to link the needs of the consumer with the products offered by the travel industry on a global scale. For national tourism industries the concern that has been expressed recently about the placing of terminals at the point of sale should be of minor consequence in comparison to the need to link vendors to these distribution channels.

A major cost element in international travel is the scheduled airfare. This problem is being addressed by the liberalization of tariffs. Governments have seen the rapid expansion of tourism as a creator of new employment opportunities and also as a generator of income. The growth in air traffic generated by liberalization needs to be linked closely with the sale of other tourism products.

It is also evident that outbound tourism is a major factor in adverse balance of payment figures. It is, therefore, important to governments to ensure that the growth in outbound travel is matched by similar or increased growth in inbound traffic.

How does CRS affect this picture? The experience in North America has been a growth in independent travel. There will continue to be a need for consolidators and tour operators, but more leisure as well as business travellers will expect their travel counsellors to put together a package through a CRS, consisting of transport, hotels or accommodation, car hire and local travel information. This would indicate that there is a need for a broader range of information at the point of sale. Most retailers are saying that travellers are becoming more knowledgeable and also more adventurous in their choice of destination. For the agent this creates similar problems to the deregulation of air travel.

The travel counsellor is confronted with the need to be able to access a wide range of information on travel and tourism facilities throughout the world. He currently has comprehensive information on airline schedules and fares, which is supported by increasing access to information on other travel products.

The sale of travel will in the future require a high level of service from the counsellor. He will then use the CRS technology to meet the exact needs and to obtain the most competitive rate for his client. For frequent travellers the systems will store details on the clients' preferences, whether they be a window seat on the flight, a room with a sea view, the booking of a non-smoking room or the hotel group preferred. This enables the agent to suggest a full itinerary for the client, which is likely to meet his requirements.

Impact and implications

Distribution systems will change the way in which travel services are sold to the customer. They will affect patterns of world tourism and this will offer tourist boards major opportunities as well as potential threats. CRS are the travel directory of tomorrow. But they are also a reservation and packaging system.

The expansion of CRS will increase the automation of retail outlets. They will provide the levels of service required by the consumer to take advantage of the investments in tourist facilities. They will be the shop window around the world for vendors.

If we consider the alliances that are now being created between Pars, Gemini, Abacus and Amadeus, one can envisage a global network of travel retailers linked to a global network of vendors. For vendors this means representation in new markets and the ability to switch marketing and reservation effort to accommodate fluctuations in demand created by currency movements. It also means that seasonal variations of tourist traffic are reduced and that additional inbound tourist traffic can be encouraged.

However, CRS are not in themselves the sole answer to a vendor or to a tourist board's marketing strategy. In order to complement their advance, vendors will need to invest in their own 'electronic brochures' to link their offerings to the distribution systems. For travel vendors this will necessitate a decision which will be whether to invest in their own reservation system, which can be linked to the CRS, or to join a bureau service. For smaller operators, consolidators or vendor cooperatives should be encouraged to provide central reservation systems. Within the UK, Hi-line and the Bournemouth Tourist Board are at the forefront of creating opportunities for their regions through this use of technology.

National tourist boards will be concerned with ensuring that their industry is encouraged to invest in the infrastructure to produce this electronic information. And information providers will need to produce electronic information on events, which might assist in tourism promotion. CRS themselves will target the larger travel vendors as their first priority. For national tourist boards wishing to encourage the expansion of inbound tourism, the need is to provide access to information and create reservations for a broad range of international and domestic outlets. There is, therefore, a need to link the vendor industry to a full range of distribution systems.

The British Vendor Industry, with the support of the British Tourist Authority, are examining the possibility of producing improved access to the UK through a coordinated approach to communication links with the CRS. The BRAVO project matches the needs of the vendor industry with the aspirations of the CRS and has the potential to create a significant boost for inbound traffic to the UK.

Conclusion

The message is clear. A marketing mix involves offering the right product, at the right price, with the right promotion. The travel industry is spending considerable sums of money on raising levels of service and producing the right product. Price will become more competitive and yield management will play as important a role for successful tourism vendors as airlines. The final touch is the correct form of promotion.

Promotion is only successful if it generates business. CRS as a distribution channel are providing us not only with the shop window through access to retail outlets but also with a powerful sales team throughout the world. The opportunity is there; it is now in the hands of vendors and tourist boards to exploit the technology.

24 Developing effective computer systems for tourism

Paul R. Gamble

The travel trade in the UK is often considered a leader in the use of information systems because of the speed with which it switched from using telephones to the use of on-line videotex systems. Yet a report by Istel Ltd[1] in 1987 revealed a large number of problems. Insufficient and inadequate training has resulted in many agents making partial, inefficient and overexpensive use of their computerized databases. Many managers and even more counter clerks have not assimilated BT's zonal pricing structure and are incurring inefficiency costs. Many expressed fear and ignorance of the methods for changing the auto dial facilities. Others were uncertain of the best way to move around databases once they have made contact. An element of under resourcing is revealed. Over two-thirds of agents have only one videotex machine and a further one-fifth have two. In the height of the season most of these agents abandon their videotex and revert to telephones, wasting staff time. A relatively trivial investment in sets and additional telephone lines could have offset this difficulty.

There appear to be two main shortfalls in management reactions to information technology. First, on the revenue side there is little hard evidence of *added value* resulting from the use of computer systems. Most of the benefits claimed in the surveys were local and short term. 'We can cope better if someone is off sick with flu.' 'Payroll now takes only two or three hours instead of a day.' There is little published hard data which relates improved levels of revenue, profitability or service standards to the use of this technology.

Second, on the cost side, reductions are sometimes claimed which do not *take into account all costs* – the capital, training and staff costs associated with information technology (IT). Where productivity gains are recorded, they are often related to sales or costs on a per employee basis after changes in staffing level. If you dismiss half the members of a football team, each person in the remainder has to make more goals, if you are simply to get the same total score. In other words, productivity may go up but there is no real gain in productiveness.

Training and organizational support for managers

Training

Research[2] indicates that levels of computer utilization by managers in the hospitality sector of the tourism industry are not markedly lower than that of other professional or managerial groups. In a way, this is quite remarkable. Until recently, hospitality managers had less opportunity to participate in appropriate forms of higher education and are generally less well qualified than other, similar managers. They are also less likely to have had formal training within their company in the use and application of information technology. However, levels of formal training are low. Although 60 per cent of hospitality managers claim to have undertaken some training in computer use, 28 per cent of managers are actually self-trained.

By contrast, Thomson Holidays[3] provide an excellent illustration of the commitment necessary to support technological adoption. Their award-winning training schemes were based on a thorough skills audit of their computer systems department's personnel. Projects were then formulated in relation to the existing skills base and the skills required for new projects. The resulting courses were eventually re-evaluated after implementation to check for quality and relevance. The cost of such thoroughness can be substantial. In the case of Thomson Holidays, which operates a total of 61 training courses, 8 per cent of its systems department's payroll budget is allocated for the purpose.

Monitoring and development of information technology

Perhaps the issue that follows from this is the question of how managers are meant to keep themselves aware of what is going on and what can be done. It would appear that even major corporations have a fairly haphazard approach to information technology, although larger companies tend to take a more disciplined approach.

Ironically, it appears that while many companies are not giving their operational managers much training about IT, neither are they giving their IT managers much business training. A report in April 1988[4] shows that only 21 per cent of IT professionals receive training about their main company activity. There is, therefore, a primitive form of justice or perhaps injustice is the more apt term. It is also apparent that many companies perceive IT people as non-management. Only 25 per cent of British companies have the head of IT on the board. Indeed, other studies have shown that Japan alone has a substantial proportion of companies with formal monitoring mechanisms for IT at board level. Most senior managers are expected to keep themselves informed in this complex area.

However, few managers establish formal mechanisms appropriate to such a task. In the hospitality industry only 10 per cent of companies have any procedure for giving managers systematic, regular briefings about developments in IT.[5] Such a lack increases the likelihood of companies having to redevelop (or reinvent) systems in the future. It also leads to the effects reported by Istel.

The nature of decision support systems

If computer systems are to be used more effectively, their application must be directed to the activities with which managers are most closely associated. Probably the main task with which managers associate themselves is decision making, in fact Stewart[6] actually defines management in these terms.

How do managers make decisions – the theory

The classic taxonomy for problem solving stemmed from work carried out by Herbert Simon in the 1960s. Essentially, Simon proposed a largely rational model of decision-making behaviour that proceeds logically in four stages: clarify objectives, isolate ends, evaluate various possible solutions based on a theoretical model, and select the most appropriate solution.

In this scheme, issues of emotion or intuition are set aside. The basic framework of these ideas has proved to be very important. Indeed, Simon was eventually awarded a Nobel prize in 1972 for work on human problem solving, which he published with a colleague.[7] However, most of the experimental research on which his theories were founded concerned special types of problems which do not fit very well with the day-to-day workings of most organizations.

How do managers make decisions – the practice

In practice another model of organizational behaviour and decision making, known as the 'garbage can model'[8], is probably more realistic.

Envisaged in this way, organizations are pictured as garbage cans for decision making. They produce results when something is dropped into the can where it is shovelled around until a decision emerges. Decisions thus produced are an outcome of four, relatively independent, streams of organizational activity.

(a)   The first stream involves identifying problems. This is to do with recognizing or defining problems. It would seem that a problem is anything which might warrant some attention. Two managers might well interpret the same intelligence quite differently. One manager might say, we need a reservations computer because we are so busy, another might say, why do we need a computer since we have all the business we need.

(b)   For this reason, problem identification is often linked closely to the second stream which involves solutions. In many cases solutions are available before matching problems can be found. For example, a travel agency might review its billing systems after its manager has been attracted by a new electronic Point of Sale (POS) system. In many cases, managers do not deal with problems until they have first found a solution.

(c)   The third stream concerns who takes part in the decision. It would appear that a participant can be anybody who comes and goes within the overall process. Participation in a decision is seen to be a function of time, attention and availability rather than how much a person might know about the problem being solved. Sometimes the person assigned to deal with a decision depends simply on who is around.

(d)   Finally there are choice opportunities, the occasions when organizations are expected to produce what is called a decision. This might be some sort of crisis (the accounting staff have walked out) or some sort of opportunity (another disastrous British summer).

Notice the key points. First, decision making is a fairly messy business. The nature of decisions may depend on who is around, what kind of background they have, how much time, how much status. The decision process itself is nothing like as organized in practice as it needs to be if conventional computer approaches are going to be useful. Second, for many decisions, the solution is often discovered before the problem. Managers encounter something that looks useful and then consider where it will fit in. This POS looks great, maybe we should examine our billing procedures? In terms of technology, computers have to be seen as solutions before managers begin to attach them to problems.

Table 24.1   The role of a computer in a decision support system

		Extent to which preferences for outcomes are shared	
		Completely	*Partially*
Extent to which beliefs in causation are shared	*Completely*	*Computation* Control invoices Cost holiday packages Analyse competing pckgs	*Ammunition* Design new brochures Fix new prices Select media schedule
	Partially	*Learning* Accept reservation Bid for tour business Manpower planning	*Inspiration* Reposition in market Change product line Modify image

Source: De Alberdi and Harvey[9]

Why computers are not seen as solutions to many management problems

The short answer is that, as they are used at present, computer systems in the tourism and hospitality industry are not being deployed effectively to deal with some of the more complex problems. Current computer systems are largely designed to deal with black-and-white problems in a world that is actually varying shades of grey.

Organizing a collection of 'facts' on a computer might be relatively straightforward. It is much more difficult to organize those facts for problem solving. In general, managers (and others) respond to situations on the basis of cognition and attitudes. Cognition refers to knowledge and the way that knowledge is organized. Attitudes refers to the feelings or values applied to knowledge. These values include preferences and beliefs which form the basis of judgements.

Many management problems potentially involve a wide range of factors. They do not lend themselves equally to quantification and are not often well understood. It would also appear that managers may respond differently, to the same information, according to the current situation and according to their preferred style of problem solving. Even when given 'facts', managers tend to use judgement to select a course of action.

Judgement and the design of decision support systems

The role of judgement affects the design of an information system in two dimensions. The first dimension concerns beliefs about the cause of a problem. Where the problem space is large or where it is not well understood, the cause of a problem may be very unclear. For example, holiday sales to a resort may be declining because of the way in which the holidays are priced, or because of changing demographics in the target market or because of competition from other resorts.

The second dimension concerns the extent to which managers share preferences about what they are trying to achieve. In the example given, the retail manager may advise a new pricing structure, the marketing manager new packaging for special interest groups and the travel buyer may want to drop the destination altogether from the programme. Since solutions are very important to problem definition, such preferences will have a major effect on outcomes.

The role of a computer system as part of a Decision Support System (DSS) (Table 24.1) varies according to the mix of preferences for outcomes and beliefs about causation:

(a) *Computation:* When preferences and causation are both certain, the role of a computer is to perform the necessary calculations.
(b) *Ammunition:* If there is some difference of opinion about preferred outcomes, the computer system must be designed to support the manager by providing ammunition for a chosen course of action.
(c) *Learning:* If there is some uncertainty about the cause of a problem, then it is the role of the computer to help the manager assimilate data or explain the situation. In this case the DSS must be designed to help the manager learn about the problem.
(d) *Inspiration:* Finally, in circumstances where neither cause nor outcome can be agreed, the DSS must somehow move into the realms of inspiration to help the manager rationalize choice.

Almost all current hospitality and travel computer applications, and not a few new applications, would be located in the top left-hand box of Table 24.1. They are primarily computational or data processing applications. The weight of usage is greatest at the clerical level, for computerized billing. The second major area is inventory applications, primarily inventories of sales in the form of reservations.

The productivity mismatch

A mismatch between where gains are expected by managers and where computers are actually used, is not unusual. PA Management Consultants[10] revealed what was described as a 'disturbing mismatch' between the expectations of top managers and their companies' information technology (IT) strategies. In fact Gallier[11] discovered IT was a fully-integrated part of the business planning process in only 10 per cent of instances. So, while many companies say they would like to use information technology for decision support, the reality is rather different:

(a) Most companies have a technical rather than a business-orientated approach to the realization of IT projects.
(b) Senior managers, especially chief executives, often have a minimal involvement in information technology strategy. Very often this is confined to final stage approval of financial arrangements.
(c) Many chief executives do not like to be first – they do not like to innovate.
(d) Innovation in other industries is often associated with product champions. In the IT area these product champions usually have a technical background, yet IT professionals are unlikely to be fully familiar with the operational and decision support needs of their organization.

Without a corresponding development of people and systems, major advances in the operation of information systems are unlikely. Various new technologies are becoming available that offer the promise of systems which learn, systems which rationalize, and maybe even systems which inspire. Each of these areas is very important for 'soft' decision making. Admittedly management decision making is a more complex area than most of those in which successes have already been scored. Yet technical advances do seem to be possible, if only managers are prepared to take advantage of them.

Methods of effective organizational change

There are all sorts of reasons why managers might resist technological change.[12] They may resent the change especially if there is no consultation. They may be anxious about their job, their promotion prospects, or their future pay rises. They may actually be frightened of appearing incompetent, especially in front of subordinates who may be more confident or highly trained. This may be associated with a sense of frustration, a perceived loss of promotion or the thought of a career cut short.

Resistance will be less if there is clear support from the top and if the change is seen as non-threatening. There are various ways to make a development more acceptable and most of these are well known.[13] Broadly they require the involvement of participants, perhaps the suggestion that the change offers interesting new experiences and clear indications that a flexible, open approach will be used. In particular, opportunities for clarification and feedback should be allowed.

Initiating technological advance

More interesting perhaps is the question of how to encourage managers to initiate their own change. How to find managers who will be effective users of information technology. People who will be able to demonstrate objectively that their applications bring quantifiable gains and maybe even competitive advantage. Three basic approaches appear to offer themselves.

(a) Mrs Beaton's recipe for jugged hare advises that you must 'first catch your hare'. By the same token, for successful use of IT you must first have the right kind of manager. This simply means a manager who is predisposed to use IT productively. Despite their popularity as a technique, personal interviews are notoriously ineffective as a tool for selecting staff. It is not possible to identify such people subjectively. Nor is it merely a question of using younger people instead of older people. There is no evidence to show that predisposition to innovate is related to age or reason to suppose that younger managers would have developed the necessary insights.

A method based on the application of repertory grid[14] techniques may be used for this purpose. The resulting cognitive map relates the way in which a person construes technology to their preferred methods of decision making. A person who thinks of a computer in the same way as they think of, say, a calculator, is unlikely to be predisposed to use computers for applications involving judgement. Psychological profiling will incur additional costs in the personnel budget but the chances of success for IT projects of all kinds will be increased.

(b) Second, existing attitudes revealed by these tests can be shaped by the use of trainers and consultants. A programme of education and communication at all levels will keep staff informed about developments in the IT world. Formal mechanisms are needed for explaining the nature of potential technical advances. This may then encourage them to come forward with ideas for applications and improvements. In particular, if a company is large enough to have one, open up the communication channels between the IT department and the operating management. Obviously both parties will benefit.

(c) Finally, managers must develop a clear understanding of what can be achieved. All the people who may influence the implementation and operation of a computer-based system might be consulted during the development phase, even the customers. It is important to allow enough time for proper planning. Many IT projects lose credibility by being ill-considered, rushed, overambitious or even oversold. If your new booking system is just an electronic version of an existing clerical procedure, then real productivity gains will only derive from managers who are able to make more effective use of available time. Maybe they will have more time to prepare forecasts or to improve merchandising. In which case they must be trained how to do it.

If management attitudes are not cultivated and management capabilities are not developed, then all that is likely to be achieved with information technology is prettier reports and bigger electricity bills.

References

1 Travel Business Group, *Technology and the Travel Agent*, Istel Survey, Redditch, 1987.
2 Gamble, P. R., *Computers and Innovation in the Hospitality Industry: A Study of Some Factors Affecting Management Behaviour*, PhD thesis, University of Surrey, 1986.
3 Vowler, J., 'Releasing Your True Potential', *Computer Weekly*, 21 April, 1988.
4 Kavanagh, J., 'Business Acumen Doesn't Reach Computer Rooms', *Computer Weekly*, 27 April, 1988.
5 Gamble, P. R. (1986), *op. cit.*
6 Stewart, R., *The Reality of Management*, London: Pan, 1979, p. 76.
7 Newell, A. and Simon, H., *Human Problem Solving*, Englewood Cliffs, NJ: Prentice-Hall, 1972.
8 Cohen, M. D., March, J. G. and Olsen, J. P., 'A Garbage Can Model of Organizational Choice', *Administrative Science Quarterly*, 17, 1972, pp. 1–25.
9 De Alberdi, M. and Harvey, J., 'Decision Systems', in Christie, B. (ed), *Human Factors of Information Technology in the Office*, Chichester: Wiley, 1985, pp. 170–85.
10 PA Management Consultants, *Survey of Chief Executives and their Perception of Office Automation*, Royston, 1985.
11 Gallier, R., 'A Failure of Direction', *Business Computing and Communications*, July/August 1986, pp. 32–8.
12 Drazin, R. and Joyce, W. F., 'Towards a Typology of Resistance to Change Behaviours', *Academy of Management Proceedings*, 1979, pp. 304–8.
13 Raia, A. P. and Margulies, N., 'Organizational Change and Development', in Kerr S. (ed), *Organizational Behaviour*, Columbus, OH: Grid, 1979.
14 Kelly, G. A., *A Theory of Personality*, Norton and Co, New York, 1955.

Further reading

Further reading on new technologies in *Tourism Management* 1980–9

Boberg, K. B. and Collison, F. M., 'Computer reservation systems and airline competition', vol. 6, no. 3, September 1985, pp. 174–83.

Booth, R., 'Automation in the travel industry', vol. 4, no. 4, December 1983, pp. 296–8.

Bruce, M., 'Information technology: changes in the travel trade', vol. 4, no. 4, December 1983, pp. 290–5.

Burke, J. F., 'Computerized management of tourism marketing information', vol. 7, no. 4, December 1986, pp. 279–89.

Crandall, D. A., 'US Recreation-information system', vol. 7, no. 3, September 1986, pp. 205–7.

Fein, C. S., 'Teleconferencing and its effects on business travel', vol. 4, no. 4, December 1983, pp. 279–89.

Shafer, E. L., 'Technology, tourism and the 21st century', vol. 8, no. 2, June 1987, pp. 179–82.

Sheldon, P. J., 'The impact of technology on the hotel industry', vol. 4, no. 4, December 1983, pp. 269–78.

Sheldon, P. J., 'Computers – tourism applications', vol. 8, no. 3, September 1987, pp. 258–62.

Willis, E., 'Low cost microcomputers and tourism marketing', vol. 5, no. 3, September 1984, pp. 236–7.

Part Nine

Third World Issues

Most of Africa, Asia and Latin America, the Caribbean and the Pacific islands, make up the Third World. In many countries in these regions tourism has been of growing importance. Its impacts, as well as other issues, have been increasingly studied and analysed. The three articles in this part of the book deal in turn with a broad overview common to all, an issue of concern to many, and a need demonstrated particularly by the smaller developing countries.

C. L. Jenkins of the University of Strathclyde, UK, provides a wide-ranging perspective of the role of development in 'Tourism policies in developing countries'. The article is a review of tourism as a development option, constraints, and government involvement, and a critique of tourism research.

Jean Holder of the Caribbean Tourism Research and Development Centre (now Caribbean Tourism Organization) in Barbados, West Indies, highlights the importance of the environment in 'Pattern and impact of tourism on the environment of the Caribbean'. Although the article examines tourism and the environment in the Caribbean context, most of its recommendations are valid for other island environments, and many for developing countries generally.

Victor Teye of Arizona State University, USA, examines 'Prospects for regional tourism cooperation in Africa'. The article considers the benefits, opportunities, existing frameworks, as well as obstacles, and puts forward regional cooperation in the Caribbean as a model for Africa.

Further articles concerned with Third World issues in tourism published in *Tourism Management* from 1980–9 are listed on page 297. See also Chapter 29 'Towards new tourism policies' and Chapter 18 'South Pacific tourism promotion'.

25 Tourism policies in developing countries

C. L. Jenkins

The objective of this article is to provide a perspective of the role of tourism in development. It is not possible within the limitations of this paper to provide a technical analysis of tourism and development – the issues raised are those suggested by the author to be of importance to any consideration of the role of tourism in the developing countries. In this article, 'development' is used to embrace economic and social progress. The 'developing countries' are those usually noted on United Nations statistical lists as being outwith OECD member countries and the socialist centrally-planned economies.

Tourism is now recognized as an important international economic activity. Before 1945, the bulk of activity was domestic and centred on a financial elite, but there are now very large flows of tourists, from all classes, crossing international boundaries. This rapid growth is readily explained by the increase in real personal disposable incomes and leisure time, and by developments in transport since 1945.

Economists have been attracted to the study of international tourism by the relatively high and sustained growth rate in tourist arrivals, and by the economic implications of this for specific countries and regions. Despite the inadequacies of tourism data it does seem that the rate of growth in international tourism receipts has been consistently above the rate of growth of world trade generally, and many traded commodities specifically.

Although international tourism is geographically concentrated, its relevance to development can be seen in the emergence of specialist organizations and institutions concerned with monitoring, supporting, and developing tourism.

Traditionally, most tourism activity has centred on the developed countries of the world. The majority of international tourist flows are between, and within, developed countries. The share of total recorded international tourist arrivals and expenditure accruing to developing countries is relatively small, and distribution is highly concentrated within this group.

Even so, there is growing evidence that many developing countries, some not traditionally identified with tourism, are beginning to promote their countries as potential destinations. A very large proportion of the signatories to the Articles of Agreement of the World Tourism Organization are developing countries. And even a casual examination of telephone directories for cities such as London, Paris and New York shows a surprising number of countries with national tourist offices or with consular and diplomatic representation. There is clearly a growing awareness in the developing countries of the potential benefits to be derived from participation in international tourism.

Why tourism is an attractive development option

As I have mentioned, the share of international tourists received by the developing countries is relatively small and highly skewed. The number of tourists that a country can attract will depend on a variety of factors – not least on the distance of the receiving country from the main tourist-generating countries. In general, the more distant the destination country, the more costly the total trip and the fewer number of tourists it will attract. Despite this obvious disadvantage, many developing countries regard tourism as being an important part of their development strategies. I suggest that seven main factors support this view.

The wanderlust

Even given the problems of seasonality and changes in destination preferences, overall visitor arrivals have increased remarkably rapidly. The oil crisis of October 1973 merely slowed the rate of increase. This remarkably consistent growth indicates that international tourism has a greater buoyancy and stability than is sometimes believed.

Of course, variation of tourist flows amongst countries will continue. But in general, the developing countries see tourism as a growth industry. And within the overall growth pattern there is evidence to suggest that, for major generating countries, long-haul tourism has shown even greater increases in departure rates. The long-haul tourist seems also to be less price and income sensitive than other 'mass' tourists. Both factors are important to the developing countries which are usually distant from the main tourist generators.

Income redistribution

The flow of tourists from developed to developing countries has the effect of redistributing income. Most developed countries have 'hard' currencies and the transfer helps to alleviate the often chronic foreign-exchange 'gaps' of developing countries. There is considerable debate on the net effect of this redistribution for particular countries; and even greater concern with identifying means of increasing the net retention of tourist expenditure in host countries.

However, at this stage in the debate I agree with Robert Erbes, who states that developing countries should not regard tourism as 'manna from heaven which can provide a solution to all their foreign exchange settlement difficulties.'[1] At first sight, there is no particular reason why tourism should be an inefficient earner of foreign currency relative to other sectors, but the particular conditions in a country should be identified and evaluated on an intersectoral basis.

Freedom from trade restrictions

Unlike commodity and other forms of trade, with their tariffs, quotas and other obstructions, international tourism has been characterized by a relaxation of barriers. The widespread abolition of visas, the modification or removal of currency restrictions on travel, and improved international relations have made tourism one of the few developing countries' 'exports' relatively unhindered by trade restrictions. Marked social changes in attitudes to holidays and travel in the developed countries make it unlikely that governments would now impose travel restrictions as part of their economic protection measures.

Demand growth likely to continue

In the developed countries, those influences which increase demand for holidays abroad seem to be strengthening. Leisure time and disposable income have increased and the impact on demand has been intensified by innovations in tour wholesaling and retailing. The development of inclusive tours and cheap charter flights continues, together with an increasing range of promotional fares made available by airlines. Improvements in aircraft have considerably reduced flying time and economies of scale have resulted in lower fares. The present buoyancy in travel demand is likely to continue as more distant countries are added to tour destinations.

At a more fundamental level, there seems to be in most developed countries a growing tendency to regard the annual holiday as a necessary rather than a luxury purchase. Insufficient research has been done in this area, but recent UK experience certainly supports this contention.

Development costs

As a development option for host countries, tourism is too often regarded as a low-cost sector, because it requires and uses the country's natural attributes (e.g. scenic amenity, beaches, climate). These basic features may be supplemented by ethnic and cultural factors. The tourist amenity of a country (the sum of its inherent attractiveness) is sometimes regarded as having a low or even zero opportunity cost, since no alternative use can be found for it. However, the country's attractiveness to tourists is rarely unique: its use in tourism often depends on expensive investment in infrastructure and buildings.

Employment

The service aspect of tourism is often seen as a benefit by developing countries, because of the jobs created, both directly in tourism and indirectly through linkages. At the initial stage of tourism development, many of the low-skill jobs can be filled by local people, with the main expertise being provided by foreign labour. The main difficulty is in moving on in later stages to the employment of local people as managers.

Tourism is sometimes described as 'labour intensive'. That may be the case in specific projects, but infrastructure is often a costly input to the tourism sector – making this description inaccurate. Where tourism does generate employment, it will clearly have an economic impact, enhanced by the multiplier effect, on incomes and government revenues.

Prestige

In some countries the development of tourism and its amenities can be viewed as a prestige sector. New hotels and related complexes may provide the sole sign of 'modernity'. That these amenities depend almost entirely on foreign capital, managerial expertise, and servicing are often ignored. In one sense, tourism can be seen as bridging the development gap between two very unequal economies and disparate societies. A sense of national pride and achievement often prevails for a development similar to those condemned by Galbraith as 'synthetic modernization'.

Constraints

Despite these seven factors and their effects, no single receiving country can influence either the growth rate or the direction of flow of international tourists. The international market is highly competitive. Most developing countries seeking to enter, or to increase their share of, the market will find themselves at a financial disadvantage with respect to developed countries in trying to influence tourist demand through advertising. Some of their other disadvantages are equally formidable.

Most studies, reports, and books on tourism in economic development are enthusiastic about the benefits, but minimize the disadvantages. Nowhere is this more noticeable than in the lack of consideration given to the international ambience of tourism within which individual countries have to operate. Robert Erbes has stressed the problems of dependency in international tourism[2], but there are other organizational and institutional factors. The most restrictive factors, over which the developing countries have little control, are exogenous (i.e. external to the countries).

Demand

A combination of influences operate in generating countries and culminate in an individual's decision to holiday abroad. The determinants of demand, the prime exogenous factor, cannot be directly affected by the receiving country. Tourism advertising is unlikely to influence the magnitude of total demand, but may affect the destination chosen. This should be taken into account by tourism policymakers in developing countries. Strong dependence on a single market will place the host country in a competitively weak position.

Air transport

A developing country with its own air carrier, particularly if it is a member of the International Air Transport Association, will at least have some influence over the type, frequency, and fare structures of services. In bilateral discussions with tourist-generating countries it can negotiate a share of traffic, and agree promotional fares if required. The developing country without its own carrier is entirely at the mercy of foreign airlines. Expensive investment in tourism plant and infrastructure could be wasted if foreign carriers are unable, or unwilling, to match capacity limits in the host country.

Seasonality

International tourism demand is seasonal, as a result of a combination of social, educational and institutional factors in the generating countries. In spite of great publicity efforts made by host countries, the traditional holiday pattern in generating countries has altered little. This fluctuating demand is an important consideration for any country embarking on a programme of tourism development: in developing countries the seasonal use of scarce investment resources poses particular problems for economic planners.

The market interface

A tour wholesaler acts as a catalyst of demand – he interprets the market needs of his clients and packages these needs into destinations. His influence on the direction of demand is particularly significant to the long-haul, relatively expensive, destinations – i.e. most developing countries. Limited market knowledge, finance, and experience force many of the more distant countries offering high-priced, low-volume tours to work with and through specialist wholesalers. This can impose serious limitations on tourism policymaking in the host country.

Endogenous factors

Amongst the endogenous factors which should be considered are the nature and type of tourism industry that is desired, the pace of development, location, investment policies and manpower planning for tourism. In most cases these will be inextricably linked with a consideration of the exogenous factors.

Government policy

In the developed world, tourism has attained its present importance largely as a consequence of private-sector enterprise and initiative. In many countries this initiative has been, and is being, supported by a wide range of government assistance. The emergence of national and international companies mainly engaged in the leisure and tourism field has been a parallel development.

However, in most developing countries the private sector is small, private investment funds are limited, and experience of tourism is negligible. Governments often have to adopt the role of entrepreneur, sometimes in response to proposed private foreign investment.

There is clearly a dichotomy in aims. Private investment criteria centre on profitability: other considerations take a secondary position. Government investment, although concerned with profitability, must also take account of non-economic ramifications e.g. social and cultural impact, land-use policy. Without government involvement in tourism policy-making, short-term developments can give rise to long-term problems: 'benign neglect' of tourism will not facilitate sound development.

There are obvious reasons why governments in developing countries should positively intervene in tourism. When funds are required to support investment in tourism, the government is often the only agency able to raise or guarantee the loan. At the macro level, the government has ultimate responsibility for the allocation of funds and resources for specific sectors. It is a government responsibility to decide on regulations and loans which can affect tourism (e.g. foreign-exchange regulations, fiscal incentives for developments, vocational training for tourism, physical planning, land-use allocations).

The governments of developed and developing countries share many areas of responsibility. But in the developing countries the problem of resource scarcity and consequently allocation is acute. Strong government control is necessary to prevent exploitation and obvious waste, and to ensure that the benefits from tourism are optimized. Tourism in developed countries can be regarded as a mainly social activity with economic consequences: in developing countries it is largely an economic activity with social consequences.

Research: a critique

As I have indicated, a wide range of factors affect any consideration of the role of tourism in development. Although there has been an increase in the literature on this subject, much of it deals with the developed countries. Studies related to the developing countries are of more recent origin.

This neglect is not hard to explain – tourism is an essentially pleasurable activity accompanied by often conspicuous expenditure. That tourism manifests itself in the midst of areas of relative poverty and deprivation is anathema to some observers. Despite these reservations, most developing countries have attempted to examine tourism as an option for development: it is largely this attempt to justify tourism which has led to the spate of economic impact studies.

Although the technical quality of some of these studies is high, their contribution to tourism research lies more in the refinement and application of techniques than in developing an understanding of tourism dynamics. Of necessity, they are concerned largely with static analysis of data largely conditioned by exogenous variables.

For example, one of the important variables affecting tourist demand for a destination country is the cost of air fares, which are either exogenously determined (e.g. by the International Air Transport Association traffic conference) or subject to bilateral agreement. In turn, the cost of the air fare is an important element in the total holiday cost (or price of tour). This total selling price influences the number of tourists who choose a specific destination, and it is the number of tourist arrivals who determine the initial level of tourist expenditure – the usual starting point for economic impact analysis. In this sense, impact analysis is static, i.e. it is determined by external variables which, because of their complexity, must often be taken as given. The main benefits to be derived from economic impact studies, therefore, may well relate to the linkage and leakage effects rather than to the computed magnitude of impact.

A second broad group includes marketing studies, 'national tourism-development plans, and feasibility studies. These 'operational' studies are usually privately commissioned, to provide development and implementation guidelines.

A further group of studies focuses on some of the theoretical aspects of the role of tourism in economic development. These studies are probably of most interest to students of tourism, since they attempt to set out a framework, within which specialist country and regional data can be analysed.

I have three general criticisms of tourism research related to the developing countries.

● Too many studies lack a comparative dimension, not only between countries but often between tourism and other sectors in an economy. This limits their usefulness for policy formulation.

- Too many studies are based on a single discipline, usually economics, occasionally sociology. As a wide-ranging activity, tourism must be approached through multi-disciplinary analytical studies.
- The neglect of the social and anthropological aspects of tourism in developing countries should be rectified.

I hope future research will reflect these needs and begin to provide a growing background of comparative studies.

Positive government action

There is an urgent need for further empirical and theoretical research into tourism and its effects on developing countries. In particular, tourism policymaking should be closely examined, preferably on an intercountry basis.

That many developing countries have benefited from tourism is undisputed. It is, however, essential that information for policymaking is improved, and that the problems of tourism management are analysed. In particular, the economic benefits derived from tourism in some countries are threatened by a growing discontent with the non-economic disbenefits.

President Nyerere has claimed that, in most developing countries, tourism is regarded as a 'necessary evil'. Only active and positive government involvement can save the industry from that criticism.

References

1   Erbes, Robert, *International Tourism and the Economy of Developing Countries*, Paris: OECD, 1973.
2   *Ibid*.

26 Pattern and impact of tourism on the environment of the Caribbean

Jean S. Holder

The future of Caribbean tourism will depend on the extent to which the Caribbean public and private sectors and the host populations understand the relationship between tourism and the environment and take the necessary steps to ensure the protection and enhancement of the natural and built environment. The Caribbean Tourism Organization's ideas on environmental issues may be summarized as follows:

● Tourism is critical to the economic survival of the Caribbean.
● The environment is tourism's resource. It is our environment, or rather the experience and enjoyment of it, that the tourism industry promotes and sells.
● A proper understanding of tourism and commitment to a lasting and healthy tourism is possibly the best method of ensuring the preservation of the Caribbean environment.
● The long-term commitment to tourism required to ensure the careful planning necessary for minimizing negative environmental effects was absent in the early stages of Caribbean tourism development.
● It is necessary that we thoroughly assess the costs and benefits of tourism development in Caribbean states. Successful remedial action will, however, require a vastly changed attitude to tourism itself.
● Because of Caribbean economic realities and increasing dependency on tourism, the region has no option but to devise sophisticated systems of management, education, research and monitoring with respect to its environment resources.

Environment constitutes tourism's resource

The environment is defined as comprising the biosphere, i.e. the rock, water and air that surrounds the earth, together with the ecosystems which they support. These ecosystems consist of communities of individuals of different populations living in a given area together with their non-living physical environment. Some are simple, some complex, but they are all interrelated – all forms of animal and plant life are included. This definition also includes the environment built by the human component of the animal species such as existing buildings, complete cities, historic monuments and archaeological sites. Finally, we include the patterns of behaviour of the people themselves – their folklore, dress, food, and general way of life that differentiate them from other human communities.

Tourism is defined from two perspectives – for the tourist it is the enjoyment of experiences gained by interacting with people and other animal life, and the natural and built environment in a location away from the tourist's normal residence. Movement is an essential ingredient. The motivations for travel are many and various although recreation is a major factor. For the tourist operator in the tourist generating country or area, and the tourist operator, both public and private sector, in the receiving area or country, tourism constitutes the packaging and sale of those experiences for profit. This article is concerned with the need for long-term tourism planning in the context of tourism's interrelationship with the environment.

Understanding and commitment

The environment is Caribbean tourism's resource and, therefore, our tourism is an environmentally dependent industry. To say that one both wants and understands tourism, is to say that one is committed to the preservation of its resource, which is the environment. The converse is also true. Far from the protection of the environment being an obstacle to tourism development, it is the only way of ensuring tourism's survival. The truth of this fact does not, however, mean that it is obvious. Many environmentalists, seeing the environmental mistakes already made through tourism development, take a fatalistic approach to tourism. They believe it to be both self-destructive and inevitably destructive of its environment. On the other hand, many tourism operators lose sight of the real reasons why people go to great expense and trouble to travel away from home, often to do the same type of things they could do at home.

This shortsightedness can lead to the sacrifice of the entire industry on the altar of short-term profit. The hotelier who grasps the reality, that for the tourist the room is only a base from which to enjoy the environment, will in his enlightened self-interest, become an environmental *aficionado*.

Self-destruct theory of tourism

However, because the Caribbean is so dependent on tourism, it should give some consideration to the following self-destruct theory of tourism. This theory postulates that tourism develops and declines in cyclical fashion in four phases:

Phase 1. A remote and exotic spot offers peaceful rest and relaxation and provides an escape for the rich who live in isolation from the resident population.

Phase 2. Tourism promotion attracts persons of middle income who come as much for the rest and relaxation, as to imitate the rich. More and more hotel accommodation and tourist facilities are built to attract and accommodate more and more tourists. This transforms the original character of the place from escape paradise to a series of conurbations with several consequences:

- the local residents become tourism employees, in many cases forsaking agriculture, and earn more than ever before;
- the rich tourists move on elsewhere;
- the growth in the tourist population makes interaction between tourist and resident population inevitable, leading to a variety of social consequences, mostly seen as negative; and
- increased tourist accommodation capacity leads to excess supply over demand and a deterioration in product and price.

Phase 3. The country resorts to mass tourism, attracting persons of lower standards of social behaviour and economic power. This leads to the socio-environmental degradation of tourist destination.

Phase 4. As the place sinks under the weight of social friction and solid waste, all tourists exit, leaving behind derelict tourism facilities, littered beaches and countryside and a resident population that cannot return to its old way of life.

There are many examples of countries with tourism facilities or even entire industries at one of the first three phases of the self-destruct theory. One way to avoid Phase 4 is to ensure that the region becomes environmentally conscious and plans as though it expects tourism to be around for the long term. This calls for long-term commitment.

Long-term commitment

Regrettably the long-term commitment has not previously been present. This at first seems surprising since tourism clearly addresses the region's two most critical economic problems: shortage of foreign exchange and high unemployment. Caribbean tourism earned US$7.5 billion (000m) gross and employed well over 300,000 persons in 1989. As regional trade problems remain unsolved, as markets for sugar, bananas and other export crops worsen, as the price for Trinidad and Tobago's oil and Guyana and Jamaica's bauxite falls, the Caribbean's dependence on tourism grows at an alarming pace. The lack of commitment, however, derives from what I refer to as the Caribbean's socio-cultural and economic dilemma.

This dilemma is caused by the Caribbean growing more and more dependent on an industry to which deep down, and often without realizing it, it has a certain resentment. This resentment is based on tourism's past performance and the unhappy associations which the characteristics of tourism tend to evoke in societies recently emerging from a colonial past. Perhaps this seems surprising but the truth is that we often confuse the fact that tourism is all pervasive, with the belief that it is accepted. Tourism has prospered in the Caribbean in spite of neglect and negative attitudes about its potential as an engine of development in several important quarters.

Comprehensive planning resources were not applied to an economic activity, which was often seen as fickle and short term, of dubious social value, and unlikely to provide a long-term solution to economic problems. These socio-economic doubts about tourism have historically restricted input from governments, international aid agencies, regional development agencies and Caribbean academics. In many cases governments felt tourism could be left to the private sector. Even now, considering the high expectation that Caribbean governments have of the tourism sector for earning foreign exchange, generating revenue and creating jobs, it sometimes appears that tourism does not receive a large enough share of government time, effort, planning and financial resources.

With respect to the private sector, left in the early days to take important decisions about tourism development, in an unrestricted and unplanned situation, the focus was naturally on maximizing profits from individual operations, and often too little attention was paid to socio-cultural and environmental concerns – some through lack of knowledge, others for short-term gains.

The future hope for the industry lies in a transformation of existing attitudes by a demonstration of the true socio-cultural, environmental and economic impacts of tourism through a realistic understanding that our beautiful and healthy environment is really what we offer as a tourism product, and what attracts our clients, should inform the focus of our efforts. Our long-term strategy must, therefore, begin with some consideration of how much tourism is too much. To preserve the goose that lays the golden egg, we will definitely have to pay attention to the carrying capacity of our small states with their fragile social systems and equally fragile ecosystems.

It is normal for tourism people, and the Caribbean is no exception, to measure their own success largely in terms of the percentage increase in visitor arrivals in one year over another. This tendency to count heads often ignores other important indicators of success, such as length of stay, bed-nights, high achieved hotel rates and visitor expenditure, and loses sight of a serious potential problem of exceeding the carrying capacity of small islands. This carrying capacity has to be defined in terms of:

- physical deterioration of the tourism resource;
- irreversible damage to the ecosystems resulting in loss of both wild-life and their habitats;
- social irritation among host populations due to competition for scarce resources and services;
- the comfort of the tourists themselves.

Regrettably there can be no mathematical formula for establishing in advance how many tourists are enough, although it becomes clear after the fact how many were too much. *First,* a pragmatic approach would suggest that *constant vigilance* be maintained over the stress on services and the impact of tourism on them and more emphasis be placed when setting goals on getting more socio-economic benefits from fewer tourists. The political will must also be present to take bold action for change where it is clearly necessary.

For example, to reduce the pressure from cruise passengers, Bermuda took the bold step of doubling the per capita tax. This resulted in the desired reduction in numbers and a significant increase in revenue.

Second, we must give our tourism industry an environmental thrust which should be preceded by an *Environmental Impact Study* covering inter alia:

1   Adequate quality and quantity of drinking water and water for domestic purposes to serve the needs of residents and tourists.
2   Sea water and beach pollution, which results where construction of accommodation outstrips the provision of adequate sewage treatment facilities.
3   Oil pollution from motor boats and increased dangers to bathers from unregulated sea activity.
4   Beach erosion caused, inter alia, by heavy concentrations of buildings and other unauthorized erections built too near the high-water mark, buildings that are often also wasteful of energy and out of character with the local landscape.
5   Removal of reefs and damage to coral formations and shells, thereby interrupting the role they play in maintaining the ecological balance.
6   Shutting out sight of the sea just metres away from the road, by using almost every coastal spot for tourist building.
7   Supplies of sea food, especially delicacies such as lobster and sea eggs, which are endangered by overfishing.
8   The disappearance of special species of sea creatures and birds, as land reclamation has taken place.
9   Noise pollution from canned music and aircraft landings.
10 Amounts of litter arising from increased consumption and specifically from canned and boxed take-away foods.
11 Changes in the character of villages.
12 Attitudes to sex, race, personal relationships, drugs and crime, and consumption patterns.
13 Desertion of agricultural employment for tourism jobs.
14 Changes in the price of land due to tourism development.

Perhaps we should also determine the extent to which *tourism development in Caribbean countries has caused or contributed to the following:*

●   improved air and sea ports, improved and increased air and sea traffic, and ground transport, which benefit the entire population in such respects as general mobility and pursuit of trade and business relationships;
●   revenues to fund better health care, education and other social services, which improve the quality of life for all;
●   improved telephone, telex and other communications systems nationwide;
●   development and upgrading of national parks, natural and manmade attractions, recreational and health facilities;
●   preservation of historical sites and monuments;
●   an appreciation of vernacular architecture;
●   beautification of public places;

● increased cultural offerings, craft development, and museums;
● a wider experience of international cuisines; and
● restoration of old cities.

Finally, there seems *need for action* in the following areas:

1   The Caribbean Tourism Organization, together with the Caribbean Conservation Association and Caribbean National Trusts, should step up educational and training programmes in the area of the environment.
2   Throughout the region, there should be comprehensive national tourism policies which include a significant section on the preservation of the physical (natural and built) and social environment as tourism's resource.
3   The administrative structure of our governments should more closely reflect the interrelationship between tourism and the environment. This suggests either a linking of ministries dealing with both tourism and the environment or implanting a significant body of environmental expertise into the Ministry of Tourism. A great deal of disparate activity already in progress in environmental matters should be rationalized.
4   The governments' environmentalists should not only have a monitoring and a regulatory function, but should also liaise with research, education, preservation and aid agencies, both private and public sector, acting as catalysts in seeing new initiatives taken.
5   Government tourism policy should be specific on such matters as:

● regional zoning of tourism facilities;
● building codes relating to construction and sewage disposal on beaches and coastal areas generally;
● identification, use and maintenance of national treasures;
● development, use and maintenance of national parks and nature trails;
● pollution of water resources, and litter generally;
● energy conservation;
● regulation of in-shore motorized boats and other craft;
● protection of certain species of plant and animal life;
● conservation of fisheries;
● noise regulation;
● stimulation of arts and crafts;
● preservation of building monuments and cities; and
● providing incentives to private individuals and groups to assist the government in its tasks.

6   Environmental impact assessments should precede approval of major tourism development projects.
7   Tourism and environmental studies should be firmly integrated into the educational systems of each of our countries.
8   Governments should legislate where appropriate to enforce their tourism and environmental policies.
9   Governments, especially in highly-developed tourism destinations, should beware of simply pursuing growth in numbers of tourists where they might employ other methods of maximizing tourism earnings without increasing danger to the environment. It is clear that fewer people staying longer and spending more per capita can achieve the same ends.

Management of our tourism resources here defined as our environmental resources, requires the wisdom of Solomon. The key word, however, is balance – maintaining, as far as possible, the natural balance between ecosystems, balancing economic and social goals, balancing the responsibilities of the state with rights of individuals and groups. It will not be easy, but through the concerted efforts of CTO and other interested agencies we can achieve a happy medium acceptable to both tourism practitioners and environmentalists.

Acknowledgement

This chapter is an edited version of a paper delivered by the author at a workshop held at the Dover Convention Centre on 6 April 1987 which was organized by the BANFF Centre of Management, the Caribbean Conservation Association, the Caribbean Tourism Research and Development Centre, and the Caribbean Community Secretariat. The workshop was hosted by the Government of Barbados and funded by the Canadian International Development Agency Management for Change Programme.

27 Prospects for regional tourism cooperation in Africa

Victor B. Teye

An increasing trend in international tourism is the desire of tourists to visit more than one destination on a trip to a long-haul (over 1500 miles) tourist region. In the case of destinations in developing regions of Asia, Africa and South America, a substantial segment of visitors from the main tourist-generating regions of North America and Western Europe prefer visiting a number of countries on a single trip. Multiple tourism-destination development which allows the creation of regional tours and multi-national circuits is only one element of regional cooperation in tourism development. Others include:

- joint promotion and marketing;
- tourism facilitation including liberalization policies for passport and visa requirements;
- currency regulation, immigration and customs controls;
- collection of uniform tourism statistics;
- investment incentives and regulations for local and foreign investors;
- transport system policies for landing rights, charter flights, and over-land international crossing;
- standardization and regional classification of tourism facilities;
- coordination of health and medical requirements;
- conservation and preservation programmes for natural, historical and cultural resources;
- personnel and manpower training;
- foreign assistance (aid) programmes; and
- international representation on foreign markets.[1]

In the case of African countries, some of the above considerations are so critical to tourism development that they require bilateral and multilateral cooperation. Malaria and cholera outbreaks, for example, can spread quickly across international boundaries. Hence, international tourism arrivals to a whole region could decline dramatically and devastate tourism and related industries. Wildlife poaching is presently a major problem threatening the tourism industries of East, Central and Southern Africa. The long and unsecured borders of some of these countries require institutionalized cooperative arrangements with neighbouring countries to deal with the complex problems of poaching. For example, Zambia shares open borders through isolated regions with eight countries, none of which can solve its poaching problems alone.

Multiple-destination marketing

Tourism marketing has provided the primary reason for whatever regional cooperation exists in developing countries. The reasons for cooperation vary from country to country. For instance, the need for a multiple-destination development in the case of Zambia derives from the recognition of serious limitations imposed by the narrow base of its tourism product, and the availability of complementary tourism products, especially those based on aquatic (beach and lakes) resources in other destinations in the Eastern, South and Central African regions, and the neighbouring countries bordering on the Indian Ocean such as Kenya, Tanzania, Mauritius and the Seychelles. Given the relative similarity of the tourism resources of the majority of West African countries, the importance of multiple-destination development for Nigeria or Ghana, on the other hand, derives from the 'total' perception of Africa by tourists from Western Europe, and in particular, from North America. The Tourism Development Plans of Zambia[2] and Ghana[3] illustrate the above point, as well as the differences that give rise to the need for a multiple-destination development.

While tourism marketing currently provides the main reason for regional cooperation, regionalism in tourism should be more comprehensive.

Regionalism in tourism development

Renninger describes regionalism as cooperation and integration among proximate states which share a sense of their own individual inadequacy in dealing with the problems of security and welfare.[4] Development of tourism at the regional level therefore means that the different states in each African region will cooperate and integrate their attractions, capital infrastructure, natural and human resources to serve the needs of the domestic and international (interregional and intraregional) tourism sectors. This integrated approach is important for a number of reasons. First, the African tourism region, occupying about 11.7m square miles (30.3m square kilometres), is endowed with physical tourism resources which include a vast array of relief forms, topography, fauna, flora, maritime and aquatic resources as well as a diverse assemblage of historical and cultural tourism resources. Second, each country in the five sub-Sahara African regions (West, North-eastern, Central East, Central, and Southern Africa) is a long-haul destination relative to the tourist-generating regions of Europe, North America and the Far East. Third, intervening tourism opportunities exist in the more developed destinations in North Africa. The large size of Africa, the diversity of its tourism resources and the locational disadvantages of sub-Sahara Africa provide incentives for regional cooperation. A group of countries acting as a unit is better able to educate the marketing intermediaries (tour operators and travel agents) in the tourist-generating countries in order to overcome some of the negative perceptions and images of Africa, a major problem hindering efforts to promote and market sub-Sahara Africa.[5] Similarly, a group of countries acting in concert has a better leverage to protect their interests in dealing with institutions such as Tourism Transnational Corporations (TTC) which play a critical role in the tourism development process.

International tourism

Africa's share of global international tourism arrivals and receipts in 1986 was a mere 2.5 per cent and 2.2 per cent respectively. Furthermore, these proportions have remained nearly the same for more than a decade. The industry is also concentrated in a few North African countries, Kenya and South Africa. Tourism in most sub-Sahara African countries is hardly an industry since the tourism infrastructure is weak, tourism organization is poor, and net revenue is meagre. Almost all tourist arrivals consist of African nationals resident abroad returning to visit friends and relatives, business visitors, and those visiting expatriate residents. The primary vacation or leisure tourism sector is undeveloped. Furthermore, interregional tourism is substantially higher than intraregional tourism, indicating that obstacles to intra-Africa tourism exist. Yet the potential for this development is great, e.g. in 1983, 3,057,939 tourists from Europe visited Africa compared with the 4,736,938 (or the 1,678,999 more) tourists who visited Europe from Africa.[6] Regional cooperation will therefore not only improve the flow of tourists from the main generating countries outside Africa, but it should also facilitate the expansion of intra-Africa tourism.

Regional development organizations

Cooperation for development is not new in Africa. In West Africa alone there are currently more than thirty sub-regional organizations which have either exclusively or predominantly West African membership. The former French colonies were joined together during the colonial period as the Federation of French West Africa. However, since attaining independence individually, the federation has been disbanded and replaced by several economic groupings. The four former British colonies in West Africa are not as contiguous as the Francophone countries but they also had a number of cooperative institutions during the colonial era. All the links, except a few like the West Africa Examination Council, were dissolved on attainment of independence. For both Anglophone and Francophone West Africa, there clearly is greater fragmentation and duplication today than during the colonial era. However, there are currently more cooperative institutions within Francophone than Anglophone countries. This difference can be attributed to colonial policies, some of which are referred to later.

The three former British colonies of East Africa had the strongest regional cooperative arrangement which survived each country's political independence. Until its break-up in 1977, the East African Economic Community (EAEC) coordinated several regional programmes and institutions including railways, harbours, telecommunications, airline and currency.[7] A key component of the community was a regional tourism industry which facilitated the establishment of a number of tourist circuits within the common borders of the three countries.

The Federation of Rhodesia and Nyasaland was a pre-independence community consisting of Zambia, Malawi and Zimbabwe. This federation operated from 1953 until its dissolution in 1963 just before Northern Rhodesia became independent Zambia. A number of existing organizations which individually or collectively have the potential to enhance regional cooperation in tourism development in sub-Sahara Africa are described next.

Communauté Economique de l'Afrique de l'Ouest (CEAO)

The CEAO, also known as the West African Economic Community, was established in January 1974, replacing the West African Customs Union. The seven member countries are Benin, Burkina Faso, Ivory Coast, Mali, Mauritania, Niger and Senegal. The community's three main areas of activities involve trade, regional economic cooperation and economic integration through community projects. Proposals for regional and rural development projects approved in 1984 included 'development of regional tourism, setting up a community shipping line, a regional transport plan, and a programme of scientific research.[8]

Counseil de l'Entente (Entente Council)

The Counseil de l'Entente is a political and economic association of four countries which were formerly part of French West Africa. Founded in 1959, it consisted of Benin, Burkina Faso, Ivory Coast and Niger. Togo became a member in 1966. Through the Mutual Aid and Loan Guarantee Fund, the council promotes economic development in the region. This is achieved through assistance in preparing specific projects, mobilization of funds from external sources (including donor nations such as France and the USA, and institutions, particularly the World Bank). While the majority of projects emphasize agricultural development, 'the building of hotels and encouragement of tourism' have received investment and technical support.[9]

Economic Community of West African States (ECOWAS)

This is the most important regional development organization in West Africa. It consists of all the countries in West Africa, both Francophone and Anglophone, except Chad. The Treaty of Lagos, establishing ECOWAS, was signed in May 1975 by the fifteen states (Benin, Burkina Faso, The Gambia, Ghana, Guinea, Guinea Bissau, Ivory Coast, Liberia, Mali, Mauritania, Niger, Nigeria, Senegal, Sierra Leone and Togo). Cape Verde joined in 1977. ECOWAS has four specialized commissions:

● Trade, Customs, Immigration, Monetary and Payments;
● Industry, Agriculture and Natural Resources;
● Transport, Communications and Energy; and
● Social and Cultural Affairs.

The organization aims to promote cooperation and development in economic, social and cultural activity, particularly in the fields of the four specialized commissions. While the focus of the organization's activities is on agricultural and industrial development, several tourism-related objectives are being implemented.[10]

South African Development Coordination Conference (SADCC)

This is the most important regional organization in southern Africa. The nine SADCC member countries include Angola, Botswana, Lesotho, Malawi, Mozambique, Swaziland, Tanzania, Zambia, and Zimbabwe. There are ten sectoral commissions located in each member country (two commissions are in Maseru, Lesotho), two of which are directly related to tourism. These are the Tourism Sectoral Commission located in Lesotho, and the Southern Africa Transport and Communications Commission with its headquarters in Maputo, Mozambique.

The main focus of SADCC's projects is transport, on the grounds that, as the Lusaka Declaration noted:

the dominance of the Republic of South Africa has been reinforced by its transportation system. Without the establishment of an adequate regional transport and communication system, other areas of cooperation become impractical.[11]

Some transport projects do have direct tourism benefits. While specific tourism development projects have low priority, as in the case of transport projects, both direct and indirect benefits to tourism could be substantial. For instance, sectoral projects for manpower development, wildlife, energy, forestry and industrial development will each have both direct and indirect impact on tourism in the region.

Other organizations

There are a multitude of other regional (African) and external organizations whose activities impinge upon tourism development and could therefore become umbrella organizations for some aspects of regional tourism cooperation. Nearly 100 other African regional organizations exist, but only a few will be mentioned here. The African Airlines Association was founded in 1968 to give African airline operators expert advice on technical, financial, legal and marketing issues. The association is based in Nairobi, Kenya, and has a membership of thirty-six national carriers. Founded in 1976, the African Travel Association promotes tourism in Africa by holding annual conferences, and sponsoring specialized trade shows and seminars. The Agency for the Safety of Air Navigation in Africa and Madagascar was founded in 1959 and has a membership of fifteen Francophone countries in sub-Sahara Africa. The Organization for

Museums, Monuments and Sites in Africa fosters the collection, study and conservation of the natural and cultural heritage of Africa. It encourages cooperation between the thirty African member countries through seminars, workshops, conferences and exchange of personnel and training facilities. Activities of the Organization of African Unity (OAU), particularly those of its specialized agencies such as the African Civil Aviation Commission (AFCAC) also have direct impact on tourism development. Since it began operations in 1966, the African Development Bank (ADB) Group has made available substantial loans for development programmes in Africa. Nearly 27 per cent of its lending approvals in 1985 was for projects in the transport sector with direct impact on tourism. Another 19 per cent was for development of public utilities with both direct and indirect benefits for the tourism sector. The potential for funding tourism projects exists but it has not been tapped.

External organizations

External organizations whose activities impinge on African tourism are also large in number. These include such United Nations specialized agencies as the United Nations Development Programme (UNDP), the International Bank for Reconstruction and Development (IBRD), and the Economic Commission for Africa (ECA). One of the ECA's eleven divisions is the Transport, Communications and Tourism division.

The United Nations Environment Programme (UNEP) which has its headquarters in Nairobi, Kenya has, since its establishment in 1972, provided major assistance in preserving some of Africa's vital and endangered tourism resources. It administers the Convention on International Trade in Endangered Species of Wild Fauna and Flora. Through the Ecosystem Conservation Group (UNEP/FAO/UNESCO/IUCN), UNEP has provided funding, training and technical support for programmes in wildlife and national park management in Africa (and also in Latin America and Asia) in a coordinated regional context.

Other external development organizations would include the Commonwealth, the United States Agency for International Development (USAID) and the European Economic Community (EEC). The EEC provides a good example of the potential for cooperative development and promotion of tourism in Africa under the auspices of an external organization. In the case of the EEC, this potential is being achieved through the Lomé Conventions.[12]

The financial resources in support of the three conventions (each with five years' duration) amount to about 3,500m European Currency Units (ECU) for Lomé I from 1975 to 1980. Lomé II from 1981 to 1985 received about 5,530m ECU, while about 8,500m ECU has been committed to Lomé III which expires in 1990. Tourism has received the least direct commitment and, indeed, Title IV 'Development of Trade and Services' under the ACP-EEC cooperation in Lomé I and II barely mentioned tourism. A major step under Lomé III in articles 95–100 are the specific references to tourism as an integral component of cooperation in the area of trade and services. In spite of the limited financial allocation to direct tourism development, some of the sectoral allocations such as economic infrastructure, transport and communication do have both direct and indirect impact on tourism. The ACP (African, Caribbean, Pacific) states specifically expressed the necessity to include cooperation in the field of tourism during the negotiations for Lomé III. Such cooperation is now designed to integrate tourism fully into the social, cultural and economic life of the citizens of the ACP states.

Obstacles to regional cooperation

It could be concluded from the preceding discussion that cooperative organizations exist with the potential for integrated planning, development and promotion of tourism on a regional basis in sub-Sahara Africa. However, a number of obstacles need to be overcome if regional tourism cooperation is to materialize.

Political instability resulting from frequent military intervention has stifled tourism development.[13] Subsequent border closures, militarization of air and seaports, dawn-to-dusk curfews, and maltreatment of foreign visitors are serious impediments to regional cooperative programmes. Protracted liberation wars also contributed to the problem.[14]

While political, economic and social legacies from the colonial era have contributed to the diversity of the continent, they are also the source of some of the problems limiting regional cooperation. The issue is more pronounced in West Africa where France and the UK pursued different, and sometimes opposite policies (e.g. direct versus indirect rule, and cultural assimilation versus limited assimilation).[15] In addition to the English and French groupings, there are three other countries that do not belong to either but stand in a more or less isolated position. Liberia has been an independent nation since its foundation in the nineteenth century. Guinea, an ex-French colony, refused to join the French Commonwealth after its independence. Guinea Bissau is the only mainland former Portuguese colony in West Africa.

A model for Africa

The Caribbean Tourism Association (CTA) which is the oldest Caribbean regional tourism organization provides a good example of the types of cooperative activities and benefits that could be realized in Africa through private and public sector interaction. Founded in 1951, the CTA evolved from the Caribbean Commission which was established by President Roosevelt and Prime Minister Churchill toward the end of the Second World War. At the outset, the CTA was envisaged as a forum in which the public and private sectors would jointly plan and work toward the advancement of the regional tourism industry. There are more than 400 allied members consisting of private-sector entities representing diverse tourism services such as hotels and guest-houses, airlines, cruise lines, tour operators, travel agents, local merchants, yacht charters, taxi and ground operators, restaurants, local attractions and operators of entertainment facilities. Presently, there are twenty-six Caribbean government members. The CTA has brought together former colonies of France (e.g. Haiti), Britain (e.g. Barbados), and Spain (e.g. Dominican Republic). Indeed, some CTA member countries are still colonies or territories of the Netherlands, USA, Britain and France. This fact points to the possibility for regional cooperation in Africa regardless of historical, cultural, political and colonial experiences. In fact, these differences should be assets, rather than liabilities, because they enhance the diversity of Africa's tourism product.

Perhaps the CTA's most important functions are those which focus on tourism marketing, particularly in North America (Canada and the USA), the main markets for Caribbean tourism.[16] Three areas of tourism marketing (publications for travel agents and tour operators, establishment of regional chapters abroad, and regularly organized travel trade expositions) are just a few examples of the host of marketing opportunities offered by a strong regional tourism association.

The CTA also works in close cooperation with the Caribbean Tourism Research and Development Centre and the Caribbean Hotel Association. The activities of the CTA and its relationships with the CTRC and CHA provide a good model for regional tourism cooperation in Africa under the auspices of the African Tourism Association.

Summary

This article has shown that opportunities and broad frameworks exist for cooperation in the field of tourism in each region of sub-Sahara Africa.

Several regional programmes provide both direct and indirect benefits to tourism. In this respect, Africa is no different from other regions such as North America, Latin America, Western Europe, Eastern Europe, the Middle East, Asia or the Pacific. The difference lies in the limited tourism-specific cooperative regional programmes in Africa. This article has also shown that a number of obstacles have to be removed as a prerequisite for successful regional cooperation in Africa.

The examination of the CTA's activities points to the need for a strong Africa Travel Association composed of both private and public sector membership with an organized and effective presence in the market regions of Africa's tourism. Similar to the CTA's activities in the Caribbean, the Pacific Asia Travel Association (PATA) has made significant contributions to the regional development and marketing of the tourism industry in the Pacific. Hence, PATA as well as the CTA provide models for tourism-specific cooperation in Africa.

A strong African Travel or Tourism Association should play a major role in solving the problems impeding tourism development in Africa.

References

1 Cleverdon, R., *The Economic and Social Impact of International Tourism on Developing Countries*, The Economist Intelligence Unit, London, Special Report No. 60, 1979, pp. 121–5.
2 Government of Zambia National Tourist Bureau, *Zambia Tourism Marketing Plan*, Lusaka, Zambia, 1979.
3 Hoff and Overgaard Planning Consultants, *Tourism in Ghana – Development Guide, 1975–1990*, Copenhagen: The Danish International Development Agency, 1974.
4 Renninger, J. P. *Multinational Cooperation in West Africa*, Oxford: Pergamon Press, 1979.
5 Nyaruwata, S., 'European market for African destinations', *Tourism Management*, vol. 7, no. 1, March 1986, pp. 56–60.
6 World Tourism Organization (WTO), 'Movement of persons from the industrialized to the developing countries', *World Travel*, May/June 1985, pp. 49–52.
7 Delupes, I. D., *The East African Economic Community and Common Market*, London: Longman, 1969.
8 *The Europa Yearbook 1987: A World Survey*, vol. 1, London: Europa Publications, 1987, p. 190.
9 *Ibid*, p. 192.
10 Lehman, A. C., 'Tourists, black markets and regional development in West Africa', *Annals of Tourism Research*, vol. 7, no. 1, 1980, pp. 102–19.
11 SADCC Secretariat, *Lusaka Declaration*, 1981.

12 Lee, G. P., 'Tourism as a factor in development cooperation', *Tourism Management*, vol. 8, no. 1, March 1987, pp. 2–19.
13 Teye, V., 'Impact of military coups d'état on tourism development in Africa: The Case of Ghana', *Annals of Tourism Research*, vol. 13, no. 4, 1986, pp. 589–607.
14 Teye, V., 'Liberation wars and tourism development in Africa: The case of Zambia', *Annals of Tourism Research*, vol. 13, no. 4, 1986, pp. 589–607.
15 Crowder, M., *Colonial West Africa*, London: Frank Cass, 1978.
16 Caribbean Tourism Association, *Caribbean Tourism Association – History, Development, Membership Services*, CTA, New York (undated).

Further reading

Further reading on Third World issues in *Tourism Management* 1980–9

Chib, S. N., 'Financing tourism development: a recipient's view', vol. 1, no. 4, December 1980, pp. 231–7.

Dernoi, L. A., 'Alternative tourism – towards a new style in North–South relations', vol. 2, no. 4, December 1981, pp. 253–64.

Heraty, M. J., 'Tourism transport – implications for developing countries', vol. 10, no. 4, December 1989, pp. 288–92.

Holder, J., 'Tourism and the future of Caribbean handicraft', vol. 10, no. 4, December 1989, pp. 310–14.

Jenkins, C. L., 'Education for tourism policy makers in developing countries', vol. 1, no. 4, December 1980, pp. 238–42.

Jenkins, C. L., 'The use of investment incentives for tourism projects in developing countries', vol. 3, no. 2, June 1982, pp. 91–7.

Lee, G. P., 'Future of national and regional tourism in developing countries', vol. 8, no. 2, June 1987, pp. 86–8.

Lee, G. P., 'Tourism as a factor in development cooperation', vol. 8, no. 1, March 1987, pp. 2–19.

Theuns, H. L. and Rasheed, A., 'Alternative approaches to tertiary tourism education with special reference to developing countries', vol. 4, no. 1, March 1983, pp. 42–51.

Winpenny, J. T., 'Issues in the identification and appraisal of tourism projects in developing countries', vol. 3, no. 4, December 1982, pp. 218–22.

Part Ten

Limits and Threats to Tourism

As this book went to print, tourism appeared set for further growth worldwide. Prospects of expanding markets and product diversification, development of new facilities and services, as well as improved marketing, were among the reasons for many growth scenarios. However, from the 1970s onwards unrestricted growth came to be increasingly questioned and the well-being of tourists and the travel industry threatened. The three articles selected for this part of the book deal with major challenges to tourism growth and development.

In 'Tourism carrying capacity' A. M. O'Reilly of the University of the West Indies, Bahamas, examines the concept and problems of measurement, and stresses the need for carrying capacity to form an integral element in tourism planning and development.

In 'Towards new tourism policies' Jost Krippendorf of the University of Bern in Switzerland, argues that unrestricted tourism growth could lead to positive economic impacts of tourism being outweighed by significant negative social and environmental effects and calls for a fundamental change in our conception of tourism and recreation.

In 'Terrorism and tourism as logical companions' Linda Richter of Kansas State University and William Waugh of Georgia State University, USA, assess the impact of terrorism on tourism and suggest how the industry and policymakers should proceed to reduce the vulnerability of tourists and the travel industry.

Further articles on limits and threats to tourism published in *Tourism Management* from 1980–9 are listed on page 327.

28 Tourism carrying capacity

A. M. O'Reilly

The word 'capacity' in its true sense suggests the ability to contain or accommodate, or the amount that can be contained in a certain space or area. Indeed, tourism capacity can be simplistically defined as the maximum number of tourists that can be contained in a certain destination area. However, there are two schools of thought concerned with the nature and interpretation of tourism capacity. These concepts go much further than the simplistic definition given above.

First, tourism capacity is envisaged as the capacity of the destination area to absorb tourism before negative impacts of tourism are felt by the host country. In other words, the capacity is dictated by how many tourists are wanted rather than by how many tourists can be attracted. Here more attention is paid to the host country and population than the tourist.

The second school of thought proposes that tourism capacity be considered as the levels beyond which tourist flows will decline because certain capacities as perceived by the tourists themselves have been exceeded, and therefore the destination area ceases to satisfy and attract them and hence they will seek alternative destinations. This has been argued by Plog in his *Psychographic Positions of Destinations*, where he divided travellers into 'psychocentrics' (the non-adventuresome) and 'allocentrics' (adventuresome and curious).[1] As a destination becomes more commercialized it loses the charm and authentic qualities, which attracted the 'allocentrics' and forces them to seek other destinations. The destination loses its true appeal, becomes more mundane, and appeals to travellers at the other end of the spectrum or those in the midcentric range.

In tourism capacity, an even balance has to be maintained, both in the physical environment and the quality of the experience of the host country to the visitor. There has to be as little disruption as possible in these two areas, and this balance hinges on the maximum number of people who can use a site, whether it be a beach, resort, or town, without negative changes being created in the environment or in the product itself. This balance relies on the carrying capacity, which as Mathieson and Wall say 'is the maximum number of people who can use a site without an unacceptable alteration in physical environment and without an unacceptable decline in the quality of experience gained by visitors.'[2]

Carrying capacity concept

The above definition only takes into consideration the physical impact of tourism on a destination, both from the environmental and experiential points of view. However, there are also economic and social qualities which may be measured. In fact, in certain destinations with fragile economies and cultures which can easily be disrupted by an overinsurgence of visitors, the overcapacity created can have great consequences not only on the physical and environmental aspects but also on the social, cultural and economic subsystems of the destinations. Carrying capacities exist for all the above subsystems, as they can all be considered to be interrelated.

> Thus the notion of economic carrying capacity – the ability to absorb tourist functions without squeezing out desirable local activities can be developed. The wear and tear of historical buildings and the contamination of beaches by untreated sewage are examples of physical carrying capacity being exceeded. It is well known that host people's levels of tolerance for the presence and behaviour of tourists has been surpassed in some locations and thus the social carrying capacity has been overreached.[3]

This suggests what can or may have indeed happened, when there is no proper planning and control of capacity.

Indeed, these problems do exist, especially in developing countries that have, in most cases, to depend on the tourist industry for economic survival. In the Commonwealth Caribbean islands, which today receive mass tourism in abundance, there has been little or no research or control as to certain areas of physical carrying capacity, namely resort developments. In some territories this has caused overcapacity in certain coastal areas resulting in physical and environmental abuse not only of the land but also of the sea, where, e.g. in the 1970s faecal bacterial counts have been high in some instances.[4] This of course was caused not only by, e.g. overcapacity on the west and south coasts of Barbados, but also by poor planning concerning waste disposal there and elsewhere in the Region.

Before regions chosen for tourism expansion are developed, they must be checked for their capacity to absorb tourist and new facilities and activities. Capacity levels are influenced by two major groups of factors:

- the characteristics of the tourists;
- the characteristics of the destination area and its population.[5]

The first group includes all the characteristics of the foreigner coming into that society, namely their socioeconomic characteristics – age, sex, income, availability of spending money; their motivations, attitudes and expectations; their racial and ethnic backgrounds and behaviour patterns. Not only are the tourists' character and personal traits important, but the level of use of the facility, the visitor density, lengths of stay, types of tourist activity and levels of tourist satisfaction are equally important 'because they all influence the magnitude, frequency and kind of interaction with the physical attributes of the destination and its people.'[6]

The second group can be summarized under the following headings:

- natural environmental features and processes;
- economic structure and economic development;
- social structure and organization;
- political organization; and
- level of tourist development.[7]

Here we see the need to take into account the interrelationships of all these factors for the proper development of the product – including all fundamental aspects of the country from the physical, economic, social and political points of view.

A tourist development may be economically feasible and desirable, but socially and environmentally damaging. Here the carrying capacity levels differ between the three subsystems and also vary among the components which contribute to any one of the subsystems. Examples of this can be if a development creates jobs and income for residents, but family and social life is disrupted and affected because of long working hours or split shifts. Or, as in the case of Barbados mentioned above, hotel developments creating pollution because of poor waste disposal made enough money to have these discrepancies corrected.

Impact interrelation – a synopsis

Therefore, we can see that 'the economic, physical, and social impacts of tourism are as a result of the interactions between the tourists and the destination area and its population.' Each segment or subsystem has a carrying capacity and 'the magnitude and direction of tourism impact is determined by the tolerance limits of each.'[8]

Physical carrying capacity, as explained before, can be defined as the limit of a beach or historical building or site beyond which wear and tear will start taking place or environmental problems will arise. Some examples are the pollution of beaches, the almost collapse of the Leaning

Tower of Pisa – the foundations of which have had to be strengthened – the wear and tear of the stones at Stonehenge due to the effect of thousands of feet and hands, trampling and touching the stones – this has been solved, at least temporarily, by the erection of fencing to prevent human contact, and thus the historic site is preserved. It is, however, ironic to see that control and management of tourism impacts have only occurred when the particular entity is threatened with deterioration and/or destruction, or when crises have arisen, and have often only occurred when carrying capacities have been exceeded. Therefore, it would seem that in most cases there is no forward planning, and only when crises arise are controls introduced.

Coupled with physical carrying capacity is the perceptual or psychological capacity which suggests the lowest degree of enjoyment tourists or users of the product are prepared to accept before they start seeking alternative sites or destinations. In other words this is the behavioural component reflecting the quality of a recreational experience, as opposed to the biophysical component reflecting the quality and the maximum capacity of the environment.

Social carrying capacity can be defined objectively from the tourists' point of view as the level of tolerance of the host population for the presence and behaviour of tourists in the destination area; or subjectively as the degree of crowding users (tourists) are prepared to accept by others (other tourists).

Economic carrying capacity, as we have seen before, can be described as the ability to absorb tourist functions without squeezing out desirable local activities.

However, because these impacts differ in degree and direction for every subsystem of the destination, carrying capacities will also differ and probably conflict.

Measurement of carrying capacity

The concepts of carrying capacity are now generally accepted, 'but difficulties in measuring and quantifying the thresholds have restricted the use of carrying capacity as a planning tool.'[9] Some factors causing this restriction are:

● that the acceptable levels of crowding can differ from one society to another;

● that certain types of developments necessitate higher densities than others, even if the sizes of the developments are the same, e.g. beaches for relaxation vis-à-vis tourism; and

● physical and environmental carrying capacities can be affected by management techniques.

However, certain projects have employed useful methodological studies, e.g. Brittas Bay in Ireland where actual densities and distributions were measured and reproduced from aerial photographs taken on a busy Sunday afternoon.[10] This was supplemented by a questionnaire survey distributed to the beach users. A comparison of the two surveys was made and it was seen that many users would accept a density of 1000 persons per hectare or 10m² per person without considering a beach overcrowded. This system was also used in France in planning the scale of new beach resorts in Languedoc–Roussillon.[11] Andronicou in his Cyprus plan has put forward certain density ratios which have been taken into account, provided that there is a balanced disbursement of accommodation.[12] Factors considered were:

● the number of tourist arrivals per 100 local people in each region;
● the number of tourist nights per 100 local people in each region;
●. the number of tourists per square mile in each region; and
● the capacity of the seashore in each region.

However, it could be argued here that Cyprus was aiming for the middle and upper market share, and not the mass tourism market which obviously makes capacity difficult to quantify, although peak volume usually determines capacity.

Carrying capacity is dependent on the goals that are specified for every development. Therefore a park used for a 'nature reserve' should have a lower density than the same park employed as an amusement park; thus the desired density is related to the use to which the development is put, and provided visitors have a good time, capacity may not be exceeded.

In the development of new projects, cost-benefit analyses should be adopted to see at what level the project will be financially viable. Even so most theme parks operate at a loss – the basic benefit is one of social benefit to the region. However, correct levels of carrying capacity must be adopted to preserve the economic, physical, ecological, social and cultural balance within the society.

Conclusion

In this article I have looked at the subject of carrying capacity in tourism, its different components, how they interplay and difficulty in measuring this concept. The term carrying capacity 'applies not only to the maximum number of tourists or tourist accommodations which seem desirable at a given time, but also to the maximum rates of growth above which the growth process itself would be unduly disruptive.'[13] As far as measurement is concerned, although there have been certain methodological studies carried out on beach capacity, capacities on the whole have been difficult to measure, although a cost-benefit analysis approach could be used to determine feasibility or infeasibility of the proposed development.

Also, capacity cannot be used as an absolute limit but as a means to identify critical thresholds which need attention and by so doing removing obstacles where possible or applying controls. However, even if capacity cannot be measured absolutely, statistical methods could be set up by planners to examine relative changes year-on-year. Finally, capacity should also be considered as part of a systematic strategy plan for the development of tourism.

References

1   Plog, S. C., 'Psychographic Positions of Destinations', *The Tourist Business*, New York: CBI Publishing, 1974.
2   Mathieson A., and Wall, G., *Tourism: Economic, Physical and Social Impacts*, Longman, 1982, p. 21.
3   *Ibid.*
4   Gooding, E., *Effects of Tourism upon the Environment*, paper presented at Regional Seminar on Caribbean Tourism, Nassau, November 1975.
5   *Op. cit.*, reference 2, p. 22.
6   *Op. cit.*, reference 2, p. 22.
7   *Op. cit.*, reference 2, pp. 22–3.
8   *Op. cit.*, reference 2, p. 34.
9   Barkham, J. P., 'Recreational Carrying Capacity: a Problem of Perception', *Area*, vol. 5, part 3, 1973, pp. 218–22.
10 An Foras Forbatha, *Brittas Bay: a Planning and Conservation Study*, An Foras Forbatha, 1973.
11 Pearce, D., *Tourist Development*, Longman, 1983, p. 36.
12 Andronicou, A., 'Case studies – selecting and planning for tourists – case of Cyprus', *International Journal of Tourism Management*, 1983.
13 de Kadt, E., *Tourism, Passport to Development*, Oxford University Press for World Bank and UNESCO, 1979, p. 17.

29 Towards new tourism policies

Jost Krippendorf

There is really nothing like walking in the country. It's just a pity that it takes so long to reach the place where I like to walk, because there is so much traffic on the main road. I have to travel by car for an hour each way, to go for an hour's walk there. But I accept this, because I find walking so relaxing and I get so agitated after the journey there in the terrible traffic that I need the relaxation of a walk to strengthen me for the journey home.

The extraordinary density of the traffic on this road is caused by the fact that so many people are going to the same spot for a walk. The road is sometimes completely blocked, so there are now plans to widen it, so that everyone will be able to reach the beautiful places more quickly. And all the more people will be able to experience the pleasure of being there, which is a good thing. It's a pity that more parking space has to be created for the increasing number of cars, and this land has to be taken from the countryside. If there were to be room for everyone's car who wanted to walk there, the whole area would have to be turned into a car park. And perhaps that would be a good idea, because then less people would want to go there, and the problem would solve itself.

Extract from *By Car for a Walk* by Klaus Mampell

Importance for tourism of environment and landscape

Taking the needs and motives of tourists as my starting point, I refer to two propositions which may be regarded as having been established by empirical observation:

1 The scenic attractions of the holiday destination stand at the central focus of tourist needs and are in fact the most important tourist motivation. The structure, beauty and mood of the landscape – its whole 'experience value' – are absolutely crucial. Travel companies often overestimate themselves. As far as the tourist is concerned they are

merely the means to an end: he makes use of the services they offer so that he is better able to 'consume' the landscape and countryside.

2   The needs of the tourist are characterized by the oft-quoted escapism – the flight from the boredom of everyday life, the need for a change of environment, the search for something different, the concept of the holiday as a 'contrast-experience'.

If these observations are accurate, these two powerful constants will be even more decisive than hitherto in determining future tourism motivations. The landscape is the real raw material of tourism. It is the reason for the existence of tourism as well as its economic driving force. From the tourist's point of view the attraction of rural areas lies in the dissimilarity and contrast which they offer to his everyday world. So long as this contrast remains, the countryside will continue to attract him.

However, the mass phenomena of modern tourism have initiated the paradoxical process 'Tourism destroys tourism'. The landscape loses its tourist value through its use, or rather overuse, by the tourist. Tourism has certainly contributed to mass awareness of the importance and difficulties of nature conservation, but only in the sense of therapeutic reparation. If there were no tourism, more cultural and natural scenery would be preserved. But on the other hand more areas would become spoiled and unproductive, quite apart from the increasing depopulation of such areas (rural exodus). In those areas where tourism supplies the only possibility for economic development, it is the financial power of tourism which keeps the land productive.

Development of tourism as a burden on environment and society

The tourist industry

One only needs to look at the travel statistics to understand why tourism has become the so-called gold mine of the twentieth century and why it has become an industry in itself – the tourist industry. It appeared as the dynamic push-factor of encumbering circumstances and also as a setback to more considerate developments, i.e. those developments more appro- .priate to the scenery and more in tune with the needs of both tourists and indigenous populations. 'One industry has taken control of our leisure. It not only offers fulfilment but also creates the wishes and desires which belong with it. It creates demand for which it already holds a supply which is constantly increasing.' (R. Traitler) 'The holiday, as a contrast-experience to the industrial environment, has become an industry in itself.' (H. Hoffman)

Tourism is the industry of the holiday companies, travel agents, transport firms, building companies, caravan manufacturers, cable railway operators, ski manufacturers, souvenir sellers, the car industry, banks, insurance companies ... an industry with its own laws, its own legitimacy. Each struggles for more turnover, for a greater share of the market. Each will sacrifice everything and operate with the most stringent marketing methods to reach its target. The countryside – especially the most popular tourist areas – offers itself to this industry as a promising playground, promising success.

In the year 2000, according to Hermann Kahn and others, the leisure industry will be the world's largest. There will always be more and more demand. Here are some quotations from the tourist industry itself: 'There will only be the Alps once'; 'Tourism is business, not charity'; 'To hell with paradise.'

All this has led to a boom in the spawning of tourism infrastructures in many rural areas, in particular the most attractive places, the so-called tourist honeypots. Every year we get countless new hotels, restaurants, apartment blocks, holiday chalets, bungalows and holiday homes, holiday villages, new transport facilities, airfields, roads, car parks, playgrounds and sportsgrounds, ski-slopes, footpaths, camping and caravan sites. They take our environment for their own use and thereby change its character.

Let us again specify the importance of the environment for the concept of tourism. In any other branch of the economy – as Werner Kämpfen once succinctly pointed out – capital can be lost and multiplied again. However, once the basic raw material of tourism – the land itself – is lost, it can never be reclaimed. It is unfortunately all too easy to conclude that the tourist industry does not and will not recognize what is in fact the most important of its tasks, namely the preservation of the environment.

Whether the tourist has visited just a few holiday resorts or has travelled the world over, he will not be able to escape this depressing conclusion: development and exploitation have triumphed over the care and protection of the environment almost everywhere, and without struggle. And this pressure on the environment is increasing exponentially ....

The tourist explosion

What are the prospects for the future development of tourism, and what consequences should we expect? All experts agree that in the German Federal Republic as in all other industrialized nations the average income per person in real terms will rise, and with it the disposable portion of income will grow. The urban population will increase, car ownership will increase greatly, and working hours will be reduced, although these trends will slow down somewhat in comparison with previous years. The underlying dynamics will, however, be marked and will show exponential effects. One would therefore be justified – all too justified perhaps – in forecasting a further explosion in holiday traffic like the one which we have already seen. Such development is also being encouraged by other factors:

- the expansion in construction of motorways and trunk roads, bringing town and country still closer together;
- the expansion of existing resorts – which many feel desirable – and the discovery of new holiday destinations for the frustrated city-dweller;
- the professional marketing men who are creating the tourist demand – they operate at all levels, from state tourist offices and powerful monopolies to the enterprising small firm. Peter Drucker once said 'Markets are not made by God, nature or economic factors, but by businessmen.'

Probable consequences of unrestricted growth

The growing tourist avalanche of the future will, therefore, for the most part pour into areas already developed for tourism and often already at the limit of their capacity, although some tourists will go into still undeveloped regions. What will be the consequences for the countless places which are already displaying symptoms of a serious environmental disease; for places which suffer from bottlenecks into which they have manoeuvred themselves, and which are desperately struggling to make up deficits in all sectors of their infrastructure; and for places which are fighting for fresh air, and fighting against the pollution of their waters and destruction of their skyline by new buildings, struggling even to provide enough water for their guests? They build car parks, silos and roads, in an attempt to master the seemingly unstoppable swelling mass of cars.

At a recent conference of Swiss tourism experts I asked: 'Can we still fulfil everywhere tourists' expectations of unspoilt countryside, of pleasant lively and small-scale places, which don't remind them of the city? Are the (Swiss) tourist regions really still holiday areas? How can we explain that even in our holiday regions we are building more and more new and faster roads, removing every obstacle from the path of the apparently sacrosanct private car, and literally encouraging the tourist avalanche with all its consequences? Why are we doing so little to prevent the urbanization of our holiday resorts by putting up buildings whose structure and style remind us so much of what is to be seen in our cities? Haven't we reached the limits of the capacity of our countryside, which our guests also feel, or even overstepped this? And who can guarantee that our resorts will really switch over to a zero-growth policy when they have reached an optimal state of expansion? Is it not the case that we do not react until we can see with our own eyes and touch with our own hands the consequences of our actions – when, in fact, it is then too late?'

But who is worried about such prospects, who is interested? So long as the short-sighted tourism companies and policymakers can reckon with increasing growth rates, that is all they are interested in. Those who are only concerned with the short term, as most of them are, feel that the consequences of growth are insignificant.

Anybody who thinks about the longer term, however, even with the most primitive concepts, does not need much imagination to picture what will happen to the holiday regions and the people who live there if the circumstances surrounding tourism do not change.

A turning point in tourism policy?

Can we find indications of a new tourism policy which will take into account the phenomena and perspectives already illustrated? A policy which is not only an emergency policy but one which, as a causative therapy, also treads new paths?

All over the world discussion has begun about the costs and benefits of tourism to the economy, the environment and society, whereas before the talk was only of benefits and the economy.

Most importantly, these discussions are now being held in many tourist resorts, and a change of attitude towards tourism is becoming noticeable in many areas. I should like to distinguish three approaches.

Phase 1   The economic approach

At the beginning of tourism development, and surprisingly right up to this current age of modern mass tourism (that is until about twenty years ago) all the participants – the tourists themselves, the people who received the tourists, and the travel companies – seemed fairly unconcerned about the tourism concept itself. In so far as the effects of tourism were analysed at all in the holiday countries, these investigations were limited to economic aspects.

Although critical voices have multiplied, the overwhelming majority is of the opinion that tourism can make a positive contribution to the economic development of a region. The most important economic effects are:

● foreign currency effect;
● income effect;
● employment effect; and
● regional equalization effect.

Opinions regarding these effects are, as I have said, very diverse. The most important socioeconomic risks of tourism are its seasonality, its relative susceptibility to crisis, and the social inferiority of tourism occupations. In general the positive economic effects should outweigh the negative ones.

Phase 2   The environmental approach

Just as the effect of tourism became tangible and the far-reaching changes became universally recognizable a few years ago, people began to try to come to terms with the effects of tourism on the environment.

Tourism growth tends to seize the countryside, its own reason for existing (hence the notion of the destruction of tourism by tourism itself). It damages the environment of the native inhabitants and thus reduces their quality of life. Demands are increasingly heard for an integrated cost-benefit approach to tourism, which emphasizes all the economic, social and environmental costs (disadvantages) and benefits (advantages).

Phase 3   Sociocultural approach

The discussion of the sociocultural effects of tourism, in particular the social effects on the population which receives tourists, has only recently found its way into practical tourism policymaking. The basic effects must overwhelmingly be classified as negative:

● The effect of increasing understanding between nations is, when one looks closely, almost non-existent, and it is possible that tourism in fact has just the opposite effect.

● Tourists demonstrate behaviour and attitudes which can evoke mistrust, resignation and aggressive dissatisfaction in the native population.
● The effect on native customs is often that of acculturation, cultural levelling and adaptation under the influence of commercialization.
● Tourism planning is usually in the hands of outside promoters – the local population are regarded merely as landowners or as a reserve of labour, not as people entitled to participate in decision-making.

Balance of advantages and disadvantages

The overwhelmingly negative effects of tourism on society and the environment are the price paid for the economic benefits derived. However, people are beginning to ask how high this price must be, and are beginning to reflect on the more or less limitless development of tourism. There is a real danger that indiscriminate tourism development could cause the fundamentally positive economic effects to be outweighed by the disadvantageous social and ecological implications, and could even change the economic advantages into disadvantages. A growing consciousness and sensitivity to these negative effects is becoming noticeable in the tourist areas.

Consequences of the critical approach to tourism

What are the consequences to be expected of this more differentiated and critical approach to tourism? The basic tendencies in brief are as follows.

1 Tourism regions are tending to shake off outside influence, to take matters into their own hands, to determine developments themselves and to participate in them. This means that they will increasingly regard their region first and foremost as the home of its native population. Lower priority is given to the role of providing recreation for others. Tourism is losing some of its importance.
2 Efforts are being made to win back the decision-making power in essential matters rather than leaving it to outside people, companies and institutions which are mostly in the cities of the industrialized nations (transfer back of decision-making processes). The will of the local population to participate will not only manifest itself in the tourist areas, but also find its way back to the countries of origin of the tourists (marketing channels).

Table 29.1   Hard versus soft tourism

Hard tourism	Soft tourism
A General concepts	
Inconsiderate	Considerate
Offensive	Defensive
Aggressive	Cautious
Fast/impetuous	Slow/thoughtful
Long strides	Short steps
Unchecked	Controlled
Unregulated	Regulated
Maximal	Optimal
Excessive	Moderate
Short term	Long term
Particular interest	General interest
Outside control	Self-determination
Least resistance	Greatest resistance
Sector-based	Entirety-based
Price-conscious	Value-conscious
Quantitative	Qualitative
Growth	Development
B Tourism development strategies	
1 Development without planning	Planning before development
2 Project-thinking	Concept-thinking
3 Each community plans for itself	Centralized planning for larger areas
4 Indiscriminate development	Concentrate development on particular areas
5 Haphazard and scattered building	Conserve land, build in concentration, keep open spaces
6 Exploit especially valuable landscapes particularly intensively	Conserve especially valuable landscapes (reserves)
7 Create new building-stock Build new bedspaces	Improve use of existing building-stock Exploit existing bedspaces
8 Build for indefinite demand	Fix limits on expansion
9 Develop tourism in all areas	Develop tourism only in suitable areas and where local population available
10 Tourism development left to outside concerns	Opportunity for decision-making and participation by local population
11 Utilize all available labour (also outsiders)	Development planned according to indigenous labour potential
12 Consider only economic advantages	Weigh up all economic, ecological and social advantages and disadvantages (costs-benefits)
13 Regard farming population only as landowners and tourist labour	Preserve and encourage agriculture

Table 29.1 *(continued)*

Hard tourism	Soft tourism
14 Leave social costs to be paid by society	Leave costs to be paid by perpetrators
15 Favour private transport	Encourage transport
16 Provide facilities for maximum demand	Provide facilities for average demand
17 Remove natural obstacles	Preserve natural obstacles
18 Urban architecture	Local architecture (building design and materials)
19 General automation of tourist resorts	Selective technical development, encouragement of non-technical tourism forms

C Policy frameworks

Retain concentration of holiday departures	Stagger holidays
Admit tourism personnel without certificate of ability	Improve education of those responsible in tourism
Spread 'stereotype' holidays on offer	Prepare travellers
Hard selling	'Heart selling'
Regard tourism as economic panacea	Seek new options within, and alternatives to tourism

Hard travel	Soft travel

D Tourist attitudes (Source: R. Jungk[1])

Mass tourism	Travel alone, with friends or family
Little time	Plenty of time
Rapid means of transport	Appropriate (or even slow) means of transport
Fixed itinerary	Spontaneous decisions
Outside-inspired	Self-inspired
Imported lifestyle	Native lifestyle
'Sights'	Experiences
Comfortable and passive	Strenuous and active
Little or no intellectual preparation	Previous research on destination country
Unable to speak the language	Learning to speak the language
Feeling of superiority	Willingness to learn
Shopping	Bringing presents
Souvenirs	Memories, diaries, new perspectives
Snaps and postcards	Photography, drawing, painting
Curiosity	Tact
Loud	Quiet

3   The readiness to replan overambitious targets and to submit to limitations will increase, to give protection against the unwanted effects of tourism. New policies of land and environmental use will develop in the tourism regions, with consideration of limits to capacity. People will increasingly try to define the economic, environmental and social-psychological limits to the capacity of a region, and adopt appropriate political measures to secure development within this framework.

This is all evidence of the development in many cases of a new 'differentiating' tourism policy. However, in other areas, the ruthless changing of countryside into tourist area, and of farmers into tourist-servants goes on in the same old, familiar way, and still as yet unpunished by market forces. The same mistakes are made again and again out of sheer ignorance or against people's better judgement. There is clearly little willingness to learn from the countless frightening examples to be found all over the world, partly because such policies are still relatively successful in the marketplace, and partly because until now there have been no spectacular collapses, which have brought about any international awareness.

A new tourism policy

All the changes described above make a new conception of tourism policy absolutely necessary. The first priority of a new human and environmentally-orientated tourism policy would read something like this:

> Guaranteed optimal satisfaction of the different kinds of tourism demand for people of all classes within the framework of efficient tourist facilities and in an unspoilt environment, consideration being given to the interests of the local population.[2]

This aim implies that new tourism policies will no longer concentrate on economic and technical necessities alone, but will emphasize the demand for an unspoiled environment and consideration of the needs of the people affected, i.e. the tourists and the local population. I would call a kind of tourism which fulfils these demands 'soft tourism', and that which obeys purely economic and technical forces, 'hard tourism'. I have tried to restructure the propositions which I put forward in my book *Die Landschaftsfresser* in Table 29.1.

As we have seen, there are many indications of changes of direction in tourism policies. The most important thing is to speed up the process, and encourage the development of soft tourism as we have described it. We must find new horizons within the available time and in the necessary areas. But for this we do not need yet more scientific reports e.g. on capacity problems – but politicians and people at all levels who possess the courage to make subjective and qualitative observations, and who have the courage to support measures which are unpopular, since they will be perceived as being against the short-term interests of many people.

If we really want to change something we will not get anywhere with anaemic theories and recommendations. It is a question of exposing all our insights, of simplifying them and making them comprehensible. We must encourage action, sometimes even opposition and disobedience, and courage itself. A change of attitude among politicians will only take place under pressure from the public, the electorate. We are therefore looking for rebellious tourists and rebellious natives!

Summary

A 'careful' tourism policy has become necessary for the following reasons; (a) the special vulnerability of the rural environment; (b) the irreversibility of certain processes; (c) the special importance of the environment as the raw material, the basis of tourism and its economic driving force; (d) the lack of evidence and the uncertainty we experience (measurement of damage to environment, see-saw effects, when they appear, etc.); (e) the sensibilities of the local population and its claims to independence.

Therefore, tourism policy should concentrate more on the understanding that ecology should be placed before economy in tourism, not least for the sake of the economy itself and all who participate in it.

References

1   Jungk, R., *GED Magazin*, 10 October 1980, pp. 154 *et seq.*
2   Krippendorf, J., *Die Landschaftsfresser, Tourismus und Erholungslandschaft – Verderben oder Segen?*, Bern, 1975, p. 86, and Beratende Kommission für Fremdenverkehr des Bundesrates, *Das Schweizerische Tourismuskonzept*, Bern, 1979, p. 58.

Acknowledgement

This chapter is a translated and edited version of the paper given to the 24th Tourism Studies Congress at Pirmasens in January 1982. It was translated from the German by Helen Tyrrell.

30 Terrorism and tourism as logical companions

Linda K. Richter and William L. Waugh, Jr

Estimates indicate that 1.8m Americans changed their plans for foreign travel in 1986, following American raids on Libya and terrorist attacks on several European airports. These figures suggest that threats of violence can have a tremendous economic impact on the tourism industry. Western European hotel and resort operators were particularly aware of this fact in 1986. International tourism is the world's largest item of trade, grossing more than twice the amount spent on global armaments and representing a major industry in over 100 nations.[1] Yet a few terrorists can have a decisive and crippling impact on travel patterns and the economies of particular locales.

Terrorism in its international and domestic forms and as practised by revolutionary, sub-revolutionary, vigilante groups and by governments has become a fact of life in the 1980s. Indeed, terroristic violence has become a familiar phenomenon of modern times. That familiarity is largely due to the mass media, rather than to the nature of the violent acts themselves or the numbers of casualties and actual property losses.

What is new about terroristic violence in the post Second World War period is the impact of its message and the distance that that message can be projected. Terrorism is a form of communication, of both the threat or reality of violence and the political message.[2] To some extent the mass media are responsible for that communication. But the high priority given anti-terrorism programmes by political leaders often is disproportionate to the terrorism's effects and, thus, the importance of the events is magnified.

However, there are also other forces at work. The increasing political and economic interdependence in the international community means that acts of violence directed at business firms or government officials or opposition leaders in one nation, can have tremendous impact on people and governments on the other side of the world. Domestic elites also may be adversely affected when foreign business interests are attacked by terrorist groups. That is no less true with attacks on tourists and/or tourism facilities. To the extent that tourism represents a significant economic activity within a nation, terrorists may find such attacks useful and effective as tools for levering resources from or gaining political advantages over incumbent elites.

One can argue that sporadic incidents of terrorism are statistically insignificant. More Americans are killed by lightning or falls in their baths each year than from acts of terrorism.[3] The attention of the media may exaggerate terrorist threats.[4] But that begs the issue. There is a need for the tourism industry and those policymakers who have invested in tourism to acknowledge the unique vulnerability of the industry both to actual terroristic activity and general perceived insecurity. Using the media as a scapegoat helps neither the industry as a whole nor those governments attempting to contain the economic and political damage done by terrorism.

Government efforts to counteract perceived insecurity are expensive and seldom successful. After the TWA hijacking in 1985, the Greek government spent over three million dollars on a 'Come Home to Greece' campaign.[5] Those efforts were negated by the Christmas 1985 bombings in Rome and Vienna airports and reports that followed in the spring concerning the lax security at Athens airport.

Relationship between terrorism and tourism

There is a logical connection between terrorism and tourism, indeed, travel has been associated with increased vulnerability to all types of crime from biblical days. Being a traveller implies being away from one's familiar environs and contacts, which also necessitates greater expense so tourists are likely to carry more money and spend it more awkwardly than they would at home. The fact that 'hotel belts' and tourist attractions concentrate travellers in particular locations also points tourists out as easy targets for criminals and terrorists.

But, throughout most of history, tourists were individual victims of crime, not symbolic targets for major acts of political violence. Warfare between nations was relatively easy to avoid and civil wars were more confined to the principal combatants. The blurring of distinctions between combatants and non-combatants and the boundaries of political conflict may draw tourists into domestic and international conflicts, nonetheless.

Tourism is frequently an early casualty of internecine warfare, revolution, or even prolonged labour disputes. Even if the tourist areas are secure, as was the case in Jamaica in the late 1970s or more recently in Haiti, Lebanon, Northern Ireland, and Sri Lanka, tourism may decline precipitously when political conditions appear unsettled. Tourists simply choose alternative destinations.

Unfortunately, many national leaders and planners either do not understand, or will not accept, the fact that political serenity, not scenic or cultural attractions, constitute the first and central requirement of tourism.

Tourism is an extremely fragile industry in societies with mercurial politics and/or histories of ethnic, socioeconomic, or regional tensions. Governments seduced by the prospect of earning foreign exchange from tourism discover that luxury hotels with imported furnishings do not convert easily to alternative uses or toward meeting basic subsistence needs of local residents.[6]

Sometimes nations which are quite tranquil may find that their own international tourism traffic may be negatively affected by regional political conditions, including terrorism. Indian and Maldive tourism, for example, have suffered from Sri Lankan terrorism. Pakistani tourism is negatively affected by the civil war in Afghanistan and Uganda coups deter East African travel even as Zimbabwe's violence discourages Zambian travel.[7] Even Switzerland, the pre-eminent symbol of domestic tranquillity and political neutrality, has seen tourism drop as a consequence of terrorist attacks in Italy, France, Austria and FR Germany.

Mass tourism itself is becoming a political issue, spawning divisive conflicts among proponents and opponents of tourism development. Terrorism against tourists has moved from the political periphery of the globe to the very centres of power and international travel. Europe and the USA are the current foci with billions of dollars at stake and the mobility of millions threatened.

To understand just how and why international tourists have become so attractive to terrorists, it is important to understand the resource needs of terrorism and the way in which tourism meets those needs.

Tourism and the objectives of terrorism

Tourist facilities are logical targets of terrorist violence because they afford opportunity and relative safety for terrorists to act. The convenience of transportation facilities, particularly international airports for foreign tourists, provides means of escape and channels for transporting weapons. The frequency of terrorist attacks within and against international airport facilities is ample evidence of the attractiveness of such facilities to terrorist organizations.

The large numbers of foreign-speaking and foreign-looking tourists provide cover for international terrorists. The diverse populations and relatively free movement within tourist areas increase the freedom of operation of domestic terrorist groups. The large concentrations of people that are attracted to tourist areas and to tourist activities, such as festivals and cultural events, also provide both cover and a choice of targets. The relatively large financial transactions, particularly in foreign currencies, facilitate transfers of money. And the hesitancy of police to restrict the movement of tourists and other persons within an area militates against strong anti-terrorist operations and effective security arrangements.

There are numerous reasons why tourists and tourist facilities are attractive targets for terrorists. One analysis[8] indicates that terrorist objectives can be categorized as long range or ideological, mid-range or strategic, and short range or tactical. That analysis in essence concludes that terrorists may seek to satisfy tactical objectives in order to sustain their longer-term efforts and to maintain their organizations. The strategic objectives may have more political meaning to the organizations and their members and represent the means of achieving the ideological objectives. The strategic objectives may be the most familiar because they are most frequently expressed as demands.

The ideological objectives, on the other hand, may not be so publicly enunciated. These may be as grandiose as the overthrow of an oppressive regime and the institution of a democratic government, or vice versa, or as limited as the removal of a few government officials or the reform of an unpopular law.

The objectives of terrorist organizations can, in short, be quite diverse. There are patterns in the kinds of objectives that terrorist organizations may have and those patterns generally indicate that tourists and tourism facilities are quite logical and appropriate targets of terroristic violence.

Tactical objectives of terrorist organizations

There are any number of logistical and personnel concerns that may motivate terrorist organizations. In fact, some of the best indicators of impending terrorist activity of a political nature are increased robberies of gun stores, banks, doctors' surgeries, constructions sites, military weapons facilities, and other sources of supplies. The money, guns and ammunition, medical supplies, explosives, and other materials collected are essential ingredients in terrorist campaigns.

Terrorist demands frequently include ransoms. The demands also frequently include requirements that captured terrorists be released. Personnel are usually a scarce resource for terrorist organizations. Prisoner releases are necessary to maintain the strength of an organization, as well as the morale.

Tourist areas are logical targets for terrorists seeking to satisfy tactical needs. In most developing nations, the tourist resorts are located in the most affluent areas. Banks, physicians, and other services in those areas may be the best in the nation. Certainly movement is easier for foreign terrorists who can blend in with other tourists. The tourists themselves would generally be more vulnerable to attack, less wary of suspicious activity and more likely to be carrying large quantities of money and expensive goods.

To the extent that resort areas may include the residences of the nation's socioeconomic and political elites, those areas would be special targets simply because of the greater potential for high gains. The poorer the nation, the more likely criminals and terrorists would find the tourist and other affluent areas attractive targets. While police and military protection may be greater in those areas, there is likely to be more hesitancy about detaining unknown persons or obstructing pedestrian and automobile traffic unless a violent event has already taken place.

Strategic objectives of terrorist organizations

The more political objectives of a terrorist organization are less easily classified. The means used to achieve the ultimate aims of the group may generally be categorized as:

● organizational;
● publicity;
● punishment;
● provocation;
● disruption; and
● instrumental advantage.

Attacks on tourists may be used to achieve all of these objectives, singly or in combination.

The organizational objectives of a terrorist organization may include engendering high levels of *esprit de corps*, ensuring conformity and discipline, maintaining unity of purpose and action, and legitimizing the actions of the group. Terrorist organizations have to be active in order to maintain interest, discipline and morale. Relatively frequent and successful operations are morale-building and capacity-building in the sense of increasing the capabilities of the group's members to carry out successful operations.

In terms of morale-building and legitimizing political objectives of the terrorists, attacks on foreign tourists are less likely to alienate popular support than would attacks on domestic targets. Americans, Israelis, and the British are perhaps the favourite targets of terrorist violence world-wide. Terrorists wish to legitimate their violence for their own vindication, as well as to engender popular support. Ideological justification for the violence often provides that vindication.

The Philippines under martial law rule of President Marcos furnishes one of the best examples of the use of terrorist tactics against the regime by way of attacks on tourists. The President jettisoned a gradual and balanced programme of tourism development in favour of a crash programme, of high-profile hotel construction, including over a dozen ostentatious hotels in Manila alone. The 'Light a Fire' movement was born in a series of arson attacks that destroyed several hotels owned by the Marcos family or their associates – tourist arrivals plummeted.

In the case of terrorism practised by governments against their own citizens or by vigilante groups protecting a status quo, the same organizational needs hold. But, vindication may come with the continuance of policies or dominance of elites. Tourists may reinforce the perception that a particular group is still in control and its actions justified. That has been the charge concerning tourism in South Africa, especially in Sun City.

Attacks on tourist areas also assure media attention and limit the ability of incumbent elites to control the content of the news about the events. Political threats and propaganda messages are conveyed by the tourists themselves and by their home governments via consular facilities. Thus, the publicity objective is achieved even in nations that may effectively control the content of domestic news.

Tourists chosen as targets because of their symbolic value as indirect representatives of hostile or unsympathetic governments, also have symbolic value for other tourists. That was the case in the mid-1970s when Japanese tourists were kidnapped in the southern Philippines by the Moro National Liberation Front, a Muslim secessionist group. The Japanese government sounded the alarm and the hotels emptied.[9] Thus political messages are magnified by the audience.

At the same time, however, the conduit provided by tourists may be used to distort international perceptions. Using agents, provocateurs and/or misinformation, governments and vigilante groups may be able to influence international public opinion in their own favour. Aside from the question of complicity and despite the lack of credibility the attempt to blame the assassination of Philippine opposition leader Aquino on communist insurgents was an example of such an action.

The punishment objective may also be satisfied in the same way as the organizational objective. Attacks on American tourists, for example, may be viewed as a punishment of the US government. Attacks on tourists, too, may be viewed as punishment of the economic and political elites that own and operate tourism facilities. Hotel and restaurant owners, tour guides, transportation operators, and other business persons catering to tourists suffer when tourists do not visit. High levels of violence may threaten the economies of entire nations. The mediating factor here may be the likelihood that high levels of violence or indiscriminate acts may endanger the livelihoods of large numbers of workers, as well as the livelihoods of the managers and owners of facilities. Terrorist campaigns resulting in high levels of unemployment or displacement would likely alienate popular support and be harder for the terrorists to justify.

Terrorists may also seek to provoke a government into overreacting to violent events. Tourists are frequently attracted to resort areas because of the freedom of movement and absence of social and political pressures. Just as tourists are attracted to resorts offering 'vices' and social activities uncommon in their own communities, often aided and abetted by lax police enforcement of laws, they may be repelled by restrictive actions by local authorities.

Anger with terrorists for violent acts can turn into anger with the police or military forces for aggravating an unpleasant situation. That is particularly true when there is a strong perception that police actions were not justified by the violent events. The reaction to media coverage of British army tanks around Heathrow airport following terrorist threats during the spring of 1986 is indicative of this kind of reaction. The presence of the tanks was less controversial than the news coverage. The image conveyed in the media was of a situation requiring a heavy military presence, although many commentators disagreed with that perception.

Terrorists may also seek to disrupt social, political, and economic activity as a means of demonstrating the incapacity of a government to maintain civil order and public safety. The expectation – the hope – is that the disruption will be so complete that the terrorists may be called on to restore order. Loosening chaos may not be effective unless a terrorist organization is strong, but history suggests that small political organizations can assume leadership during turbulent times under the right circumstances. Notwithstanding those lessons of history, disruption can satisfy a number of needs from limiting the ability of police forces to respond to discrediting particular political leaders. Governments have fallen for less reason.

The disruptive potential of attacks on tourist facilities is quite large. The lack of effective emergency management plans in many – if not most – resorts suggests that responses to widespread, frequent, or high-casualty violence will not be adequate to maintain order. Inadequate medical facilities and ineffective administrative agencies in developing nations could compound those difficulties.

Lastly, in terms of the strategic objectives, terrorists may find that tourists are surrogates for other more appropriate targets. Instrumental advantage may be gained by reducing the economic and political strength of their adversaries. Police, military, and governmental powers may be lessened by disruption, propaganda, alienation of support, coercion of enemies, and so on. Tourists may provide camouflage and assistance in direct attacks on government authorities.

Ideological objectives of terrorist organizations

To the extent that the tourist industry in most developed and developing nations is controlled or managed by socioeconomic and political elites, tourists and facilities may be targeted by any group in opposition to those elites. Certainly the most familiar pattern would be communist opposition to capitalist hotel and resort owners. Other patterns of political opposition may be more likely, however.

The tourist industry is often blamed for exploiting and destroying indigenous industries and cultures. The availability of hard currency lures farmers away from their land and crops. The demand for exotic products, including foodstuffs, influences what is produced. The promise of low-skill, service jobs draws rural and small-town residents to the large cities and resorts. The patterns are generally familiar in Third World tourism development. The point is that such development creates problems that may lead to terroristic violence.

In the big picture, in the competition for the minds of men and women in a national struggle, tourists and foreign business travellers are logical and appropriate targets. They normally do represent some value to incumbent elites and they are often unpopular among the residents. As 'foreigners' they can be attacked without necessarily posing a threat to others in the nation. They can also be used as representatives of their home governments, permitting terrorists to attack a foreign government without leaving their own state or by doing so in a more hospitable state.

That conflict may assume a more personal, less indiscriminate cast when a government leader has invested a considerable amount of prestige in stopping the violence. All attacks then become personal affronts to that leader – which is likely to attract terrorist violence rather than dissuade it. Uncompromising positions taken by authoritarian leaders in their own states or self-righteous world leaders, often backfire when they cannot enforce their policies and when terrorists view the policies as challenges to be overcome.

Conclusions

In conclusion, the relationship between terrorism and tourism is important not because the problem is new but because the political and economic ramifications are immense and likely to grow larger. As this article
suggests, effective control over the problem will require more than
trained commando units or increased security. What is needed is:

- an appreciation of the reasons why tourism is especially vulnerable;
- an understanding that risk analysis and emergency management
  procedures must be considered before, not after, extensive state and
  private investment;
- a pro-active policy to make tourism less controversial; and
- the development of specific ways to prevent terrorism against tourists
  and combat it once it occurs.

References

1 Plog, S. C., 'Psychographic Positions of Destinations', *The Tourist Business*,
   NY, USA: CBI Publishing Co Inc, 1974.
2 Alexander, Y., 'Communications aspects of international terrorism', *International Problems*, vol. 16, Spring 1977, pp. 55–60.
3 Clarke, J., 'Hopes dim as Americans stay away from Europe', Wichita, Kansas, *Eagle-Beacon*, 2 March 1986, p. 12D; and Dillin, J., 'Putting terrorism in
   perspective', *Christian Science Monitor*, 22 April 1986, pp. 1 and 4.
4 Waugh, W. L., Jr, *International Terrorism: How Nations Respond to Terrorists*,
   Documentary Publications, Chapel Hill, NC, 1982; and Waugh, W. L., Jr,
   Terrorism and Emergency Management: Policy and Administrative Perspectives,
   New York and Basel: Marcel Dekker, 1987.
5 *Morning News*, 13 March 1986.
6 Samarasinghe, S. W. R. de A., 'Sri Lanka in 1983: ethnic conflict and the
   search for solutions', *Asian Survey*, vol. 24, February 1984, p. 255.
7 Teye, V., 'Liberation wars and tourism development in Africa: the case of
   Zambia', *Annals of Tourism Research*, vol. 13, no. 4, 1986, pp. 589–607.
8 Waugh, W. L., Jr, 'The values in violence: organizational and political objectives of terrorist groups', *Conflict Quarterly*, Summer 1983, pp. 1–19.
9 Richter, L. K., 'The political uses of tourism: a Philippine case study', *Journal of
   Developing Areas*, January 1980, pp. 337–57.

Further reading

Further reading on limits and threats to tourism in *Tourism Management* 1980–9

Edgell, D., 'Barriers to international travel', vol. 9, no. 1, March 1988, pp. 63–6.

Emery, F., 'Alternative futures in tourism', vol. 2, no. 1, March 1981, pp. 49–67.

Gajraj, M., 'Warning signs', vol. 10, no. 3, September 1989, pp. 202–3.

Krippendorf, J., 'Ecological approach to tourism marketing', vol. 8, no. 2, June 1987, pp. 174–6.

Krippendorf, J., 'The new tourist – turning point for leisure and travel', vol. 7, no. 2, June 1986, pp. 131–5.

May, V. J., 'Tourist health – taking action', vol. 10, no. 4, December 1989, p. 341.

Millman, R., 'Pleasure seeking v the "greening" of world tourism', vol. 10, no. 4, December 1989, pp. 275–8.

Petty, R., 'Health limits to tourism development', vol. 10, no. 3, September 1989, pp. 209–12.

Romeril, M., 'Tourism and the environment – accord or discord?', vol. 10, no. 3, September 1989, pp. 204–8.

Wall, G., 'Cycles and capacity – incipient theory or conceptual contradiction?', vol. 3, no. 3, September 1982, pp. 188–92.

Appendix:
Tourism Management journal articles

The list below gives detailed references to the journal articles included as chapters in the book. It also indicates whether the article has been edited, shortened and/or has a postscript added.

Book chapter	Tourism Management *article* Volume	Issue	Date	Pages	Edited	Shortened	Postscript June 1990
1	3	3	Sep 1982	149–66	x	x	
2	3	4	Dec 1982	236–41			x
3	7	3	Sep 1986	154–67	x	x	
4	2	2	June 1981	113–20	x	x	
5	5	1	Mar 1984	48–56	x	x	x
6	4	3	Sep 1983	216–19	x	x	x
7	10	2	June 1989	100–10	x	x	x
8	8	2	June 1987	106–11			
9	10	1	Mar 1989	4–8	x		x
10	8	3	Sep 1987	217–22	x		
11	10	1	Mar 1989	9–14	x	x	
12	10	2	June 1989	125–37	x	x	
13	9	3	Sep 1988	187–98	x	x	x
14	10	2	June 1989	111–24	x	x	x
15	8	4	Dec 1987	291–305	x	x	
16	8	3	Sep 1987	195–204	x	x	x
17	9	2	June 1988	137–44	x	x	
18	10	1	Mar 1989	15–28	x	x	
19	10	4	Dec 1989	279–84	x	x	
20	8	4	Dec 1987	351–4	x		
21	4	1	Mar 1983	3–11	x	x	
22	8	2	June 1987	115–20	x	x	
23	10	2	June 1989	86–8	x		
24	9	4	Dec 1988	317–25	x	x	
25	1	1	Mar 1980	22–9	x	x	
26	9	2	June 1988	119–27	x	x	
27	9	3	Sep 1988	221–34	x	x	
28	7	4	Dec 1986	254–8			
29	3	3	Sep 1982	135–48	x	x	
30	7	4	Dec 1986	230–8	x	x	

Index

Authors

Places

Subjects